VOLUME II: THE WAY OF THE SEEDED EARTH

PART 3

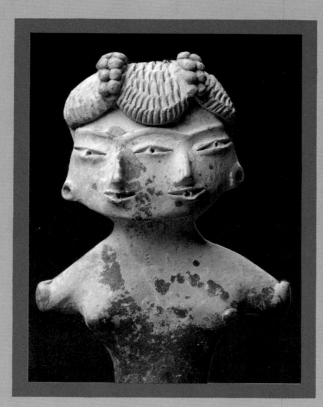

MYTHOLOGIES OF THE PRIMITIVE PLANTERS: THE MIDDLE AND SOUTHERN AMERICAS

JOSEPH CAMPBELL

HISTORICAL ATLAS OF WORLD MYTHOLOGY

VOLUME II

THE WAY
OF THE SEEDED
EARTH

PART 3

MYTHOLOGIES OF
THE PRIMITIVE
PLANTERS:

THE

MIDDLE AND

SOUTHERN AMERICAS

HARPER & ROW, PUBLISHERS NEW YORK

GRAND RAPIDS, PHILADELPHIA, ST. LOUIS, SAN FRANCISCO
LONDON, SINGAPORE, SYDNEY, TOKYO

FRONTISPIECE

1. Yamunā Devī, goddess of the river Jumna. Elūrā, Kailāsanātha compound, A.D. 750–850. Standing among lotuses, supported by a great tortoise, the goddess of the river Jumna appears within the frame of a *makara torana*. The makaras (crocodilelike monsters symbolic of the sources of the flowing waters of life) are ridden by dwarf *yakshas* (earth spirits of fertility and wealth), while pouring into their open mouths from the mouths of two back-to-back makara heads above, streams of the waters of her life-supporting river shape the gateway (*torana*) of the deity's beneficent apparition.

Library of Congress Cataloging-in-Publication Data
Campbell, Joseph, 1904–1987.
Historical atlas of world mythology/Joseph Campbell. p.   cm.   Bibliography: p.   Includes index.
Contents: v.2. The way of the seeded earth. pt.3. Mythologies of the primitive planters : the Middle and southern Americas.
ISBN 0-06-055159-3 : $.—ISBN 0-06-096352-2   : $
1. Mythology. I. Title.
BL311.C26 1989
291.1'3—dc20 89-8387

89 90 91 92 93 10 9 8 7 6 5 4 3 2 1
89 90 91 92 93 10 9 8 7 6 5 4 3 2 1 (pbk.)

TABLE OF CONTENTS

APPENDIX

AGRICULTURAL

DEVELOPMENTS
IN THE
MESOAMERICAN MATRIX

Mesoamerican Agricultural Matrix

Regions of initial formative agricultural development

Regions of early expansion of agricultural skills and practices

Regions of subsequent expansion of agricultural skills and practices

CACAO
LLAMA
Approximate geographic regions of initial plant and animal domestication

maize
alpaca
Approximate geographic regions to which domesticated plants and animals were taken

Culture area boundary

Boundary between types of agriculture

Focal regions for dispersal and diffusion

Region of the Gran Chichimeca

Approximate pre-ceramics route, c. 5000–3000 B.C.

Approximate undecorated ceramics route, c. 2000–500 B.C.

Approximate decorated ceramics route, c. 1500–30 B.C.

Principal routes of Trans-Caribbean Passage

Trade corridor

Archaeological site

Present-day city or town

THE TIDE OF HISTORY

Draw a line from San Francisco to Wichita; drop two verticals to the Tropic of Cancer: enclosed is an area that the Aztecs knew as Gran Chichimeca (Great Land of the Chichimec), the meaning of Chichimec being, Son of the Dog. It has been suggested that this may be a depreciatory term, about equivalent to the Greek βαρβαρία "land of the barbarians" (land of those strange to Greek manners, foreign, not speaking Greek). However, the Huichol Indians of the Sierra Madre Occidental, in Nayarit (just south of the Tropic of Cancer), speak of themselves as lineal descendants of "the Dog" and survivors of the Great Flood, from which only one man and one woman escaped.[1] Of all the peoples of that still largely undeveloped mountain area which lies directly along an ancient trade route from south to north, the Huichol have held most tenaciously to their pre-Columbian heritage. The name Chichimeca, therefore, may carry positive mythological, rather than (or, at least, as well as) negative sociological, implications.

Evidences are every day increasing of a substantial trade carried on over centuries between the peoples of Chichimeca and the civilizations of Mexico. Excavations conducted since the early 1970s at Casas Grandes in Chihuahua, for example, have unearthed there a large trading outpost established specifically for the conduct of this Chichimecan trade, which was in full career from c. A.D. 1050 to 1350, the very period known to the archaeology of the Southwest as Developmental Pueblo (see pages 274–276). Charles C. Di Peso reports that his own findings at this station have included "warehouses holding literally millions of shells…perforated and strung to make necklaces," brought apparently from a site near present-day Guayamas, in Sonora. "Another type of shell," he continues, "…was a large univalve, which could be used as a trumpet…to make the deep, resonant sound associated with the horned or plumed serpent—the god Quetzalcoatl."[2]

The commodity that the Casas Grandes merchants required from the north, evi-

339. A mythological theme outstanding throughout the range of the early planting cultures is of death as the generator of life. Excavated from a grave site at Tlatilco (see pp. 255–257), a mask of baked clay showing life and death as one. The principal and most characteristic early planting culture rendition of this paradoxical theme is in the mythological scenario of a divine being, slain and buried, from whose remains the food plants grow.

Across the Pacific, in Cambodia, seventh century A.D., an equivalent image fashioned in stone was of a Hindu mythic savior known as Hari-Hara, who in one person united Vishnu the Preserver (the left side) and Shiva the Destroyer (the right). Still further westward along the tropical belt, we find the East African Basungwe, once from the neighborhood of Zimbabwe, with a legend of the Lord of Life and Death as a royal presence in the Underworld, his right side alive and comely, the left rotting, crawling with maggots.

In Haitian voodoo lore (originating in Nigeria) the possessing-god Ghede, Lord of Cemeteries and Death, is equally Lord of Sexuality and a patron of children. Souls of the dead enter the Underworld by the passage that he guards, and the deities of life emerge by the same road from the same depth. As Death, he is a glutton; as Life, his dance is of copulation. He is wise with the knowledge of both worlds; and when he appears (by possessing — or "mounting" — someone at an invoking ceremony), he wears a pair of dark glasses, from which he knocks out the right lens: for with his right eye he watches those present, lest anyone steal his food, while with his left (protected from the sun's glare) he surveys the universe.[1] Of especial interest is the testimony of Ghede; for when this god mounts his carriers (or "horses"), they are bereft of any sense of self, behave and speak compulsively, and, recovered, know nothing of what they did or said. Their bifocal (life/death) behavior and knowledge are, thus, not of themselves individually, but compelled from an inner transpersonal "vision center" of which their intellects know nothing.

dently, was turquoise, an indispensable component of much of Middle American religious art. And in exchange for this, their second trade staple was birds acquired from the South: parrots, scarlet macaws, and green macaws. "The natural habitat of these birds," Di Peso notes, "does not extend north beyond Veracruz. Yet their remains were found in abundance at Casas Grandes, some 800 miles north, and in sizeable numbers in Arizona and New Mexico."[3] In fact, at Casas Grandes the remains of breeding pens have been found: "adobe boxes open at the top, which in use were covered over with fabric matting. The hutches were equipped with roosting holes. Eggshell remains and remains of skeletons of birds as young as two weeks were also found at the site, leaving little doubt that it was a breeding center."[4]

Copper bells, or crotals, of the kind known to the Hohokam culture were another item of the commerce. "Strictly speaking," states Di Peso, "a bell has a clapper; a crotal has a loose object inside an enclosed space. The copper crotals were made by the 'lost wax' method. …Copper work is found first in South America," he points out, "later in Mexico, and still later in the U.S. Southwest. Looking at the dates of copper artifacts, one can almost see knowledge of copper metallurgy working its way up the west coast of Mexico to Casas Grandes."[5]

The elaborate irrigation systems found both at Casas Grandes and in the Hohokam Gila and Salt River areas (see Map 29) add to the impression of direct connection. Di Peso is even of the opinion that the Hohokam may have been immigrants from Mesoamerica into the Southwest. As he writes: "The Hohokam's knowledge of irrigation, and their expertise in working shell, stone, and bone mark them as aliens in the Chichimecan sea. Their settlements are set apart from the villages of the indigenous Qotam. And the Hohokam built such Mesoamerican-style structures as ball courts and truncated mounds. There were religious similarities as well. For example, the Hohokam appear to have included in their pantheon the Mesoamerican war god of the black shining mirror, known as Tezcatlipoca."[6]

Map 26.

253

This enterprise, however, was late in the long history of the passage of Mesoamerican influences into regions north of the Rio Grande. Not only was it late, but it was organized and deliberate—an enterprise, as Di Peso suggests, like that of the Hudson Bay Company in the seventeenth and eighteenth centuries, as an outpost in northeastern North America of the interests of Great Britain. Among the Aztec there was a hereditary guild of armed merchants known as *pochteca*, who traveled into distant lands seeking luxury goods for the royal house. The lands of the hostile tribes they would take by force, or if unable to do so, they would provoke incidents that would lead to the intervention of the Aztec army. It has been suggested that both the Toltecs and the pre-Toltec builders of the Early Classic metropolis of Teotihuacán (c. A.D. 100 to 600) must also have known such

340. From the fifteenth-century Mextec *Codex Borgia* 55, Aztec *pochteca*, symbolic illustrations allegorical of eternally wandering stars: (**a**) the Wanderer of the North, and (**b**) the Wanderer of the South. Members of an influential and respected guild of international travelers — combining the qualities and functions of merchants, army officers, and cultural propagandists — they bear the traveling-pack (*thamamalli*) supported by the broad head-strap (*mecapalli*); a quetzal bird is perched upon one of the packs.

341. La Venta Monument 19, a sculptured stone tablet c. 800 B.C. Olmec, Tabasco, Mexico.

The prominence of the serpent in the mythologies of agriculturally based societies — whether of the primal, tribal class (such as are dealt with in this volume) or of the later, historical orders (the biblical, for example) — is a mystery of profound psychological and sociological import. Repeatedly shedding its skin to be born again, the serpent — like the moon that sheds its shadow in rebirth — typifies life-energy and consciousness locked within temporal space, delivering and suffering births and deaths.

Fluent in movement as the waters flowing over and fertilizing the earth, yet with their fiery forked tongues flashing tirelessly as lightning from a storm-laden sky, serpents appear to incarnate the elementary mystery of life, wherein apparent opposites are conjoined. In the grandiose symbolic theatre of Nature's spectacles, however, where a striking contrast can be seen between the serpents' bondage to the earth and the release of birds to untrammeled flight, an irreducible may be inferred as between earthly and heavenly powers. (Compare I.1:**68**.) In Genesis 3:14–15, for example, the serpent is cursed by a sky god and set at enmity to "the woman," with whose mystery, in most agriculturally based traditions, it is identified and thus revered. The aim of Indian yoga, in contrast, is to bring the female "serpent power" (*kundalini*) — which is to say, the will in nature as known to temporal consciousness — to knowledge of itself as identical with unconditioned being. Such a realization is what is connoted iconographically by any conjunction of lunar and solar symbols, of which the serpent and sunbird are everywhere primal examples.

Quetzalcoatl, the Aztec "Feathered Serpent," who as Evening Star dies with the sun but then as Morning Star is resurrected as herald of the light, is the best-known Mesoamerican symbol of this life-fostering realization of eternity as incarnate in the forms of time. In the unexpectedly early appearance of this archetype in Monument 19, a crested rattlesnake supports on its prodigious coils a priestly figure wearing a jaguar mask and holding in his extended right hand a little bag or basket (probably a container of powdered copal, used in Mexico to this day as incense), while the left hand, awkwardly turned palm out at the wrist, is in a position that everywhere in the Orient would be interpreted as the "boon-bestowing hand posture" (*varada-mudra*) of a divinity (see II.1:**49**). That the Olmec artist even overstrained his art to render this gesture in profile suggests that already in earliest Mesoamerica, long before its appearance in the East, the gesture must have had some such meaning.

aggressive merchant colonists and explorers. One cannot but think of Queen Elizabeth's princely pirates, Sir Walter Raleigh and Sir Francis Drake. In any case, the extent of the commerce and commercial empires of Teotihuacán and Toltec Tula (c. A.D. 900 to 1200) throughout the first millennium A.D. is only now coming into view. We see the signs of influence from Chaco Canyon (New Mexico) to Kaminaljuyu (Guatemala) and Yucatán.

Very much earlier influences out of Mexico into and across the Chichimecan north have been traced along the corridors represented in Map 26. They begin with the very beginnings of plant domestication in Middle America, and continue with increasing effect, through millennia, to the period of the Aztec empire.

The first signs already appear during what is known to American archaeology as the *Period of Incipient Agriculture (c. 6500 to 1500 B.C.)*, when in Middle America the transition was made from Paleolithic hunting and foraging to a settled Neolithic style of village life and farming (see pages 254–256).

The *Mesoamerican Formative Period (c. 1500 B.C. to A.D. 100)* is characterized by two distinct yet intermeshing developments. The first is of the native farming villages now everywhere appearing—in the highlands, in the lowlands, in the temperate northerly zones, and in the rain forests of the south—each essentially self-sufficient, yet exchanging goods (and no doubt ideas as well) over wide ranges. The second, altogether distinct development, is to be seen in the sudden appearance and flowering in tropical Tabasco and Veracruz, of a constellation of symbolically structured ceremonial centers governed by a priestly elite and of the order not at all of a Neolithic village culture but of a hieratic, literate civilization: the Olmec (see pages 260–267). Its dates (c. 1200 to 200 B.C.) parallel those of the Formative folk villages of the era, but its rise, flowering, and decline are not of the same order of life as theirs. Moreover, the mythologies and ritual styles of the subsequent Middle American Classic and Postclassic Periods, from A.D. 100 to 1519, cannot be understood as developments simply out of the folk base. They are continuations, with new inspirations and applications, of the impulse of the Olmec. The major cult, for example, of the Feathered Serpent (Kukulcán of the Maya, Quetzalcoatl of the Toltec and the Aztec) is already announced in Olmec art from c. 800 B.C. (see Figure 341).

The art of the Early Formative villages, however, was typically of ceramic figurines, not at all monumental, but with a lifelike charm, vitality, and humor. Olmec influences can be identified, here and there, but in the main the statement is of a healthy and joyous popular culture. Our

342. Dual-faced "Pretty Lady" figurine of terracota, from Tlatilco, Valley of Mexico, Middle Preclassic Period, c. 1200 to 700 B.C.

first clues to the dominant mythological archetypes structuring the works and days of these earliest of America's planting communities come to light in these clay figurines, the most numerous and best preserved of which are from the site of Tlatilco, in the great clay pit of a brickyard twenty minutes by automobile from the heart of Mexico City.

Here in the early 1940s, a bonanza find was uncovered of prehistoric graves filled with ceramic figurines of an elegant local style (Figure 344). As elsewhere in Early Formative Middle America, the most typical image is the standing female nude. There is no point in pretending—like so many exact scholars of these matters—that we do not know who she is. What we do not know exactly are the uses to which her images were applied and by what names she was invoked in her various manifestations and functions. But that she is the great goddess-mother of us all and in the context of a planting culture's inevitable order of interests was associated with the earth, we can surely know. A comparable series of ceramic female figurines from sites of a comparable culture stage (some 5000 years earlier, c. 6000 B.C.) is perfectly understood from both Asia Minor and southeastern Europe. At Tlatilco her double-headed forms are interesting and may refer (as they do in Old Europe and the Ancient Near East) to the dual domination of the goddess in the worlds of the living and the dead (as Demeter and Persephone, Inanna and Ereshkigal). Support is given to this probability by the findings at Tlatilco of forms that are half skeleton and half alive (Figure 339). The statement here is obviously of life and death as one—life out of death and death out of life—a dominant theme throughout the dominion of the planting cultures, underlying the frenzy of human sacrifice along their whole range, from Mexico, through Polynesia and South Asia, to Equatorial Africa. No evidence has yet turned up, as far as I know, of human sacrifice in the villages, but in the Olmec ceremonial centers it was apparently the central occasion, as it became and remained, certainly, throughout the Classic and Postclassic stages of Mesoamerican civilization.

343. Uncovered, 1942, at Tlatilco, a site near the center of Mexico City, were burials in which the corpses had been interred with caches of pottery and ceramic figurines (dated c. 1200–700 B.C.), the products of a prosperous early-agricultural community, whose ancestors had occupied the site from as early as 1500 or even 1700 B.C.[2] They cultivated maize, squash, and chili peppers; hunted deer, rabbits and waterfowl with

javelins propelled by spear throwers; caught fish and shrimp in the lakes; and fattened for food a breed of small dog. Their remains betray connections with other early communities far removed, "some," according to Miguel Covarrubias, who supervised the excavating, "extending as far north as the Ohio Valley, as far south as Honduras, and all the way to the Peruvian north coast."[3]

344. About the Tlatilco artifacts Covarrubias has written: "Their art was simple and unassuming, but gay and sensitive, free of religious themes. This is evident in the effigy vessels, in the clay figurines, some as large as a baby, finely modeled and highly polished, which must have required considerable skill in the potter's art, and particularly in the small, solid figurines, even if, to judge by their uniformity and large numbers, they were made by mass-production methods.

"Hundreds of complete figurines and thousands of fragments have come out of the earth at Tlatilco in a most varied range of styles; most of them are of women with small breasts, short arms, slim waists, and large, bulbous legs; some are standing, some seated, others carrying babies on their hips or caressing a small dog held in their arms. The figures of women are invariably naked, and it seems that feminine coquetry was limited to painting the face and body and wearing elaborate headdresses, of which there is an unlimited variety. Occasionally they wear abbreviated garments, such as turbans and short skirts, which seem to have been made of grass in some cases, of cloth in others, worn low at the hips. Figurines of exceptionally fat women wearing such skirts are shown in dance poses, and it is possible that these skirts were worn for dancing. The feminine figures generally show the hair shaved off in patches or worn bobbed in the back, with a long lock on each side reaching down to the waist in front. Another lock of hair was worn over the forehead, held in place by a band or garland decorated with leaves or tassels and placed at a jaunty angle like a modern lady's hat. The hair is usually painted red, suggesting that they dyed their hair, perhaps bleaching it with lime as among the Melanesians or tinting it with red achiote (*bixa orellano*) seeds, as is still done by the Colorado Indians…

"They also made representations of men, considerably rarer than those of the women, wearing loincloths (and sometimes leggings and skirts), as well as vests, garters, turbans, and helmets. A pair of figurines found in a Tlatilco burial perhaps represent shamans: each is accompanied by a dwarf, and each of the shamans wears a small mask. Ballplayers have also been found, with the characteristic belt, helmet, and knee pads, the right hand bound with a rope, perhaps to hit the ball [a striking example of these stalwart fellows is pictured in the lower right corner]. Apparently they used beds or sofas rather like ours, and from Tlatilco came an amusing group in painted clay, showing a chief or warrior comfortably reclining in bed, with a woman coyly seated at his feet. Both men and women painted their bodies in characteristic patterns with red, black, yellow, or white paint, supposedly by means of clay seals and roller stamps, decorating their thighs with geometric designs, concentric circles, and patches filled with cross-hatching. They also painted their faces with symmetric patterns over the mouth and cheeks and across the eyes. A peculiar fashion was to decorate one side of the body, leaving the other unpainted.

"The Tlatilcans were apparently little concerned with religious symbolism, though the figurines must have served a ceremonial purpose; the motifs on their pottery and clay stamps were purely decorative, and little in their art could be called representations of deities. However, a rather unusual and fascinating concept is found in certain feminine figurines with two heads or, stranger still, two sets of features on a single head: two noses, two mouths, and three eyes, reminiscent of certain paintings of Picasso, perhaps connected with the idea of twins. There are also figurines of jaguar-like beings or persons wearing jaguar masks; old crouched men, probably representations of the fire god; and strange masks of clay, one of which (**339**) shows a face of which half is contorted with a hanging tongue and the other half is a human skull, perhaps representing the idea of life and death; there are also half-human, half-jaguar faces that have a strange counterpart in the probably contemporary Chavín culture of Peru."[4]

257

345. Mushroom stone with jaguar-based stipe, from Kaminaljuyu, Guatemala. **346.** Ceramic from Colima, Mexico, of celebrants encircling a mushroom (likely *Pslocybe mexicana*) as if it were the *axis mundi*. **347.** Mushroom stone from Guatemala.

A stone image from an important site on the Guatemalan Pacific Coast, Kaminaljuyu, near Guatemala City (see Figure 345), provides a clue to the possible existence already in the *Late Formative Period (c. 300 B.C. to A.D. 100)* of another constant Mesoamerican interest—namely, in the inward, visionary transformation of consciousness produced by hallucinogens. A number of these so-called mushroom stones have been recovered from sites in highland Guatemala, and although their function is a matter of speculation, their relevance to a still-surviving Mesoamerican cult in which hallucinogenic mushrooms play a central role is not unlikely.[7] In the north, the dominant hallucinogen is mescaline, as rendered in peyote, though other plants are also used, often with more dangerous effects—for example, jimson weed (*Datura stramonium*), which the Huichol personify as the wicked enemy, Kieri, of the peyote champion, Kauyumari (see Figure 348).

The Formative Period ended with the Olmec civilization dissolving into the beginnings of the Mayan in the south and, in the north, in the Valley of Mexico, with the abrupt appearance at Teotihuacán of what has been termed the first fully urban culture in the New World. An elaborate hieroglyphic script, an extremely complex calendar, an architecture of great pyramid temples, and a social order symbolically structured marked the rise during the *Classic Period (c. A.D 100 to 900)* of the great Aztec civilization.

348. *The Power of the Tree of the Wind (Kieri)* by Hakatemi, beeswax and yarn on plywood, c. 23.5" × 23.5". The Huichol believe Kieri — their personification of jimson weed (*Datura stramonium*) — to be a wicked and dangerous sorcerer to whom offerings must be made to ward off evil.

It was during the *Early Classic Period (c. A.D. 100 to 600)* of the flowering of Teotihuacán that there were established in northern Mexico, at about the latitude of the Tropic of Cancer, two trading outposts for commerce with the Gran Chichimeca. One we have already noticed (see II.2:124) at the root of the two eastern corridors of Map 26, in southwestern Tamaulipas and San Luis Potosí, at the edge of the desert habitat of the hallucinogenic cactus, peyote. The other was at the base of the two Sonoran corridors, in what is now the state of Dur-

ango.[8] The passages of goods, techniques, and ideas to the north before the establishment of these early trading outposts had been fortuitous and piecemeal. The bottle gourd, as we have seen (II.2:124) reached Tennessee and Kentucky before 2500 B.C., apparently by way of the early eastern Mexican corridor, yet the same gourd arrived in the Chichimecan southwest only c. 300 B.C., by way of the corridor of the Upper Sonoran Complex. In c. 2000 B.C. pottery appeared in Georgia, Florida, and Alabama, but had to wait until 200 B.C. to appear (by trade) at the Koster site (I.2:210) together with maize, which by c. 300 B.C. had already appeared in the Southwest (without pottery), and by around 200 B.C. was known to the Cochise desert tribes of Utah and Colorado. Beans came next to that area, and by A.D. 500 the maize-beans-squash symbiotic complex was established throughout the region. By that time, cotton and turkeys had been acquired by the Anasazi Basket Makers, and the more intentional, commercial, introduction of Mexican products and ideas had begun.[9]

When, at last, pottery arrived in the Southwest, between c. A.D. 1 and 500, it appeared in as many as four different forms, all anticipated by ceramics to the south. From c. A.D. 500 to 700, another kind appeared, resembling in detail the Chupicuaro pottery of the Mexican west coast, and by that time the Hohokam with their Mexican ball courts had arrived.[10]

Comparably, in the East, but more

remotely and with a greater contribution of local forms and adaptations than ensued in the Southwest—also, with contributions by way of the Caribbean seaway—the great complexes of Adena (c. 800 B.C. to A.D. 800) and Hopewell (c. 200 B.C. to A.D. 500) were not miscellaneous assemblages of fortuitous odds and ends, but total and consistent structures (see I.2:212–214). The bent knees of the figurine of the Adena stone pipe (I.2:346) suggest an Olmec form; its earspools, a Mexican. Pipe-smoking, however, was an Eastern Woodland invention, unknown to Mexico until brought there as a return gift, by way of the Gilmore Corridor in reverse. Tobacco, on the other hand, does not appear on the scene until c. A.D. 1000, at two Missouri River drainage sites: Mitchell, South Dakota, and Brewster, Iowa. The origins of this weed, however—which has been called "The Red Man's Revenge"—are unknown.[11]

Finally, with the culminating *Postclassic Period (A.D. 900 to 1519)* of the expansive Toltec and Aztec military empires, we see the rise and flowering of the Mississippian Civilization in the East, c. A.D. 700 to 1700 (see I.2:210–218), and in New Mexico the phenomenon of Chaco Canyon, c. A.D. 1050 to 1350 (see pages 274–279). It is interesting to compare the numerous absolutely straight roads of that development (see Map 31) with the highways of the South American Incas (see Map 42), c. A.D. 1200 to 1532, their great coastal road of 2520 miles, from Tumbes in the north of Peru to Talca in central Chile, and the Andean Road of 3150 miles, from Quito in Ecuador again to Talca.[12] Whatever the explanation may be, one has the sense, in contemplating the incredible ruins of the civilizations of America that are gradually coming to light, of a majesty and spiritual force yet to be fully recognized and appropriately interpreted. For, as Spengler has written of the manner of its extinction: "This is the only example of a Culture ended by violent death. It was not starved, suppressed, or thwarted, but murdered in the full glory of its unfolding, destroyed like a sunflower whose head is struck off by one passing. All these states—including a world power and more than one federation—with an extent and resources far superior to those of the Greek and Roman states of Hannibal's day; with a comprehensive policy, a carefully ordered financial system, and a highly developed legislation; with administrative ideas and economic traditions such as the ministers of Charles V could never have imagined; with a wealth of literature in several languages, an intellectually brilliant and polite society in great cities to which the West could not show one single parallel—all this was not broken down in some desperate war, but washed out by a handful of bandits in a few years, and so entirely that the relics of the population retained not even a memory of it all. Of the giant city of Tenochtitlán not a stone remains above ground. The cluster of great Mayan cities in the virgin forests of Yucatán succumbed swiftly to the attack of vegetation, and we do not know the old name of any of them. Of their literature three books survive, but no one can read them.

"The most appalling feature of the tragedy was that it was not in the least a necessity of the Western Culture that it should happen. It was a private affair of adventurers, and at the time no one in Germany, France, or England had any idea of what was taking place....A few handguns and cannon opened the tragedy and brought it to conclusion."[13]

349. Cortés and his army marching on Mexico City, a color copy of an original painting by Father Pichardo from *Histoire Mexicaine depuis 1221 jusqu'à 1594*, a seventeenth-century manuscript.

THE OLMEC ENIGMA

"Coming suddenly to light within a few decades from the depths of time, a civilization totally unknown to us has emerged, with its compelling evidence and its mysteries, with its style and its gods, forcing us to recognize it as being the earliest of all those that man has built on the American continent, and perhaps as the 'mother civilization' of the New World."[14]

Thus the distinguished French Americanist, Jacques Soustelle, describes the recent archaeological discovery and reconstruction of a civilization that appeared abruptly, c. 1200 B.C., in a region of tropical rain forest, sluggish rivers and extensive swamps, along the southern shore of the Gulf of Campeche, in Tabasco and Veracruz.

"The Olmecs were the first," Soustelle declares, "to construct vast ceremonial centers, to sculpt bas-reliefs and statues in the round, to group together horizontal monoliths or 'altars' and stelae, to carve hard stone. They invented symbols that remained in use until the Spanish Conquest, more than two thousand years after them, and probably a system of writing and a highly perfected calendar as well. Their civilizations flourished from Veracruz to Michoacán, from Guerrero to Costa Rica."[15]

The first notice of the remains of such a civilization, lost to history, resting hidden in an apparently pristine wilderness, had been chanced upon at Tres Zapotes, in 1862, by a laborer clearing jungle for an hacienda. What looked to him like the bottom of a prodigious pot buried upside down proved to be, when the earth was dug from around it, the top of a colossal carved stone head (Figure 350a). Archaeological excavations in the region were not undertaken, however, until the late 1930s, when one astonishing monumental complex after another came to light.

The most imposing of these was at La Venta, situated on a parcel of elevated land,

350. Discovered in 1862 and first excavated in 1864, the Colossal Head (*in situ,* above) known as Tres Zapotes Monument A was in 1868 the first Olmec monolith to receive wide attention, when a drawing of it was published (by José Maria Melgar y Serrano in *Semanario Ilustrado*). Forgotten for a time, this marvel was re-excavated in 1938 by Matthew Stirling (whose expedition gathers around it, above). At least a dozen similar gigantic sculptures of heads have to date been identified from several different sites in the Olmec heartland (see **Map 27**).

Fashioned from basalt, Monument 1 (left) from San Lorenzo is 9 feet 4 inches tall and dates c. 1200–900 B.C. The stone, according to Michael D. Coe, is from Cerro de Cintepec, "70 kilometers northwest of San Lorenzo and a great deal further by the circuitous water route by which the monuments must have reached their final destination."[5] The pitting is of the period and intentional. Why? Many monuments at this site and at La Venta were deliberately mutilated. Coe has suggested a popular revolt c. 900 B.C., after which, in his words, "an entire Olmec state fell into disarray....San Lorenzo," he observes further, "is subsequently abandoned, but La Venta goes on to even greater brilliance, and so does Tres Zapotes."[6]

A second suggestion has been of ritual destruction to deprive the monument of its mana after the death of the personage portrayed.[7] A third might be of the vandalism of some rival cult, like that wrought by the zeal of the early Christians upon such great sanctuaries of antiquity as Eleusis, Delphi, and Epidaurus.

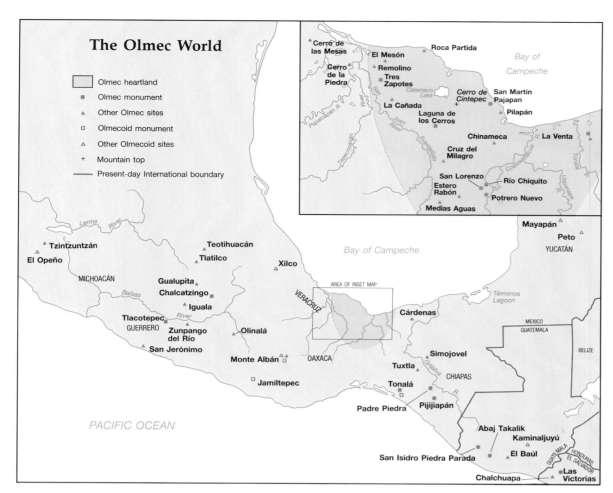

The Olmec World

- ▢ Olmec heartland
- ■ Olmec monument
- ▲ Other Olmec sites
- □ Olmecoid monument
- △ Other Olmecoid sites
- + Mountain top
- — Present-day International boundary

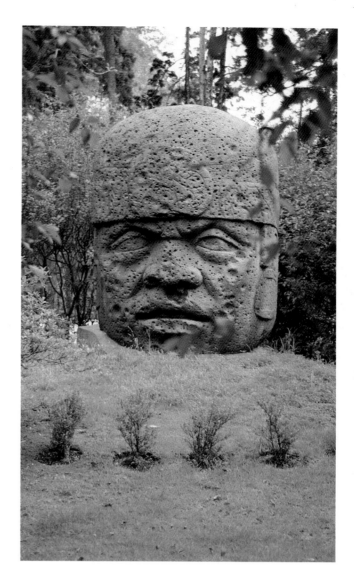

Map 27. The unannounced and unexplained appearance in the swamplands of Veracruz and Tabasco of the Olmecs' masterful sculptural tradition—from huge basalt heads to tiny jade figurines—is a phenomenon unmatched in the history of civilizations.

352. Although the Colossal Heads evidence subtle yet significant stylistic variations, their distinctly similar physical features and headgear suggest to some that they were raised to honor dead (perhaps Negroid) chieftains.[8] At right is Monument 2 from San Lorenzo.

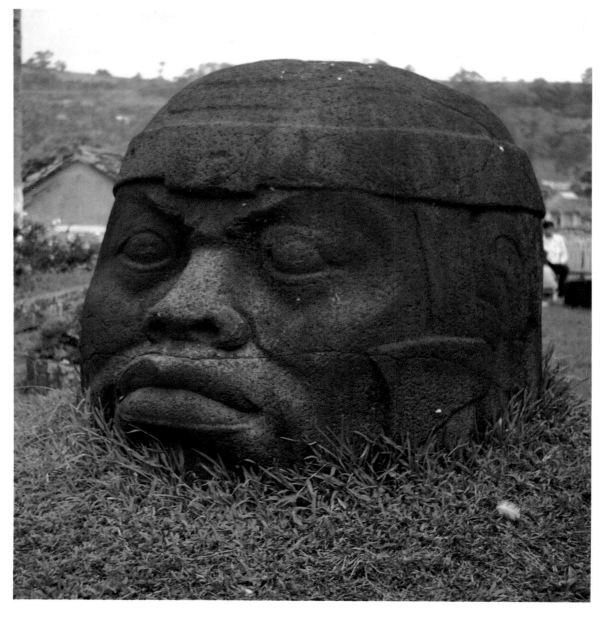

351. Since most of these huge basalt heads were in ancient times relocated and subsequently suffered over the years additional displacements, discussions about the significance (if any) of their original placements and geographic orientations remain at best a speculative exercise; but that these magnificent creations demonstrate an extraordinary mastery of the art of carving stone (carving, moreover, without the use of metal tools) is incontrovertible. Above is an eroded specimen, originally from La Venta and now in a museum; at right, another example, this one from Tres Zapotes, seems to be emerging from the ground.

353. Throughout Mesoamerica it was customary to bury offerings in a systematic relationship to either the buildings or a courtyard or a center line that bisected the site (see **Map 28**). This custom made it possible for so-buried offerings later to be easily located, examined, and, if circumstances dictated, removed. The famous figurine offering (above) from La Venta, for example, was so precisely marked that years after its burial beneath several floors of clay (variously colored clay floors, in fact, a feature that seems to have been unique to the La Venta site) "the Olmecs themselves were able to open a pit of exactly the right size on the precise site in order to inspect these figurines."[9]

Three interpretations of the arrangement of this mysterious scene have been proposed by the excavators. The first possibility is that the figurines of jade and serpentine be viewed as facing the one made of a conglomerate of granite sand. Dark buff in color, this exceptional piece contrasts strongly with the greens and grays of the rest. Its present gritty appearance may have been caused, the excavators suggest, by chemical action of the soil. There is evidence, in fact, that another figurine originally stood beside this one, backed against celt number 3, where two pieces of badly decomposed schistose material were recovered, which, when cleaned, appeared to be fragments of a figurine's arms.[10]

The second suggested view of the arrangement of figurines envisions the five characters numbered 8, 9,

10, 11, and 22 as being central to the composition and dominating it. Number 7, accordingly, may represent a captive or other important presence, but the main figure of interest, by this interpretation, is number 22, who appears to be confronting the oncoming file. "It is worth noting," the authors remark, "that this figurine was the most spectacular in appearance of all this group, being made of bright green jade with numerous black inclusions which gives a very striking appearance. The features of this figurine were also most haughty and commanding."[11]

The third suggested interpretation of the organization of this mysterious offering has to do with an apparent arrangement of figurines in pairs: 8–9, 10–11, 12–14, 13–15, 16–17, 18–19, and 20–21. The figures numbered 7 and 22, then, stand alone, and again, number 22 appears to be the real center of the action.[12]

The figurines range in height from 6⁵⁄₁₆" to 7⁵⁄₁₆". Many of them had traces of bright red cinnabar paint on their feet and their legs. Some appear as if they may have been painted all over.[13] The tall heads may reflect the practice of intentional cranial deformation by tightly binding the head during infancy. The slightly bent-knee or slouching stance of the figurines is a trait characteristic of carved images throughout Oceania and in equatorial Africa. The absence of genitalia may represent an extension to earliest Mesoamerica of the shamanic practice of ritualistic sex-change or transvestism (see I.2:173–175 and **Map 38**).

354. Carved jade mask discovered at La Venta, Olmec Preclassic, dated c. 800–200 B.C.

Map 28. Note the precise and systematic orientation of the major buildings along a hypothetical center line that bisects the site.

about two square miles in area, in the midst of a swamp some ten miles up the Tonalá river, which flows between Tabasco and Veracruz. The dominant feature at this site is a roughly conical pyramid of built-up clay, 103 feet high, fronting a long rectangular plaza oriented eight degrees west of true north (Map 28). Along the line of this orientation, as well as at other undoubtedly symbolical positions within what is clearly a ceremonial compound, there have been uncovered no fewer than nineteen deeply buried "massive offerings" (as they are now called), of which the most extraordinary is a cluster of standing, beautifully finished, eunuchoid figurines (Figure 353), two of jade and thirteen of serpentine, arranged in a semicircle facing a sixteenth, of a reddish-brown or buff conglomerate stone, standing with its back to an array of six tall slabs of polished jade.[16]

Is the company listening to an address? Or is the sixteenth about to be sacrificed?

The basis for a possible answer may be implied in three more of the discovered "offerings," which are, namely, three separately buried, yet almost identical, rectangular mosaic panels (Figure 355), each measuring approximately 15½ feet by 20¾ feet, and each composed of close to five hundred small, polished blocks of serpentine arranged to suggest a jaguar mask.[17]

355. Unearthed at La Venta were three nearly-identical mosaics (below and at right), each of which seems to represent a stylized jaguar face (see the schematized drawing at left). Excavation evidence indicates that immediately after these intricate constructions were initially completed, they were "buried," that is, covered over with a layer of clay. Given what has been learned about similar Olmec practices in other contexts, it seems reasonable to conclude that the creators of these jaguar mosaics clearly intended them to be, not part of a practical floor, but rather an elaborate ritual offering.

263

356. Some intimation of the ceremonial secrets of La Venta can be gleaned by a close examination of the mysterious iconography of Altar No. 5 (height: 5'1"): (**a**) South side, featuring glyphs of helmeted figures holding jaguar-masked boys; (**b**) front view, of a cross-legged figure with a boy supine in his lap; and (**c**) details from the North side.

357. Olmec jade figurine of standing man holding (presenting as an offering?) a "were-jaguar" child, c. 8⅝" high, Southern Mexico, c. 1000–500 B.C.

Throughout the ranges of both Middle and South American religious art the figure of the jaguar, in the form especially of the ornamental jaguar mask, appears and reappears like an obsession. The were-jaguar, furthermore, is a prominent figure in Middle and South American folk mythologies. And in every one of the recently excavated Olmec ceremonial centers unmistakable indications have been found of offerings to a jaguar god. A clue to the mythology of this god is suggested by two greatly (and apparently deliberately) damaged images of stone from two neighboring sites, Rio Chiquito and Potrero Nuevo, some fifty miles southwestward of La Venta. As interpreted by their discoverer, Matthew W. Stirling, these appear to represent a woman lying on her back with a jaguar in intercourse on top of her;[18] and since many of the most characteristic Olmec figures and figurines portray a distinctive type of were-jaguar boy, it has been suggested that these ambiguous little fellows may have been regarded as representing the progeny of that miraculous conception.

A hauntingly suggestive monument of uncertain meaning at La Venta is the carved monolith known as Altar No. 5 (Figure 356), which, in fact, may not be an altar, but a throne. From a deep hollow on its anterior face a mitred personage emerges, bearing on his arms a child, as though in offering. The northern face of the same block shows another such dignitary, clasping a child that seems to be struggling to break free. And on the opposite, southern face are two more elaborately ornamented functionaries, each with a child in his arms. A jade figurine (Figure 357) now in the Brooklyn Museum suggests that at some moment in whatever

ceremonial these images represent, both the celebrant and the presented jaguar-boy were naked. Figures 359a–d, are of celts, hachas or "votive axes" on which anthropomorphic representations of the jaguar-god himself appear, while in Figure 358, which is of a jaguar-child, zoomorphic and anthropomorphic features are indistinguishably conjoined.

Was the ritual represented in these finds of an actual child sacrifice? Or was it, as Ignacio Bernal suggests, a ceremony with "a dynastic meaning, showing the importance of the child as heir to the throne?"[19] Michael D. Coe suggests that "the feline element in Olmec art" anticipates the mythology of the Aztec jaguar-god Tezcatlipoca, pointing out: "1) that the main point of Mesoamerican theogony [myths of the origin and genealogy of the gods] was to confirm royal power, and 2) that the entire origin myth, like the Memphite Theogony of the Egyptians, was recited at the accession of a new king so that he, chosen by Tezcatlipoca himself, might know who he was and that his people might know him."[20]

In the folk-beliefs and mythologies of both Middle and South America the jaguar has inherent shamanic associations; in fact, as Peter Furst has defined the case: "shamans and jaguars are not merely equivalent, but each is at the same time the other."[21] At a critical moment in the history of the Olmec sites, as registered and even illustrated in their magnificent monuments, a dominating shamanic elite evidently assumed charge of a cultural and related spiritual transformation that amounted, as Jacques Soustelle has described it, to a "prodigious mutation that took the Olmecs from tiny hamlets to cities, from culture to civilization; and we use the word 'mutation,'" he adds, "deliberately, for there is no evidence of a 'formative' evolution, a gradual maturation over several centuries. This indeed constitutes," he concludes, "the very heart of the Olmec mystery. The sudden passage to a superior level thanks to individuals of genius? Innovations suddenly brought in from the outside?—but if so, by whom and from where?"[22]

The critical date of the Olmec event is c. 1200 B.C., which nicely matches that of the Late Shang dynastic capital at An-yang (Honan), c. 1384–1025 B.C.; also, that of the legendary fall of Troy to the Achaeans (destruction by fire of Troy, c. thirteenth century B.C.), as well as the entry into northwest India of the Vedic-Aryans. Evidence of an earlier occupation of a number of the Olmec jungle sites from possibly c. 1500 B.C. has suggested to some that a local formative development may have anteceded the abrupt appearance in the area of both great and small stone monuments in a sculptural style fully achieved.[23] No signs, however, have yet been found of formative beginnings of any kind. Moreover, great styles in art do not evolve, they appear, as manifestations of intelligible insights, after which, as in the course of time the originating impulse fades, there is a devolution to secondary interests, applications, and effects. Likewise, in the history of any mythologically structured

358. Tantalizing insights into Olmec mythology are suggested by this three-inch-high jade figurine (pierced for use as a pendant) of a polymorphous "were-jaguar" boy, in the throes of transformation.

359. Ceremonial celts with incised anthropomorphic representations of the "jaguar-god" abound in Olmec Mesoamerica: (**a**) specimen probably from Oaxaca, c. 7¹³⁄₁₆″ tall; (**b**) the jadite Kunz celt, first described in 1889, 10³⁄₁₆″ high; (**c**) "votive ax" from the region of Veracruz, 11″ in height; and (**d**) hacha from La Venta Tomb E.

civilization (and there is none known that was not originally so structured), as the initiating metaphysical insight fades and the connotations of the metaphoric customs are forgotten, practical political and economic purposes take over, the integrative principal no longer holds, and the civilization goes to pieces.

At the Olmec sites, from c. 600 B.C. onward, there are signs, increasingly evident, of a decline of this kind, until by c. 100 B.C. the civilization was extinct and its heritage of symbolic forms had been passed on to the Maya. Bernal has termed this season of devolution, Olmec III. His Olmec I is of the period from c. 1500 B.C. to the epochal "mutation" or "quantum leap," as it has also been called, of c. 1200 B.C., after which, during Olmec II, for a period of six centuries, there flourished in the torrid swamp and river lands of a Mesoamerican jungle the first monumental civilization of the New World.

One of the most remarkable aspects of the Olmec phenomenon is the very wide diffusion of the evidences of its influence. On the west coast, in the highlands of the Sierra Madre del Sur, in both Oaxaca and Guerrero, these evidences are such as to suggest an Olmec colonial presence exerting a formative influence on the local agricultural populations from as early as c. 1000 B.C.[24]

At Tlatilco, for example, among the figu-

a

b

c

d

265

rines of a local style were other objects of a distinctly Olmec cast (Figure 361), "establishing," as Miguel Covarrubias, who had supervised the dig, declared, "the contemporaneity and relationship of these two puzzling cultures."[25] The period of the burials from which the objects were retrieved was c. 1200 to 900 B.C.,[26] exactly that of the sites in Guerrero and Oaxaca. Also, as Soustelle has shown, at a succession of sites southward, along the coastal way from below Tonalá in Chiapas to the Peninsula de Nicoya of northwestern Costa Rica, monuments have been identified of distinctly Olmec craftsmanship and origin: at Pijijiapan, Ojo de Agua, El Sitio, San Gerónimo, Abaj Takalik, Piedra Parada and, in El Salvador, Las Victorias.[27] "In the southernmost border region of Mesoamerica, in Costa Rica," Soustelle suggests, "the jade deposits of the Nicoya Peninsula perhaps served as a pole of attraction drawing to this region Olmec traders or explorers—half traders and half warriors—traveling down the Pacific coast from Tonalá and Pijijiapan by way of Las Victorias."[28]

"If we observe on a map the areas occupied by the Olmec world," Ignacio Bernal has remarked, "we see that they cover most of Mesoamerica...."[29] And yet, the Olmec cannot be said to have been the masters of an empire. The explanation generally proposed and accepted for the broad reach of their influence is of trade, undertaken in the first instance to establish and maintain a

360. Concave mirror of polished hematite, pierced to be worn as a pectoral, from La Venta.

This remarkable mirror is one of eight that have been recovered. According to a technical report published by the excavators: "The polish of the specimens is excellent and probably represents the limit of perfection that the material will allow....The radius of curvature becomes progressively greater as the edge is approached. The effect is almost identical with the modern practice of parabolizing optical reflectors. This outer flattening improves the performance of a reflector that focuses radiant energy."[14]

The focal length is so long, however, that it is impossible to concentrate enough heat to ignite a fire.[15] Instead, "an even more fantastic use could have been as a 'camera obscura.' These mirrors can throw a picture of the landscape on a surface placed near the principal focus. All that is required is some shading of the screen on which the picture is to be projected."[16] Some sort of magical or symbolic use may have been made of such reflections. Whatever the case, as the excavators unequivocally remark, these mirrors "stand out as the most unique pieces of precision stoneworking of the La Venta culture."[17]

flow of jade, magnetite, ilemite, and the other luxury goods required for the fabrication of the status symbols of an elaborately ornamented theocratic aristocracy: decorated cotton mantels, earrings, lip-plugs, pectorals, and the like.[30] Protection of the trade routes required the establishment of guardian "gateway communities" at critical points along the way, while in stations of major concern, colonial factoring communities would have come into being.

For there was already in America at the time of the Spanish Conquest a well-traveled system of highways that with hardly a break extended from Chaco Canyon, New Mexico (see pages 276–277; Map 31), to Santiago in Chile (see pages 369, 375–376; Map 42); and, as it now appears, the beginnings of the type of interregional trade and traffic represented by these foot-worn thoroughfares must be ascribed to the earliest centuries of La Venta, when basalt and other materials not to be found in the surrounding swamps were already being turned into symbolic monuments on that astonishing little island of but two square miles.

Nor was all the traffic by land: see Map 26.[31] In the course of a discussion on the dating, form, and function of the pyramid at La Venta, Gordon Willey called attention to the fact that at Poverty Point, Louisiana (about 250 miles up the Mississippi River), there stands "the earliest pyramid in the eastern United States....It is enormous,"

361. That a significant Olmec influence was widespread in Mesoamerica is demonstrated by the proliferation at various non-Olmec sites of so-called Olmecoid figurines (that is, figurines that are suggestive of those made by the Olmec), such as: **(a)** seated figure of white slip, 6½" high, from Tlapacoya; and **(b)** cross-legged figure from Tlatilco.

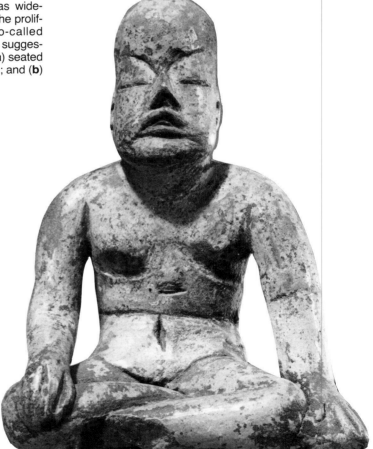

he declared, "and its radiocarbon dates are just about the same as those from La Venta."[32] And from a much later period (not determined), at a site on the savannahs around Lake Okeechobee, Florida, there has been retrieved a silver jaguar mask (Figure 363) which also points to Veracruz.[33] As envisaged by Soustelle:

"It is still too early to try to understand exactly what the Olmecs were doing when they left their normal habitat and ventured forth into regions so distant and so different from their own. They were seeking, as we have said, raw materials such as jade and serpentine, and perhaps certain varieties of obsidian as well: artifacts made of extremely rare green obsidian, scarcely ever found outside of the region of Pachuca (state of Hidalgo), in the northeast of Mexico, were discovered at Ayotla and at San Lorenzo. If, as we may suppose, Olmec travelers or colonists engaged in trade—like the Aztec *pochteca* many centuries later—they must have brought from their place of origin objects or goods that would pique the interest of the peoples who dwelt on the central plateau: the feathers of tropical birds, rubber, cocoa, carved jade pieces perhaps. These Olmec traders may thus have initiated a certain current of exchanges between *Tierra Caliente* and *Tierra Fría*—the Hot Lands and the Cold Lands—that, practically speaking, has continued uninterruptedly ever since and that serves to explain in particular how it happens that precious feathers, balls of rubber, tropical plants such as cacao trees, and jade pieces are shown in the fresco paintings on the walls of the palaces and sanctuaries of Teotihuacán."[34]

"Certain portions of this immense zone of diffusion of Olmec civilization were probably administered by individuals (priests? government functionaries? military personnel?) who had come from the 'metropolitan area,' representing, for example, the leaders of La Venta. Other regions might well have been peopled by Olmecs but allowed to administer themselves. Still others doubtless preserved the basic features of their traditional culture, their language, and their gods, but assimilated, more or less profoundly, certain traits of the more sophisticated civilization that had reached them.

"Although we know so little about Olmec religion, it is legitimate to presume that it played a large part in the dynamic expansionist thrust of these people. In world history, proselytism is always a powerful factor in cultural diffusion. Perhaps Olmec 'missionaries' journeyed along the long routes of Mesoamerica in order to spread the cult of the jaguar god....

"More cultural and religious than military, more commercial than administrative, the spreading over a wide area of a civilization rather than a power, what we call the 'Olmec empire' was chronologically the first, in this part of the world, of those great human edifices, of those groupings of peo-

362. The lower fragment of Tres Zapotes Stela C was discovered by Matthew Stirling in January 1939. Depicted on one side is a "weeping-jaguar" (arguably Cocijo, the Zapotec rain god), and on the other, signs that are of numbers, the notation being the same as that used later by the Maya: each bar is a 5; each dot is a 1. The lowest element is a day-sign corresponding to the Mayan "6 Etz' nab" (something very like "Thursday [Thor's day] the 6th"). The upper numbers represent this weekday's position in the month, the year, a cycle of twenty years, and (beyond that, see below) a megacycle of twenty such greater cycles of ever-cycling time. Hence, the designation, "Long Count" that has been given to this type of Mesoamerican calendar.

When restored with the addition of a second fragment (the upper, discovered about 1972), the inscribed date on Stela C now reads: 7 Baktuns, 16 Katuns, 6 Tuns, 16 Uinals, 18 Kins. Considering that, in the Long Count, 1 Baktun = 20 Katuns and 1 Katun = 20 Tuns and 1 Tun = 20 Uinals and 1 Uinal = 18 Kins and 1 Kin = 1 day, the signs on Stela C accordingly add up to 1,125,698 days from the base date of the Long Count calendar. Now, if the base date of the Mayan Long Count was, as some suppose, October 4, 3373 B.C., then the date here inscribed would, according to that reckoning, be November 4, 291 B.C. If, however, the base date of the calendar was, as others believe, August 13, 3113 B.C., then the date recorded on Stela C would be September 2, 31 B.C.[18] Both dates are for the Olmec, however, very late. Soustelle has therefore suggested that the Long Count of the Olmec may have been based on an earlier date than the Long Count of the Maya.[19] The question has not been resolved.

ples, that successively bore the imprint of Teotihuacán, of the Maya cities, of Tula, of Tenochtitlán. For the first time, a dynamic outpouring of thought and action, of art and of commerce, a religion, and a style transcended the narrow limits of a village. This was the decisive step, the threshold approached but not crossed by other Indians such as the Pueblos: the transition, or rather mutation, that two thousand years after the first faltering steps in the domain of agriculture, transformed the life of the Mexican peasant by inventing the city, the crucible of new ideas."[35]

363. From the Fort Center site, Lake Okeechobee, Florida, comes this silver mask (or tablet), depicting either a jaguar face or a "spider motif."[20]

267

AGRICULTURAL RITES

AND MYTHS OF
MIDDLE AMERICA

Map legend

- ⬭ Anasazi culture area, c. 100 B.C. to 1900 A.D.
- ⬭ Fremont culture area, c. 500 A.D. to 1350 A.D.
- ⬭ Hohokam culture area, c. 100 B.C. to 1400 A.D.
- ⬭ Mogollon culture area, c. 100 B.C. to 1400 A.D.

cultural tradition areas shown at maximum geographic extent

- Tribal boundaries
- Tano / Ute / Pima / Piro — Tribes and their cultural traditions
- ☐ Present day Indian Reservations and their cultural traditions
- Present day State and International boundaries
- ■ Archaeological site
- ○ Indian village
- ● Town
- △ Missions

The Desert Cultures

The Desert Cultures

From as early as 8000 or 7000 B.C., the whole area from Oregon to northern Mexico and from the Pacific Coast to the eastern foot-hills of the Rocky Mountains was occupied by a scattering of so-called Desert Culture tribes subsisting, not by big-game hunting, but by plant gathering; and whereas, over the rest of the continent, the prime signs of the time were Clovis, Sandia, and Folsom points (see I.1:35–36), the distinguishing stone artifacts in this region were milling stones for the grinding of wild seeds. The atlatl, or spear-thrower, also appears, however, and, as the animal remains suggest, small-game hunting must have contributed to the economy. Caves and rock shelters were inhabited, and by about 4000 B.C. the domesticated dog had arrived—like the atlatl, from Asia. Among the characteristic manufactures were baskets, nets, the crude milling stones, simple bone tools, and small stone projectile points, stemmed or notched.

By c. 300 B.C. in Arizona and western New Mexico the people of a specific local desert culture known as the Cochise had begun practicing a form of agriculture based on maize, beans, and squash which had been developed in Mexico between 6500 and 1500 B.C.[1] and was to become in time the characteristic agricultural form of North America. As described by Carl Sauer, this cultivated triad formed a "symbiotic complex," without an equal anywhere. As he describes it: "The corn plants grow tall and have first claim on sunlight and moisture. The beans climb up the corn stalks for their share of light; their roots support colonies of nitrogen-fixing bacteria. The squashes or pumpkins grow mainly prone on the ground and complete the ground cover. In lands of short growing season, all three may be planted together at the same time, the corn then being of early maturing kinds. In lands of long season, the corn was planted first, the other two later in the hills of the corn. With few exceptions all three were grown together. By long cultivation varieties of all were selected, able to grow to the farthest climatic limits of Indian agriculture."[2]

Map 29.

A second new appearance in the Cochise area at that time was the pit-house dwelling: huts of poles, bush, and clay, built over pits of from ten to forty inches in depth, entered by way of a stepped tunnel. There is no known evidence of any such building style either in Mexico or in the eastern United States. One suggestion is that it may be a reflection in the New World of a Late Paleolithic (Gravettian) mammoth hunters' house-form of c. 25,000 years ago.[3] Be that as it may, its sudden appearance in the American Southwest, c. 300 B.C., was in the Cochise Mogollon area (southwestern New Mexico and southeastern Arizona), after which it spread through the rest of the culture.

Farther west, in the more arid parts of what is now central and southern Arizona (largely along the Salt and Gila rivers), a remarkable local development out of the general base arose that is known to archaeology as the Hohokam culture. Its most striking feature was a network of irrigation canals, of which the first element, three miles long, was already functioning, watered from the Gila River, in the first centuries A.D. By the fourteenth century there were over 150 miles of such canals in the Salt River valley alone. Ball courts, resembling those of the Mayan ceremonial centers in Guatemala, appeared here between A.D. 500 and 900, and the art of casting copper bells in wax molds, between A.D. 900 and 1100, after which date the villages of pit-houses, which had occasionally been walled for defense, gave place to large, multiple-storied communal buildings. Early in the fifteenth century, for reasons unknown, this extensive organization of interdependent settlements broke down, and the Hohokam culture disintegrated. The modern Papago and Pima, both of which tribes are of a Uto-Aztecan language stock, are believed to be its descendants.

The Pima, who have remained in their traditional locales—the valleys of the Gila and Salt rivers—still practice a form of agriculture made possible only by controlled irrigation. They have returned, however, to the one-room dwelling, and during years of drought (which are frequent) are reduced to the ancient desert resource of small-game hunting and seed collection (largely of jackrabbits and mesquite beans). The Papago, who appropriately call themselves the Bean People (also, Desert People, in contrast to the Pima as the River People), are even more dependent on primitive desert-foraging than their relatives. Dwelling as they do in the arid hills of southernmost Arizona and northernmost Sonoma, they are thrown back upon what is known as flash-flood farming. Immediately following the first rains, they plant what seeds they have in the alluvial fans at the mouths of washes.

And yet, the elegant little fragment of myth that was confided to Natalie Curtis,

364. Reconstruction, based on posthole patterns and fallen timbers from various structures, of a typical pithouse of the Late Pithouse period.

365. The Pima pithouse tradition continued into the twentieth century: *Ceremonial Ki-Pima*, 1907 photograph by Edward S. Curtis (1868–1952).

around 1904, by the old Pima chief Hovering Hawk may well have been a particle of ancient Hohokam mythology from the great periods of the ceremonial ball courts, c. A.D. 500 to 1400. ''I will sing an old, old song,'' he told her, ''a song sung by the Creator at the beginning of the world.... The story tells of the beginning of all things, and there are many songs in the story. To tell it rightly and to sing all the songs would take all night and longer. So I will only tell you, shortly, just a part of it, and sing you the one song.... White people say that our dances and our songs are not good. We are glad that you say it is no harm for us to sing.... It is well that you have come to do this thing for us, but we have not much money to offer you in return. The white people living up above us on the river have taken all the water, so that our fields are dry. We are poor.''[4]

A history closely parallel to that of the rise, culmination, and abrupt dissolution of

the Hohokam village complex between c. 300 B.C. and c. A.D. 1400 unfolded in the Mogollon culture area as well—there where the pit-house dwellings had first appeared. That was a culture notable especially for the beauty and variety of its potteries. Already in its earliest appearance, Mogollon pottery (the first in the Southwest) was graceful and expertly made. The Mogollon villages were at first of circular pit-house dwellings, which by A.D. 700 had become rectangular. From c. A.D. 1, however, there were in many of the villages very much larger structures which served apparently as ceremonial chambers, and these were of various forms: circular, bean or kidney shaped, square with rounded corners, **D** shaped. Generally regarded as ancestral to the Pueblo Kiva, twenty-three or more have been identified in the area, and seven have been excavated and described.[5] Stress-bearing walls of masonry were introduced to the Mogollon

271

a

c

b

366. Throughout the North American Southwest, an extraordinarily diverse profusion of prehistoric paintings adorn isolated rock outcroppings, desolate caves, and seemingly inaccessible canyon bluffs. Although increasingly endangered by the passage of time, the ravishment of the elements, the maliciousness of vandals, and the encroachment of civilization, these iconographic treasures nonetheless still provide invaluable intimations of ancient ways. Herewith, a selective sampling: (**a**) 1930 photograph of anthropomorphic figures in Classic Vernal style, from Dry Fork Valley, Utah; (**b**) from Barrier Canyon, these pre-Fremont pictographs are suggestive of aboriginal Australian ancestral figuration (see I.2:**246**); (**c**) an eight-foot-long, horned and plumed, Mogollon serpent, decorated with stepped motifs that possibly represent clouds, from the Diablo Dam site in Texas; and (**d**) a colored transcript of a composition that Campbell Grant, author and illustrator of a comprehensive study of Chumash rock painting, considers to be "the most elaborate and colorful pictograph in Chumash territory." Grant continues, "It shows considerable overpainting to the right, where cruder work is overlaid with beautifully executed designs. This painting originally covered most of the cave walls, but the wind has eroded all but these paintings on the roof."[21] The Chumash, a great Indian nation that in pre-Colonial times occupied a substantial territory along the coastline in southern California, by 1839 had virtually ceased to exist.

d

culture zone c. A.D. 900, and during the classical, so-called Mimbres period, c. A.D. 1050 to 1200—which was graced by an especially striking pottery (see Figures 367–368)—pit-house dwellings gave place to apartment buildings of from forty to fifty rooms, one to three stories high, constructed around a plaza. But then again, as in the Hohokam zone (and again for reasons unknown), these substantial settlements were abandoned, and all trace (in this case) of the population has disappeared.

367. Hohokam red-on-buff pottery, Sacron phase (c. A.D. 900–1100):

(**a**) Gila shoulder olla with plaited and spiraling decorations, c. 13″ × 18⅓″, Casa Grande, Arizona.

(**b**) Shallow plate with crane, c. 1½″ deep × 9″ diameter, Middle Gila River Valley, Arizona.

368. Classic Mimbres (c. A.D. 1000–1150) Black-on-white hemispheric vessels, Mimbres River Valley, New Mexico. All have had a hole punched in them (that is, been "killed") before being placed over the face of a corpse; depicted are (**a**) anthropomorphic reptile figure, c. 3¾″ × 8¾″; (**b**) opposing pronghorn antelope, c. 4⅞″ × 11⅛″; (**c**) anthropomorphic bird with fish, c. 4″ × 9″; and (**d**) male figures with a feline in a "cornfield," c. 3½″ × 10″. Barbara L. Moulard provides a context: "Mimbres constitutes both a regional branch as well as a chronological period of Mogollon development…concentrated along the upper Gila, San Francisco, and Mimbres River valleys. Classic Mimbres Black-on-white pottery was adumbrated in…the final phase of the late Pit House Period [c. A.D. 750–1000, when] the Mimbres region experienced direct contact with the highly developed Hohokam [who] appear to have been most accessible early in their development to influences from Mesoamerica. Mexican traits continued to diffuse into the Hohokam region and the culture grew in power until c. A.D. 900–1100. The development of Mogollon pottery painting prior to the Classic Mimbres Period closely resembles that of the Hohokam from A.D. 700 to 1100. During the eleventh century, Hohokam influence gradually withdrew from the Mimbres region. At the beginning of the eleventh century, the Mimbres area underwent major social and organizational changes reflected in the move from pit house dwellings to surface cobblestone masonry pueblos."[22]

The Kiva

The third and only enduring flowering out of the early Cochise ground was that known as the Anasazi, of which the Pueblo are the inheritors. The geographical center of this development lay northward of the Hohokam-Mogollon zones, in that still magnificently beautiful area (studded today with national parks and monuments) where the four states of Utah, Colorado, Arizona, and New Mexico come together. The name Anasazi is from a Navaho noun meaning Ancient Ones, and indeed the history of this region, as it now appears, tells of the force of a single, ancestral, *cultural* continuity, which took into its fold and shaped to its own archetypes peoples of a number of distinct racial and linguistic stocks. The Navaho, Apache, Athabascan, and various Pueblo communities, for example, are of at least four separate stocks: Uto-Aztecan, Penutian, Tewa, and Keresan.

Yet all share, as though it were their own, the origin myth of an emergence from the womb of the earth (usually by an ascent through three subterranean stages), the legend of a tribal wandering before settling in their present station, and an adventure cycle of the heroic deeds of young, twin, monster slayers, whose miraculous lives are rehearsals of a series of standard mythological motifs: virgin birth, father quest, perilous journey (to the Sun) with magical aid (from Spider Woman, from the daughter of the Sun, and from various spirit messengers), paternity tests and recognition followed by initiation to self-knowledge, return to the earth with augmented powers (lightning arrows, arcane knowledge, and so on), and a series of culture deeds of Herculean type that clear the land of threatening presences. There are, furthermore, a number of other standard elements associated with these narrative motifs: colors of the four directions, one central and four cardinal mountains, sunwise circumambulation, and the ritual use of sandpaintings and of prayer sticks—all of which, by the way, were also features, until 1959, of the Tantric Buddhist ritual arts of the monasteries of Tibet.

The primitive Cochise inhabitants of the Anasazi area were a people known as Basket Makers, dwelling in caves or in shelters of poles and adobe, cultivating maize and pumpkins, and fashioning, as their name suggests, excellent baskets. Then around A.D. 500, turkeys, bean crops, and cotton were added to their holdings, and pottery (sun dried) was introduced; along with these, from the Mogollon area, came pit-houses, both as domiciles and as ceremon-

Map 30. With its impressive pueblo ruins, its network of arrow-straight roadways, and its rich ceramic tradition, Chaco Canyon offers ample evidences of what has become known as the Chaco phenomenon, a major cultural influence in the prehistoric North American Southwest.

ial chambers. At Juniper Cove, at the foot of the Black Mesa, six miles south of Kayenta, there has been excavated a large structure of the ceremonial kind, situated about one hundred feet from a late Basket Maker pit-house village. It was thirty-six feet in diameter, with a continuous bench encircling the interior, an entrance with descending steps, four large posts near the corners, which had supported a flat roof, and a central fire pit on a raised platform; the date was c. A.D. 650 to 700.[6] Through the following three and a half centuries (the period known as *Developmental Pueblo*, also as *Pueblo I and II:* c. A.D. 700 to 1050), the interiors of these Anasazi "great kivas" became standardized in arrangement and greatly enlarged. There is an example in Cahone Canyon, near Ackman, Colorado, of a date c. A.D. 855 to 872, showing a diameter of no less than eighty-one feet.[7] And among the great system of ruins at the site known as Pueblo Bonito in Chaco Canyon (New Mexico), there is a prime example from this period, known as Kiva Q (see Figures 369–370), the floor plan of which[8] presents a readily read statement of the standard main features (all mythologically symbolic) of an early Pueblo kiva.

The only exceptional element in this kiva is the entrance from the south, instead of

the north; the other elements are standard for the Developmental Pueblo period. The columns are not only structural, but also (undoubtedly) symbolic of the mythic mountains of the four quarters below ground, which support the plane of this earth. For the kiva is itself the underworld, and those initiates within it, seated on the encircling bench or in action performing ritual tasks, are in imagination identical with the world-supporting and world-generating cosmic and ancestral powers that are personified and made visible in their ceremonials. Within the kiva they have stepped back, as it were, behind the veil of time of the beginning, as well as down below the floor of sunlit space, and their flickering light now is of the "old god," fire, the sun's terrestrial counterpart, a beloved and major god throughout Middle America.

The presence of the sipapu in the floors of these first kivas of the Anasazi pueblo culture gives tangible evidence of an emergence myth already central to the ritual lore of that otherwise undocumented period of exclusively oral transmission. The symbolized Place of Emergence, furthermore, is today interpreted—as we have learned (see I.2:241–243)—as the womb of a living mother earth, who is the mother, not only of mankind, but also of the beasts and birds. The sipapu in the kiva, therefore, is an altar symbolic of the female power, as the other altar, the raised firebox, must have been of the male as engendering fire: the "old god" *huehueteotl*, as the Aztecs termed this prime giver to mankind, not only of the fire of life, but also of the hearth-fires of civilization. Thus through archaeology it appears that the reverence in these sanctuaries was of the two great mysteries of the boons of life and culture: the *yin* and the *yang* (to use the Chinese terms), the dark and the light, moist and dry, female and male. The informing mythological tradition was specifically of an emergence myth of all life arising from a female earth. And already, there was a governing society or priesthood of initiates (not individual shamans) charged with the maintenance and celebration of relevant rites.

369. Photograph of Kiva Q looking south. The arrows indicate the depth of probable rebuilding of the outer wall. Specialists doubt that the antechamber is of prehistoric construction.

North

0 4 8 12
SCALE IN FEET

370. Plan of Pueblo Bonito's great Kiva Q (Pueblo Bonito II): Its interior diameter averages forty-four feet. Its floor is nine feet below the plaza level and six feet four inches below the level of the entrance chamber (**J**), descent from which must have been by a ladder. The chamber is encircled by a permanent stone bench (**B**) against the wall (**A**). Four columns (**D**) once supported a flat roof. Two vaults (**F**) — for the storage, possibly, of ritual gear — abut the southern columns, and between them is a raised rectangular masonry firebox (**G**), with a rectangular draft opening to the north. The dimensions of the vaults are six feet eight inches (north to south) by four feet eight inches (east to west). The original height of the firebox may have been about two feet. A floor slot (**H**), which when uncovered was found to be filled with shale up to the floor level, has been interpreted as being a base for some kind of fire screen. And approximately mid-way between the two northern columns is what is known as a *sipapu* (**C**), a hole symbolic of the Place of Emergence. Circular in form the *sipapu* is fourteen inches in diameter and nine inches deep, features well-made masonry walls, and is floored with a stone slab through the center of which there is a circular hole (compare the hole in the center of a Huichol *tepari*: Figures **417** and **418**). The *sipapu* is directly in line, on the north-south axis, with the firebox and the fire screen.[23] Although Kiva Q is larger than the other kivas at Pueblo Bonito, its interior arrangement can be seen as prototypical of the architectural features of most other kivas.

Cycles of the Sun and Moon

Pueblo Bonito, five stories high with some 832 rooms and kivas, was but one of a number of Developmental Pueblo and *Classic Pueblo* (*Pueblo III*, c. A.D. 1050 to 1300) settlements centered in a vast ceremonial and commercial complex around Chaco Canyon, New Mexico. A related ruin some fifty miles northwestward, on a milelong mesa near Newcomb, New Mexico, nearly covers the mesa top with at least 1200 rooms.

In those centuries the entire canyon floor was laced by numerous roads, many as wide as thirty feet, running perfectly straight for miles out to the north, south, east, and west, with stairways cut into rock walls to ascend and descend obstructing mesas and with causeways across the low spots. Trodden only by sandaled or bare human feet — since there were neither beasts of burden nor wheeled vehicles in pre-Columbian North and Middle America — they supported what must have been a lively traffic of porters bearing produce from the surrounding farms, household goods, and luxury articles for the wealthy, as well as the tens of thousands of timbers from forests twenty to thirty miles distant to serve as beams for the building and repair of the numerous multiroom dwellings. There is evidence, also, of an import and export traffic, with itinerant merchants arriving from and departing for the great capitals to the south: Pre-Toltec Teotihuacán (c. 100 B.C. to A.D. 650), Toltec Tula (Tollan) (c. A.D. 750 to 1168), Aztec Tenochtitlán (c. A.D. 1150 to 1521).

Regulation of the public affairs of a civilization of this magnitude, dependent on agriculture for its life in a marginal agricultural zone, demanded as a first necessity a binding of the whole to the seasonal tasks of the local agricultural year, and this in turn required the maintenance of a seasonal watch on the heavens. The binding of the community was then to be achieved by way of a year-round calendar of festivals articulated by this watch. And as in every other known early agricultural society, so here in the North American Southwest, the sense of an essential spiritual accord between the social and celestial orders, with the well-being of the community understood as a function of this accord, contributed to the flowering of a mythology of personified cosmic powers functioning simultaneously in the heavens and on earth. Conformance with their celestially announced order yielded health, wealth, and progeny, whereas the slightest deviation broke the connection.

The annual passages of the sun northward and southward, back and forth, as marked by the movement along the horizon of its points of rising and setting, were

the first and most obvious signs to be watched. To this day in the Hopi village of Walpi, Arizona, for example, the festivals preceding the winter solstice (about December 21, when the sun turns to its southward course and days begin to grow longer) are determined by sunset-horizon observations; those before the summer solstice (about June 21, when the northward turn is made and the nights begin to grow longer) by sunrise horizon. Sunset observations are conducted from the rooftop of the Bear Clan's matriarchal house, which is in the center of the main house group of the pueblo; those at sunrise, from the tip of the First Mesa. As the critical day approaches, observations of the controlling celestial body (sun or moon, depending on the festival) are made each day by the chief of the particular kiva in charge of the occasion, and on the relevant evening (when the sun has reached a specific position or the moon has entered a specific phase), this watcher calls for a smoke talk. There the leading members of the society settle upon a proper date, and at sunrise of the following day this date is announced

by a crier chief. Preliminary exercises of prayer, meditation, and fasting from salt and meat are undertaken in the kivas while the altars, prayer sticks, and other elements of the ceremony are being prepared, and the public ceremonials then commence either four or eight days after the announcement and continue for either five or nine days (four or eight sleeps). On the final day there is a culminating performance, usually featuring a dance by the sponsoring kiva or kivas.[9]

A remarkable invention, unique (as far as is known) in the history of astronomical observation, has been lately recognized in the apparently casual arrangement of the three stone slabs shown in Figure 374.[10] Their site is a narrow ledge about thirty feet below the summit of an isolated sandstone butte some 475 feet high, Fajada Butte (Figure 373), which stands guard, as it were, at the southern gate of Chaco Canyon. On June 29, 1977, a week after summer solstice, a young artist in search of petroglyphs, Anna Sofaer, of Washington, D.C., having made her way up to this rocky shelf by way of a narrow chimney inhabited by

372. A sense of timelessness surrounds Walpi (seen here in an Edward S. Curtis photograph), where the Hopi of today still maintain their ancient tradition of harmonizing their daily lives with the cosmos through a ceremonial cycle set in accord with observations of sunrise-sunset horizons.

371. Pueblo Bonito, largest of Chaco Canyon's eight prehistoric towns (pueblos), is **D**-shaped, covers three acres, and contains between 650 and 800 rooms — as well as five large kivas and thirty-three smaller ones — all stacked around a large central plaza, dominated by a great kiva and bisected by a row of rooms. Across its straight-walled front, entrance to the plaza is blocked by a single-story row of rooms forming a continuous wall that rises to perhaps five stories, in the rear, where the ancient town curves into the shadow of the mesa cliff. Large logs from the highland areas (forty-seven miles away) were carried to Pueblo Bonito for use as timbers in its roofing. Ring-dated logs indicate that the construction was begun c. A.D. 919 and was completed by c. A.D. 1085.[24]

Map 31. Enhanced aerial photography of Chaco Canyon and environs has established the existence of a network of straight roadways, many thirty feet wide, interconnecting towns within the canyon and linking it to various outliers up to sixty-five miles away. When cliffs were encountered, the road was not rerouted; instead, stairs or footholds were carved. Since the Chacoans had no wheels and, further, the roads neither accommodate draft animals nor facilitate foot travel, it is surmised that they had some symbolic or ceremonial significance.[25]

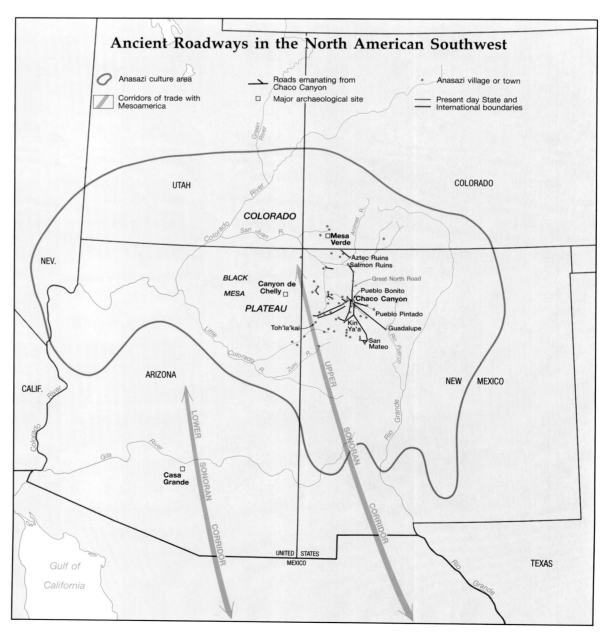

rattlesnakes on the west side of the butte, worked her way around to the southeast face and, having arrived at this arrangement of slabs, looked behind them. It was about eleven in the morning. And what she saw was a daggerlike, vertical shaft of sunlight moving slowly, as though alive, down through the center of a spiral petroglyph. In about twelve minutes the dart of light had passed completely down the spiral and disappeared.

Ms. Sofaer and her colleagues have since assiduously studied the construction, both by day and by night, for the summer and winter solstices, for the spring and fall equinoxes, and by moonlight.[11] They have found that the construction is both a solar and a lunar calendar. On the rock face behind the vertical slabs are engraved two spirals, a larger of nine and a half turns and a smaller, to the left, of two and a quarter. Toward noon on the day of the summer solstice, a dagger of living light passes through the center of the larger spiral while, in a related effect, a small spot of light, hardly noticeable, shines for but two minutes somewhat to the left of the lesser spiral.

Through the following months of July, August, and September, these two beams move steadily, day by day, to the right,

373. On isolated Fajada Butte, at the southern edge of Chaco Canyon, Anna Sofaer in 1977 discovered a unique Anasazi solar-lunar calendar.

until on the day of the fall equinox, September 21, the leftward beam, now much longer than at first, cuts through the center of the lesser spiral. Thereafter, the rightward movement continues, and this second beam ever lengthens. By noon on December 21, the day of the winter solstice, the two darts, now of equal length, perfectly frame the larger spiral, after which the movement, day by day, is from right to left. At noon on March 21, the day of the spring equinox, the positions of the light beams are exactly as they had been September 21, and by the summer solstice the cycle is completed.

As for the moon, the research teams studying these petroglyphs have established that the patterns formed by moonlight shining between the slabs are as clear as those of the day, and when the moon's declination is anywhere between the solar extremes of plus 23.5° and minus 23.5°, the patterns formed are the same as those of the sun. However, in the course of a cycle of nineteen years, the moon's declination, for a part of that time, goes beyond these solar limits. This periodic extreme was not reached again until 1987, when photographs taken on November 8 (the night when the moon attained the most northerly extreme of its nineteen-year excursion) confirmed predictions by Sofaer and others that the rising moon, shining on the verti-

cal slabs, casts a shadow which is tangent to the left edge of the spiral.[12] It has been noticed that the count of the lines of nine and a half turns crossing any diameter is 9 + 10 = 19, and we know that once every nineteen years there is a full moon on winter solstice eve.

The dating suggested for this extraordinary observatory is c. A.D. 950 to 1150, the period of the greatest population density and architectural development of the canyon.[13] Ms. Sofaer and her colleagues have recently undertaken studies of the roadways and architecture of Chaco Canyon that suggest that Chacoan involvement with cosmology also influenced the construction of their Great North Road,[14] which heads from the ceremonial buildings of Chaco Canyon directly north for a distance of some thirty-five miles to Kutz Canyon, an abyss of eroded badlands. The road seems to have been built primarily as an expression of the Pueblo belief in the north as their place of origin, where they emerged from the worlds below and where the spirits of the dead return. Chacoan cosmological involvement is also evidenced in the orientations of individual pueblos, as well as in interpueblo alignments.[15] Moreover, the large Chaco pueblos form a complex regional pattern that displays the Chacoans' sense of harmony between their society and the cosmic order.[16]

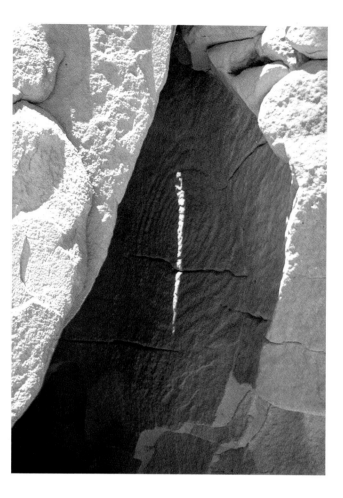

374. The Anasazi calendar utilizes three large rock slabs (**a**) to baffle and focus both the sunlight and the moonlight (**b**), so that significant celestial intervals are marked by a sliver of illumination (**c**) that falls upon and traverses one or another of the spiral petroglyphs on the adjacent cliff face.

375. A seasonal calendar showing the position of the light dagger on the petroglyphs at each equinox and at the summer and winter solstices.

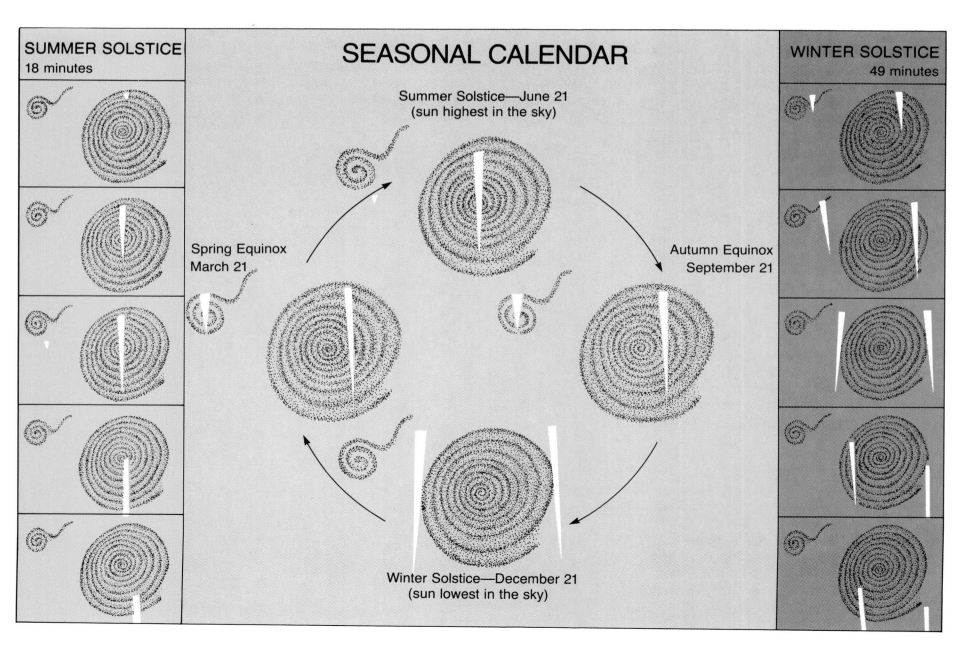

SUMMER SOLSTICE
18 minutes

SEASONAL CALENDAR

WINTER SOLSTICE
49 minutes

Summer Solstice—June 21
(sun highest in the sky)

Spring Equinox
March 21

Autumn Equinox
September 21

Winter Solstice—December 21
(sun lowest in the sky)

The Spirits of Life

The sense of a play of transcendent energies into the round of the seasons and their labors comes to expression with especial clarity in the annual cycle of solar and lunar festivals of the Hopi. Remote on their desert mesas, these have been, of all the Pueblo inheritors of the Anasazi, the least affected by Europeans. Many of the Rio Grande ceremonies (at Santo Domingo, San Ysidro, San Ildefonso, San Felipe, and Santa Ana, for example) were early converted into Christian festivals, their dates determined, consequently, not by signs in the heavens, but by the calendar—for it has already been 400 years since, in 1540, the Spanish entered the Southwest and in 1598 made it their own. In 1629 their priests established a Hopi mission at Awatovi, but the Pueblo Revolt of 1680 ended that adventure and, although Spanish authority was reimposed in 1694, the Awatovi mission was not resumed. Drought, smallpox, and Navaho raids have wrought their devastations; U.S. Indian agents arrived about 1870, and in 1897 a government boarding school was opened, to break traditional patterns and assimilate Indian children into the white community, with trade goods replacing native arts and the Christian myth, native thinking. Yet even today, without fail, every year at the time of the winter solstice, the first kachinas appear from their invisible homes. Others follow in increasing number, until by February all are present in the kivas, generating life anew. And at the turn, then, of the summer solstice, with harvest time drawing near, the kachinas, having served, are bidden farewell in a ceremony of departure, and dismissed to their homes for another year.[17]

The breakup of the Classic Anasazi civilization, of which the Pueblos today are the inheritors, followed two decades of drought at the end of the thirteenth century, 1276 to 1299, just when the Navaho and Apache were moving in. There followed a period known as *Regressive Pueblo* (*Pueblo IV*, c. A.D. 1300 to 1700), which saw a scattering of Anasazi populations southward and eastward. The great Classic centers were abandoned, and new pueblos arose in central New Mexico, along the Rio Grande, and in western New Mexico and Arizona. The languages now spoken are of four unrelated stocks: Uto-Aztecan, Tewa, Zuni, and Keresan. The eastern are patrilineal, the western, generally matrilineal.[18] Clearly, the peoples today are not of one strain. Yet all participate in what appears to have been the fundamental Anasazi heritage of an emergence mythology associated with kiva priesthoods and a ritual art of prayer sticks and altars, sand paintings, wall paintings, symbolically masked per-

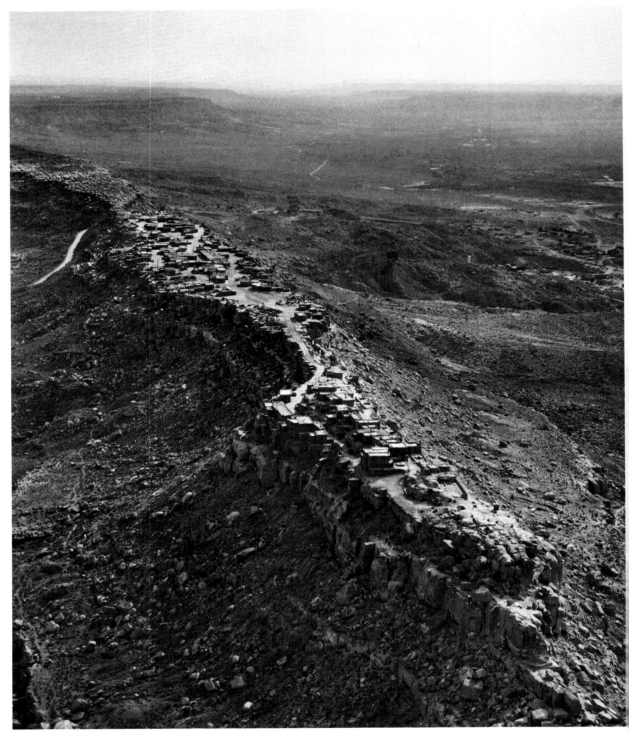

376. First Mesa, with Walpi in the foreground.

377. About the Hopi annual ceremonial cycle (events and times of which may vary at First, Second, and Third Mesas), Barton Wright, a noted authority on the Hopi, comments: "The rich tapestry of Hopi ceremonial life is interwoven by the belief that nature and God are one and that the universe is totally reliable if properly approached. Every object possesses a spirit or animus of its own which can be coerced to intercede for the Hopi in his dual world of the natural and the supernatural. This balanced cosmos is envisioned as the natural world, where objects have mass and solidity, and a preternatural world of spirit beings, substanceless shapes of evanescent mist, the physical world's mirror image. The important forces of this universe are given living form in beings who will, through the performance of ceremonies and rituals by the Hopi people, be obligated to assist them."[26]

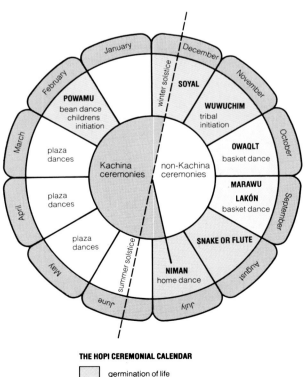

THE HOPI CEREMONIAL CALENDAR

- germination of life
- development of life
- fruition (women's societies)

formers, and a calendar governed by cycles of the sun and moon, as well as a distinctive body of folktale motifs, story plots, and popular mythic characters.

The opening festival of the Hopi ceremonial year is called Wúwuchim (from *wu,* "to germinate," and *chim,* "to manifest").[19] Its season, known as the Initiates' Moon, is the lunar month just prior to that of the winter solstice, and its first major ceremonial is the making of the New Fire in the secrecy of the Two Horn Society's kiva. "Life began with fire. Thus we begin," a Two Horn chief explained to the author Frank Waters,[20] whose *Book of the Hopi* is a compendium of information from thirty-two Hopi elders. "The Two Horn Society's symbol of two horns," states Waters, "designates knowledge of, and remembered experiences in, the three previous worlds as well as in this present Fourth World. Their six directions altar represents the First World at the time of Creation, with colored sands spread to the four primary directions: yellow for the West, blue for the South, red for the East, and white for the North. An ear of dark mixed corn is laid for the Above, and an ear of sweet corn for the Below. The wooden backdrop of the altar is

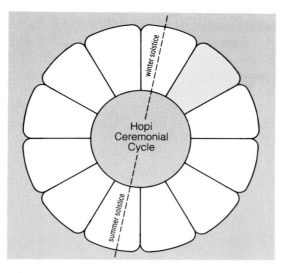

WÚWUCHIM (Tribal Initiation)

During Wúwuchim, a most sacred ceremony that begins (and ends) the annual ritual round, young men are initiated into tribal societies responsible for the performance of the ceremonial cycle, thus insuring the survival, not only of the Hopi's village life, but also of their religious traditions.

379. Enroute from Sichomovi to Walpi, Two-Horned Society members in traditional garb carry flat trays of cornmeal. Photograph by Joseph Mora.

380. Inside the One Horn Kiva at Oraibi, *plaques* (baskets) filled with cornmeal in which *pàhos* (prayer sticks) have been planted. Photograph by H. R. Voth, purportedly the only person ever permitted to photograph inside the kivas.

378. Two-Horned Society "priests" in their kiva at Oraibi, photo by H. R. Voth, a Mennonite clergyman who lived with the Hopi, 1893–1902, and amassed a vast pictorial record of ceremonies.

painted with the corresponding colors of the successive four worlds, and there are symbols of the primary elements: fire, earth, water, air represented by eagle down."[21]

It may surprise the reader to recognize here the same four elements known to the Greeks. They are represented, also, on the Aztec Calendar Stone which was dedicated in 1479, over a decade before the landing of Columbus.

Within the Two Horn kiva the First Fire is struck from flint, caught by native cotton, and kept burning with coal from the nearby desert outcrops, while prayers are addressed to Mácaw, the god of death, but also of the fire of life, which bursts from his domain in volcanic eruptions. The flame is then carried to the other kivas responsible for this festival: the Wuchim, the One Horn, and the Flute.[22]

Of especial interest here is the society of the One Horns. In contrast to the Two Horns, whose knowledge is of the previous worlds as well as of this fourth, the authority of the One Horn kiva is of this earth alone. On its altar the symbolic forms are the figure of a woman holding a child and a six-foot lance with a sharp flint point. The Twin War Gods are its patrons. The elder sits at the northern pole and the younger at the southern of the world axis, keeping the earth properly rotating. They give warning of anything going wrong by sending along the axis vibrations to which the One Horn members are attuned. And on their altar is a little bell of baked clay symbolic of this attunement.

The second major Wúwuchim ceremonial, celebrated on the fifteenth night of the moon and known as the Night of the Washing of the Hair, is of the initiation of young men. It is so profoundly meaningful and holy that for its celebration the pueblo is magically sealed off from the world for that night by a member of the One Horn Society, who, when evening falls, emerges from his kiva in full ceremonial attire and symbolically closes all four roads of access to the mesa by drawing four lines with sacred cornmeal across each. No one dares to cross these. Beasts and birds that do are found dead, they say, the next morning. In the village every door is closed, every window is hung with blankets, the streets are empty, and all is quiet and dark.

The kiva in which the youths are assembled is called the One Way Trail. It is the underworld, from which they are to emerge like the First People. In its floor is the sipapu of emergence from the two lower underworlds, and the ladder upward through the opening in the roof is the One Way Trail. There is a fire in the fire pit, by the dim light of which the young men are watching a priest who is recounting to them the history of mankind's rise through successive worlds. With fire, life began in the first. A tabu was broken; that world was destroyed and mankind mounted to the second, where again a tabu was broken and a perilous ascent made to this third world of the kiva, where the initiates are now assembled.

His narrative concluded, the priest partly covers the fire pit with a flat rock, so that there is only a faint red glow, when down the ladder, dimly appearing as though from the sipapu, members of the other kivas arrive, ceremonially robed and with large white four-pointed stars over their faces. They gather and stand around the dim fire pit, sounding a low hum and a strange blowing of breath. Both the pitch and the volume slowly rise as, down the ladder, a silent, white-robed, lone figure descends with an immense star over its face. "I am the Beginning and the End," this apparition declares, then ascends as quietly as it came.

The visitants now become agitated and noisy. The flat rock is shoved completely over the fire pit and the kiva is absolutely dark. A yell sounds and the company, in wild confusion, throwing off its stars and robes, rushes naked for the ladder, to escape before this world, too, is destroyed. The rungs extend to each side beyond the ladder poles, so that two or three can climb at a time, the terrified initiates among them, contending for the exit. On emerging, each is drenched with a bucket of water and greeted by the village chief, called Father of the People. The Crier Chief is there as well, and a member of the Coyote clan, called Guardian of the People, whose function it is to "close the doors." And when all have come out, the Father calls down into the dark hole of the empty kiva, ordering anyone there remaining to come up.

Wet and naked as newborn babes, the initiates are gathered to a nearby home, where their hair is washed in nine successive bowls of yucca suds, which represent (as Frank Waters was told) the seven stages of the Road of Life (three worlds already passed, this the fourth, and three to come) plus the realm of Sótuknang (the god governor of the universe, creator of all ceremony) and that of Taiowa (the Creator, whose light blazes in the sun).[23]

The final event of Wúwuchim is a public dance by the associated kivas, whose members appear in the village in two long parallel lines. Between them is the drummer, and on the outside the asperger with his bowl of water and eagle feather who sprinkles each dancer. It is noticed that the four leading Two Horns are maintaining a rhythm out of accord with the rest. With their knowledge of previous worlds, they are keeping time to an unheard rhythm, unbroken by time and space. The dance threads through the village four times, and on the fifth appearance all but the four leading Two Horns are naked save for breechcloths—in anticipation of a Bath Ceremony now administered by the women, who all come running to pour buckets of cold water (and not all of it clean, by any means)[24] over everyone but the Two Horns, taunting the dancers and being taunted in turn, with all terminating in a roughhouse around the kivas.

Finally, out of their kivas come the One Horn members, striding without voice to the brittle clatter of the small clay bells in their hands. They circumambulate the pueblo countersunwise, signifying an earthly, in contrast to the heavenly, sunwise round. The sun is now setting. A few minutes later the Two Horns make the same circuit, and so the festival ends.[25]

381. Four priests (Tawȧkwaptiwa in the lead), carrying cornmeal in *plaques*, prepare to follow Mastop Kachina to the Flute Spring, where the Soyál Chief will present him with a special *páho* before he departs to the west. This simple sequence of events begins Soyál, a ceremony of world renewal celebrated during winter solstice.

Soyál, the winter solstice festival, is announced already the next day by the appearance on the desert, coming from the east, of a kachina in turquoise helmet and white robe, staggering like a child learning to walk. This is Soyál Kachina, the first kachina of the year, signifying life reborn and to be followed next day by a terrifying figure, Mastop Kachina, whose black attire and mask, showing white stars on each cheek, tell of the interstellar distances from which he has arrived. He is the unmitigated power of male energy. (Compare his Mandan counterpart, described by Catlin, I.2:228.) Entering the village, he grabs a married woman from the crowd and simulates copulation, then descends into the Soyál kiva and, after bestowing there his blessings for the coming year, departs westward to his shrine at the bottom of the cliffs.[26]

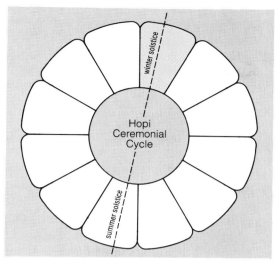

SOYÁL

384. During Soyál, seed corn (carried here by Kachina Mana) is sanctified to increase its yield, the village is ritually cleansed of all misfortune, and the sun is turned back from its southern course so that it might come again to the Hopi.[27]

The term *kachina*, as understood today, has four references, the last three of which are inflections of the first: (1) a personified charge of the energy of life, (2) a ceremonial costume and mask representing such a personification, (3) a ceremonial celebrant wearing such a costume and mask, and (4) a doll representing the personification, fashioned originally for the instruction of children, now also as an *objêt-d'art*, for pleasure, or for sale to tourists, museums, or collectors.

The holy season, which in the West is a celebration of the birth of the world savior, is on the Hopi mesas welcomed chiefly within the kivas with symbolic rites, "establishing," as they say, "life anew for all the world."[27] Its season is of the full moon around the moment "when the sun is turned back," which is a conjunction (as we have seen, page 279) that occurs once

382. Barton Wright's painting of Soyál Kachina, the first kachina to appear each year.

383. Mastop Kachina, the second to appear, c. 6⅛" tall, made of pine, paint, and owl feathers.

every nineteen years. There are no spectacular public dances. Prayers are addressed to the sun, who is the deity of this festival, and prayer sticks placed before an altar six miles to the east. Formerly, every four years, a virgin (usually of the Soyál chief's family) was sacrificed at this season. Today, the Hawk Maiden, ceremonially attired, simply sits for a time in the Soyál kiva, watching rituals for the germination of crops. After sixteen days of such rites, the festival is concluded with a four-day rabbit hunt, followed by a feast and a ceremony of blessing.[28]

Through the following two lunar months kachinas arrive in increasing number, both to empower the seeds now being planted and to instruct and discipline children in the knowledge of the laws of their own nature. Kachinas do not visit the Rio Grande pueblos, where there is sufficient water for crops. The only other favored

a

385. Joseph Mora's paintings of some of the kachinas appearing during Powamu, when children of proper age are initiated into the mysteries of the kachinas, whose cooperation the Hopi seek during the coming growing season: (**a**) Wupamo, who is a guard; (**b**) Owangazrozro, an ogre clown, among whose functions is that of inter-kiva messenger; (**c**) Tumas (Crow Mother), who leads both the Powamu procession and the children's initiation; (**d**) Powamu, who performs the dance during which the kachina dancers are shown to be men; and (**e**) Avachhoya, the distinctively costumed Speckled Corn Kachina.

pueblo is Zuni, but the Hopi say that since these spirits emerged from the underworld with themselves, those that the people of Zuni know must have been originally of the Hopi. They all live, it is said, to the west, on the San Francisco Peaks, and their appearances at Oraibi, Walpi, and the other Hopi-mesa villages are to ensure the timely occurrences of the rains which in those parts are the *sine qua non* of life.

b

e

d

c

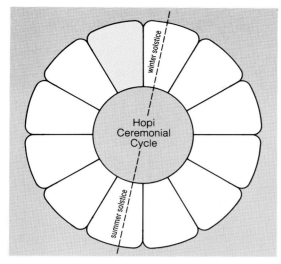

PAMURTI

At the start of the festival of Powamu, during the lunar month (mid-January to February) of the full presence in the pueblos of the kachinas of that year, beans are planted in the kivas at the first appearance of the new crescent moon. They are diligently watered, ritually smoked over, and sprinkled with sacred meal, so that by the eighth day the first sprouts have appeared. In the kivas, meanwhile, and in public, there has been ceremonial dancing: as many as two hundred kachinas together appearing on some of these occasions, praying, singing, and dancing, both to help the corn, beans, and other crops to grow, and to confirm the Hopi themselves in their faith in the power of the life-force represented in these masks to bring health and beauty to their lives.

Children between six and ten are being at this time initiated into their own kachina societies. They are given little gifts by the masked dancers. But there also are brief but painful whipping rites to which they are subjected, while for those who are disobedient, there are warnings of monstrous Scare Kachinas, for whom they had better watch out.

By the time this festival is approaching its end, the bean sprouts in the kivas have grown and been cut. Tied into small bun-

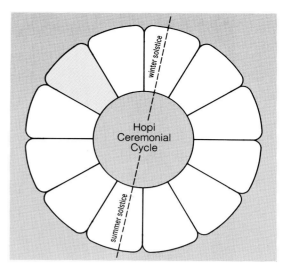

POWAMU (Bean Dance)

dles, they are carried by kachinas to all the homes in the pueblo, together with presents for the children: kachina dolls and plaques tied with bean sprouts for the girls, and for the boys, moccasins and painted bows and rattles. A final, grandiose procession in the village plaza of all the kachinas and initiates brings the whole occasion to a climax with singing, dancing, and various kachina appearances. Then a Kachina Father cries out for all the mothers to cover the eyes of their uninitiated children, one of the kachinas yanks off his mask, and they all disappear into the kivas. So the festival ends. The bean plants, which have been blessed, are carried to various shrines and then home, for a concluding feast.[29]

386. Performed during Pamurti (Jan. to early Feb.) are so-called social dances; many, such as this Buffalo Dance, have religious overtones.

387. An 1893 assembly of kachinas of Powamu.

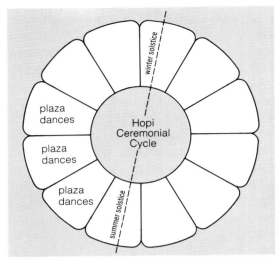

PLAZA DANCES

In the spring and early summer the Hopi hold performances of the Plaza Dances: Line Dances, in which all kachinas are the same (as in **388**, below, where Ota line dancers are accompanied by the White-Faced Kachina Girl [Alo Mana] and a side dancer), and Mixed Dances that involve a variety of kachinas, all differently masked and costumed. Now, regardless of outward appearances or what they might otherwise represent, all kachinas are believed to be rain-bringing supernaturals and, although each offers its own special blessing, their dances now bring to the mesa the moistures of the underworld. Prominent during the Plaza Dances are Hopi clowns, both the "Mudheads" (Koyemsi Kachinas, see **389**) and the striped Hano Clowns (Koshari Kachinas, **390**).[28]

389

390

388

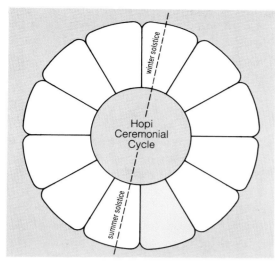

NIMAN (Home Dance)

The ceremony of departure at the time of the summer solstice, when the crops have matured and the kachinas' work is done, is called Niman Kachina (Home Dance) and assigned to the lunar month Niman-muya (Home-going Moon). Earlier in the spring, a number of eagles' nests will have been identified in the sides of nearby cliffs and marked with prayer sticks, inviting the great birds to come willingly to the villages to be sacrificed after this ceremony. The hunters, then, either lower themselves on ropes or climb by perilous ledges to remove from the nests the birds too young to fly (in former years, sometimes as many, they say, as twenty-five), which then are brought with great honor to the village and tied by the feet to eagle platforms on the rooftops.

A second preliminary to the celebration of this season is the pilgrimage by three selected men for the gathering of spruce.

They carry special male and female prayer sticks some forty miles northeastward to Black Mesa and into a long, desolate canyon, where there is a cave at the top of a rocky, spruce-and-pine-covered ridge, and within the cave, a sacred pool that is known as Kisiwu (Spring in the Shadows). The cave is approached with ritualized precautions. The prayer sticks are planted, prayers are recited, and next morning, to a selected spruce tree the leader prays: "O Spruce Tree, we have come for your leaves, to be used for our clothes, so come with us!" They bless the tree, leave a prayer stick before it, and without touching it, turn to other trees and gather from them their branches, for the spruce tree is thought to have a special magnetic power that draws to it the rainclouds. As John Lansa of the Badger Clan, Oraibi, who had performed the pilgrimage twelve times, explained to Frank Waters: "It is the spirits of the spruce, the clouds, and the rain who give this life to us, you understand. So we offer our prayers again to the male and female branches, and we invite all the spirits to our village to take part in the ceremony."[30]

At dawn on the morning of the Home-going Dance, two fresh spruce trees, a male and a female, are standing in the otherwise empty plaza. From a nearby housetop a tethered eagle screams, and the kachinas enter in single file, led by the Powamu Chief, who is unmasked, wearing an embroidered kilt and a single eagle feather. The Kachina Father and his assistant follow, with some thirty Hemis Kachinas (Far-away Kachinas, a reference to the distant realm from which these presences have come and to which they are now to return) and eight or more Kachina-manas (Kachina Mothers) behind. Their bodies are black and their masks are yellow on the left side and blue on the right, with blue cloud-terrace crowns rising high above, tufted with heads of wild wheat and eagle feathers. Deer-hoof and turtle-shell rattles adorn their right legs, straps of bells their left. Spruce branches hang from their belts; spruce twigs are stuck in their arm bands; in the left hand each carries a feather and a twig of spruce, in the right a rattle; and there is a ruff of spruce around the throat. In contrast, the face masks of the Kachina Mothers are orange. Each wears the classic squash-blossom hair whorls of the Hopi unmarried maiden, a black manta, a red and white blanket, and white deerskin boots. Each carries, besides a pumpkin shell, a notched stick and the scapula bone of a sheep or deer, with which to accompany the music.

"After entering the plaza, they stand silently," states Waters, "the *kachinas* in a long line, the *kachina-manas* behind them. The Powamu Chief sprinkles each with cornmeal from a sack worn on his breast. The Kachina Father encourages them with talk. Then suddenly the leader of the *kachinas*, standing in the middle of the line, shakes his rattle. The powerful legs lift and stamp; the low, strong voices break into song—a day-long dance and song, beautiful and compelling, but with infinite variations in which are found its deepest meanings."[31]

391. In preparation for Niman, early in the spring, the Hopi clans go to special eagle-hunting grounds (each has its own), where, with proper ceremony, they remove from nests fledglings that they bring with great honor back to the village, where they are tied by their feet to rooftop platforms. There the eaglets remain and flourish, until the Niman ends, and they are with ceremonial reverence "sent home."

392. At first light, into the plaza file the Hemis Kachinas, spruce-adorned and bearing children's gifts (here, cattails), and the Home Dance begins.

The line is along the north side of the plaza. Dancing, it moves westward, curves southward, and breaks before a circle is formed, "just as the pure pattern of life was broken," Waters states, "and the First World destroyed." The line moves to the west side and again curves and breaks, signifying the dissolution of the Second World. All move, then, to the south side, and again the pattern breaks, in the way of the World before this. But there is no fourth position taken, because in this Fourth World we do not yet know whether its circle is to be broken or formed.[32]

The cosmological pattern of three with a fourth implied and open is suggested, also, by the day's program of three appearances of the dancers, at sunrise, mid-morning, and late afternoon until sunset. Armloads of significant gifts are again distributed to the children. At the closing dance the year's brides attend, attired in their wedding robes. And when it ends, the Kachina Father delivers a word of farewell:

"It is now time for you to go home. Take with you our humble prayer, not only for our people and people everywhere, but for all the animal kingdom, the birds and insects, and the growing things that make our world a green carpet. Take our message to the four corners of the world, that all life may receive renewal by having moisture. I am happy that I have done my small part in caring for you this day. May you go on your way with happy hearts and grateful thoughts."

The leader of the kachinas shakes his rattle to show that the message is accepted and will be delivered. The spectators step forward to pluck twigs of spruce from the kachinas to carry home, and separate to let them file from the plaza and away. The two spruce trees are carried from the plaza. At the same time, as Waters tells, "the great proud birds waiting on their platforms are 'sent home' with the kachinas. No blood is shed during their sacrifice. The clan leaders ascend to the housetop platforms, wrap a blanket around the head of each and as gently as possible snuff out its life."[33]

It is supposed that the kachinas in their distant world experience winter and spring during our summer and fall, so that on returning home they will again be engaged in ceremonials. Here on earth, meanwhile, it is important to bring a final burst of rain, so that the flooded washes will deposit fresh soil for new crops. And in this function the famous Hopi Snake-Antelope Ceremony alternates from year to year with a Flute Ceremony, during the lunar month known as the Big Feast Moon (Nashanmuya) of late August.

393. In this 1901 photograph taken at the Hopi village of Shungopovi, Hemis Kachinas dance the farewell ceremony that "sends the spirits back to their various homes and encourages them to continue to send their benefits to the Hopi although they will not return again till December."[29] As the sun sets, they file silently westward, out of the plaza. No one follows. When the kachinas arrive at Kachinki (Kachina House), their cliff-edge shrine, there is a disrobing and unmasking ceremony. Then, members once again of the human community, they return to the village. The next day, the Powamu Chief leads the final *tangave* (religious plan act), the closing of the kivas.

394. Simultaneously, clan leaders reverently enfold the eagles in blankets and "send them home."

Inside the house, when the eagle's body is cold, its feathers are gathered for ceremonial use, and

the body is ritually "buried, head to the west, with cornmeal, *piki*, tobacco, and prayer feathers."[30]

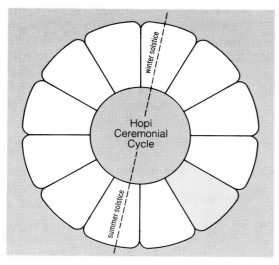

ANTELOPE-SNAKE/FLUTE DANCES

Preparations for the Snake Dance commence in the kivas of the Antelope and Snake societies with the usual preparation of prayer sticks, fasting, and setting up of altars. The Snake Society's altar carries the images of two Snake Maidens. That of the Antelope Society—set up on a sand painting of the four directional colors with at each corner a small cone of sand (called a cloud mountain) into which a hawk feather is stuck—represents the world as formed by earth, air, water, plant life, and mankind. These preparations require eleven

days, after which the Snake members set out on their four-day task of searching the desert for rattlesnakes, sidewinders, gopher snakes, bull snakes, and the rest, coming back with some fifty or sixty.

Meanwhile, in the Antelope kiva there has been ritually consummated a symbolic *hieros gamos* ("sacred marriage"). A young virgin already initiated into the women's Snake Society—her forehead, chin, and throat painted white, the rest of her face painted black; her hair loose, with a small eagle-down feather attached to it; and wearing the customary woman's black manta and a red and white cape, to which there have been added a Snake Dancer's kirtle and a necklace of turquoise and shell—is conducted by the Snake chief into the Antelope Society's kiva, where, in the role of Snake Maiden, she is the living counterpart of the two Snake Maiden images on the altar of the Snake kiva. In her hands she carries an earthen jar containing prayer sticks, corn, melon, squash, and bean vines. And she is greeted in the kiva by the Antelope chief and the Antelope Youth, a young man in whose hands are an Antelope fetish and a snake. His hair, too, is loose, with a small downy feather tied in front. And his chin, too, is painted white. He is wearing a white cere-

monial kirtle, and his body is ash grey, but with white zigzag lines drawn on the torso, arms, and legs.

The Snake Maiden is seated on the south side of the Antelope kiva's symbolic altar, and the Antelope Youth on the north. Between the altar and the fire pit is an earthen bowl full of yucca suds, and before the altar, a woven plaque full of many kinds of seed. The maiden and the youth are conducted by their chiefs to the bowl, and there a full wedding ceremony is performed, after which the Snake chief washes the maiden's hair in the yucca suds, and the Antelope chief the youth's. The two chiefs exchange places and the Snake Maiden's hair is washed by the Antelope chief, the Antelope Youth's by the Snake chief, following which exchange, the wet locks of the couple are braided together and the two conducted to the northern bench, where the maiden is seated on the plaque of seeds that the Antelope chief has just placed there. It is midnight. Through the ladder-opening in the

395. Late in the afternoon on the final day of the Snake-Antelope Ceremony, as Antelope Dancers (painted ash-gray) await beside the cottonwood kisi filled with snakes, the Snake Dancers enter the plaza and begin their climactic circling dance.

kiva roof the bright stars of Orion's Belt can be seen. A chanting begins, which drones on until the same stars are at the western horizon. Trying not to fall asleep, the Antelope Youth and Snake Maiden remain seated together until the chanting stops, when they are blessed, separated, and taken by their guardians to their separate homes.

The ritual obviously is of the mystery of the two that are spiritually one though physically two, as symbolized in the mythological image of the androgyne. This is an image known, not only to most planting-culture mythologies, but also to every mystical tradition of the world (see I.2:142, Map 33). In the context of a planting society's interests, the function of a ritual reestablishing this image is to reactivate, through what James G. Frazer called "imitative sympathetic magic,"[34] the energies of what is conceived to be the creative ground of all temporal conditions. In the context of a mystical tradition where the same image is proposed as a theme for contemplation, its function is to release the mind from the bondage of the body by uniting it with an image transcendent of temporal conditions. Obviously, the two functions are related. And by analogy, of course, the biological act of a male and female in the union out of which a new life is born gives evidence beyond question of the life-producing power of this mystery.

Now, for a planting culture, which is necessarily committed—in contrast to its hunting-and-gathering neighbors—rather to generating life than to killing and collecting, this mystery of the two that are one and the one that makes two and the one-plus-one that makes three, is of unrelent-

ing importance. Moreover, since there is everywhere a tendency for the practical, magical aspect and the inward, mystical aspect to run together, we find—as among the Hopi, for example—disciplines of fasting and spiritual exaltation (in the kivas) integrally associated with the conduct of the public ceremonials. In fact, according to native belief, it is the set of the mind of the performers, no less than the patterns of their rites, that determines the results.

A second matter of essential concern is the precise coordination of the natural and

396. Each dancer carrying a snake (in his teeth, its body symbolically aligned with his own) is guided around the dance ground by a partner (a so-called hugger), who all the while strokes the snake with his eagle-feather snake whip.

ritual orders, and this involves not only attention to the intermeshing of the lunar, solar, and various stellar cycles, but also associated interpretations of the flora and fauna of the neighborhood. In the case, for example, of this Hopi marriage in the Antelope kiva of the Snake Maiden to the Antelope Youth, the snake, as Waters points out, which dwells deep in the earth out of which mankind originated, is equated with the lowest of man's psychological centers, that associated with the generative organs, whereas the antelope is associated with the highest center in man; for "its horn," as he tells, "is located at the top or crown of the head, the *kópavi*, which in man is the place of coming in and going out of life, the 'open door' through which he spiritually communicates with his Creator."[35] Also: "Running Antelopes make the sound of thunder whose vibration stimulates the clouds to come out of their shrines."[36] The clouds come out of their shrines to send rain; the Serpent Maiden, out of her kiva, to incubate the seeds of life! And in both instances it is the antelope that functions as the summoner, the awakener, of the life-bearer. The antelope here is male and associated with the head and consciousness; the serpent is female and associated with the generative energy of life. The ritual of her

397. When every snake has been danced, they are placed in a circle of cornmeal, and the Dancers quickly gather up handfuls to take back to the desert, where they are released to carry a message of renewal to the four corners of the earth.

marriage is an appeal, as it were, to the energies of life to come out, as she has come, from their unawakened virginal retreat.

The serpent is associated also, it appears, with the moon, which sheds its shadow to be born again, as the serpent its skin, to be born again. And the antelope, then, as of the head and consciousness, is symbolically an agent of the sun. The marriage, accordingly, is of the solar and lunar energies, which, though apparently two are in fact one, as in the Navaho version of the legend of the twin heroes, where, although the elder was begotten of the Sun and the younger of the Moon, Where the Two Came to Their Father was the house of the Sun.

Waters has noticed what is indeed a remarkable likeness of this Hopi system of symbols to that of India's Kundalini Yoga (see pages 378–379),[37] where the energy of life—all life—is symbolized as female, a female serpent coiled upon itself in a spiral of three-and-a-half turns and lying asleep, not only deep within the earth, but also, in the same way, deep within the lowest energy center of the body. The aim of the yoga is to wake this Serpent Maiden, coiled in upon herself, and bring her up the spine to full consciousness, both of herself and of the spiritual nature of all things. She is awakened by the sound of the energy of the light of consciousness (the sound of the syllable "om"), which is brought to her first

on the rhythm of the breath, but fully heard only when she has uncoiled and ascended to the center of the heart, whose animal symbol (remarkably) is the antelope— swift as the wind and thus, the vehicle of the wind, the breath (Sanskrit, *prana*; Latin, *spiritus*), the spirit. The Serpent Maiden, Kundalini, has thus left three worlds to rise to this spiritual center: the first, of her home base; the second, at the level of the genitals (sex); the third at the level of the navel (will to power, aggression), and this the fourth world, where, as the Wúwuchim initiates within the kiva heard, there is the "sounding of a low hum and a strange blowing of breath," the sound of the syllable "om." Awakened, the Serpent Maiden will now pass on along the One Way Trail of this fourth world, through three more, to the crown of the head, the seventh ($3\frac{1}{2} + 3\frac{1}{2} = 7$), as the initiates at the Washing of the Hair learned of three worlds already passed, this fourth, and three to come.

The high moment of the Snake Dance arrives on the sixteenth day of the festival, when the performers, one by one, step up to the kisi (the evergreen shelter housing the tangle of gathered snakes) and, stooping low, straighten up with a snake between the teeth, caught and held just back of its head. With the dancer's left hand the upper part of the snake's body is held level with the heart, and with the right hand the lower length of the reptile, level with the waist. The illustration of the idea of the Kundalini could hardly be improved: the serpent energy to be uncoiled from its place of rest in the lower pelvic centers (position of the right hand and lower length of the serpent), by virtue of an awakening at the center of the heart (left hand and upper body of the serpent), leading to the knowledge of a higher order of life and consciousness in the centers of the head, the inner eye and the opening at the crown (position of the serpent's head by the head of the dancer). Also relevant to this reading of the Hopi rite is the Hindu idea of two secondary nerves running alongside and crossing to right and left of the central

spinal trail up which the Kundalini is to rise. One is known as *ida* and carries lunar energy; the other, as *pingala* and carries solar energy. Before the Kundalini can be waked and brought up the central way of the *susumna*, the energies of these two have to be brought together and recognized as of one transcendent source, as in the mystic marriage in the Antelope kiva of the Serpent Maiden and Antelope Youth before, in the dance, the serpents are lifted and carried in the dancers' mouths.

Next day the snakes are returned to their desert, to carry back to their hidden homes the good tidings of the ceremonially confirmed accord of the Hopi with the natural order.

On alternate years, the ceremonial celebrated in this place is, in its public phase, a simple enactment of the Emergence. Known as the Flute Ceremony and conducted by the Blue Flute and Gray Flute societies (*ida* and *pingala*?), the members gather at Flute Springs at noon on the sixteenth day of the moon and come in a winding procession up the mesa into the village. Leading all the way are two small girls who, at intervals, toss little rings upon cornmeal lines drawn on the ground. In the plaza the people sing to the music of the flute and then simply disperse.[38]

Finally, there follow the three terminating festivals of the whole ceremonial round—Lakón, Márawu, and Owaqlt— performed by the women's societies.

398. Watercolor of a Snake Priest—not a kachina; rather, member of a Hopi warrior society—by Joseph Mora, who, living with the Hopi from 1904 to 1906, labored to document accurately (in authentically detailed paintings and in several series of sequential photographs) the rich tapestry of ceremonial life that he feared would soon disappear.

399. The Flute chief carries *paho* and cornmeal to the Flute Spring during the Flute Ceremony. Frank Water notes: "No Hopi ritual is as simple and mystifying to the casual visitor as that portion of the Flute ceremony he is allowed to witness. It is simply a procession winding up the mesa and into the village, headed by two small girls who periodically toss little rings upon cornmeal lines painted on the ground. In the plaza the people sing to the music of a flute, then silently disperse. That is all. Yet this simple ceremony embodies in song and symbolism the whole pattern of man's Emergence to the present world."[31]

WOMEN'S SOCIETY DANCES

400. During the afternoon public ceremony, the Lakón Manas, carrying baskets, form a great circle. Chanting,

Lakón, of which the meaning of the name has been lost, is celebrated in two sessions. The first is at corn-planting time in late May and early June, when four women and the Lakón chief (a man) enter the kiva for eight days of prayer, fasting, and singing, while the chief makes and consecrates prayer feathers. The second session, also of eight days, begins on the day in late September when the sun is seen to rise over a point between Oraibi and Hoteville, known as Where Two Rocks Lean on One Another. For four days the members pray, sing, and eat no salt or meat. On the seventh night, when the Lakón chief, who is watching the sky, sees the Pleiades rise, he enters the kiva, where the women are singing. From their altar they take up lightning sticks, cloud sticks, prayer feathers, and corn (leaving only the sand painting on the floor), elevate these four times ceremonially, and after replacing them, file from the kiva. The Pleiades are now at the western horizon, and daybreak is near. The women, each holding in one hand cornmeal and in the other hand three prayer feathers, follow a trail along the mesa top, pausing for prayer at certain shrines, then proceed down the rocky face of the cliff to a huge volcanic boulder whose top is covered with small brown nodules surrounded by curious whorls, which are taken to represent the embryo within the fetal membranes of the womb. The maiden members rub their hands over these whorls, offerings are left at a shrine below the boulder, and the company files up the cliff to prepare for the public ceremony.

Four maidens are chosen to represent the cardinal directions. With their feet and faces powdered yellow and wearing cloud headdresses of eagle feathers and the feathers of tropical birds, each receives four ears of corn appropriately colored: yellow for the Maiden of the West, blue for the Maiden of the South, red for the Maiden of the East, and white for the Maiden of the North. The others of the kiva have formed a circle in the plaza, and when the four appear a cloud design is drawn with corn-

401. A Joseph Mora watercolor of a Lakón Mana.

they raise them—first to one breast, then to the other—then lower them to their groins.

meal on the ground before them. In its center is placed a small ring of cornhusks, at which each in turn tosses her ears of corn. This they do four times, after which they are led into and around the singing circle and stationed at their cardinal points. The Maiden of the West rolls the cornhusk ring toward the east and quickly throws her corn at it. The remaining three follow in sequence, and then joining the other women in song, they fling plaques and baskets over the singers' heads—west, south, east, and north—as gifts to the crowd.[39]

Márawu—the word means Leg Decoration—follows in September and October. The first four days are spent in the kiva by the four leaders, two of which are men, fashioning prayer sticks, fasting, and praying. On the fifth day, the other members come in, and on the seventh a ritual is performed before the altar of specially blessed sand supporting eagle feathers alternating with a number of wooden figures and painted slabs (representing Márawu women and their guardian spirits, as well as clouds, rain, and corn of the four directions). Corn of the colors of the four directions is laid upon the altar, and in the center is a bowl of water that has been blessed. The ritual is of songs recapitulating the story of world creation: first the earth, then the vegetation, animals, and man, at the end of each of which stages the world is blessed. Dawn now is showing through the ladder opening, at which time the Village Chief and Crier Chief come down into the kiva and announce: "I want all of you to come out of this kiva. We must all come to the light." Holding hands in a long chain they climb, unable to touch the ladder except with their feet and so with difficulty and slowly, to simulate the difficulties of mankind's emergence to the Fourth World. They go to the east to greet the sun and then return to prepare in the kiva for their public appearance.

All wash their hair and dress in the usual black manta and red and white ceremonial cape, except three young virgins selected to be the Márawu Maidens. One is to be the Caller, to sing more loudly than the others, directing the changes of the songs. She wears eagle feathers in her hair, and each cheek is painted with a brown stripe down from the eye. In her left hand she carries a long rod with two eagle feathers on the top and a long streamer of horsehair, dyed red; and on her right wrist, a fox pelt that hangs to her ankles. Each of the other two selected maidens wears part of a decorated wedding dress that falls below the hips and

a kirtle that reaches to the knees. Two circles, like garters, are drawn, one high on the thigh, the other just above the knee, from which four vertical stripes, front, back, and sides, are marked down the legs. (From this, the name of the ceremony.) On their heads are fastened four upright blue sticks joined at the top with eagle feathers. Down feathers are bunched at the back of the head, and each cheek is painted, like the Caller's cheeks, with a brown stripe from the eye.

The woman leader then conducts the company out of the kiva to the plaza, where they form a circle with an opening to the east. The three Márawu Maidens follow, each carrying a small hoop or ring made of cattails, which they toss onto lines of cornmeal drawn on the ground before them by one of the two male leaders. Having tossed the rings, they throw at them their feathered sticks. This they do four times. On arriving in the circle, they are given bowls of water and of sweet cornmeal, of which each kneads two rolls of dough. One goes to the west and then to the south, throwing a roll each time over the circle of singing women to the men outside, who try to catch it. The second maid

goes tossing to the east and then the north; the older women, meanwhile, dancing and singing, throw gifts of food to the spectators. And at intervals throughout the day this pretty little game is repeated.

Owaqlt, meaning Melons on the Vine, is the last and least important of the women's ceremonies. It may be given any time between Márawu and Wúwuchim and is referred to, commonly, as the Basket Dance. Its altar, kiva rituals, and public dance repeat, essentially, the forms of Márawu, except that its maidens wear a horn on the right side of the head and a squash blossom whorl on the left, and throw to the bystanders, not food to eat, but baskets.[40]

And so, it is with the bountiful, playful joy and generosity of the women's ceremonials that the annual cycle is carried on from harvest time to Wúwuchim. The mood and flavor throughout is erotic, of maidenhood and motherhood, their charm and readiness to bear, yield, and provide for the future. And with that the cycle rolls to another round.

402. Singing, the Lakón Manas shield their faces with the beautifully woven food baskets that have given to the Lakón Ceremony the name by which it is popularly known: the Basket Dance.

The Land and Fruit of Eternal Life

Dwelling in the highlands of Nayarit, just below the Gran Chichimeca, exactly at the entrance to the Lower Sonoran corridor (Map 26), where in pre-Conquest times there were settlements from the coast to the Sierra,[41] the Huichols are the inheritors of a substantial Mesoamerican tradition. The whole rich area was almost completely destroyed, as Carl Sauer and D. D. Brand report of its archaeological remains, "because it was overrun in 1530 and 1531 by about as hard a gang of killers as Spain let loose anywhere in the New World and because in those days there was no stay upon the killing propensities of conquerors."[42] Their introduced diseases did the rest, so that, as Betty Bell reports of Nayarit, Jalisco, and Colima: "Within a few years of the Spanish conquest the Indian population had declined sharply.... Moreover, many Indians abandoned their settlements and fled into the mountains of northern and eastern Jalisco, and into the Sierra de Nayarit. These areas remained unsubjugated for many years after the conquest."[43] Such is the area in which the Huichols now dwell.

They are of the Uto-Aztecan linguistic stock, related in speech to the Hopi, Toltecs, and Aztecs, and thus of the Gran Chichimeca in origin. Their legendary place of emergence, *Wirikuta,* is the desert between the Rio Grande and San Luis Potosí, where grows the plant of eternal life, *hikuri,* the desert-cactus peyote. Annually, pilgrimages are undertaken by small parties under the leadership of a shaman (*mara'akame*) to harvest this fruit of the knowledge of immortal being. It is a journey of some three-hundred miles each way, along a route punctuated by holy sites, a passage to be accomplished during the dry season between the harvest festivals of October and rain ceremonies of February. In December 1966, two anthropologists, Peter Furst and Barbara Myerhoff, joined such a party under the conduct of Ramón Medina Silva, who besides being a *mara'akame,* was an artist (creating yarn paintings) and

Map 32.

Huichol Lands

- [filled] Present-day range of the Huichol
- [open] Legendary ancestral home of the Huichol
- [shaded] Probable areas and tribes of origin of the Huichol
- – – – Southern boundary of the Gran Chichimeca
- → Probable routes and directions of convergence
- ----- Annual present-day pilgrimage to "Wirikuta" (300 miles)
- ■ Archaeological sites
- ● Present-day Huichol sites and communities
- ● Present-day cities

a musician (playing the fiddle). The preferred manner of travel would have been to walk; but with all the photographic and recording gear a compromise was granted, namely, transportation by camper to the edge of Wirikuta. Each member of the party had an established place in the vehicle, and the decorated antlers symbolic of *Kauyumari*—the Sacred Deer Person, who is identical with the hallucinogenic cactus plant itself—were attached in front to the foremost part of the camper.

The party gathered at Ramón's little rancho and there engaged for three days in last-minute preparations. "Every *peyotero* works for weeks," states Furst, "to prepare his or her own prayer objects, ceremonial arrows, and decorated votive gourds, or even a miniature version of the large folk-art yarn paintings."[44] While the others sewed, strung beads, adorned hats, and so on, Ramón occupied himself preparing Kauyumari's antlers, wrapping them with colored yarn, and attaching ceremonial arrows along with eagle and hawk feathers hanging freely to blow in the wind; every now and then he put his hands to his mouth to make the call, or whistle, of the deer.[45]

To return to Wirikuta, all had to become gods, and on concluding his preparations, Ramón revealed the names he had dreamed for them. He would himself be Grandfather Fire, who in the beginning raised the heavens by placing four great trees in the corners of the world. His paternal uncle, Carlos, who had already gone on pilgrimage eight times, would be Our Father Sun, and another relative, Sebastián, who in his youth had failed in his aspiration to become a shaman and now was afraid of becoming a sorcerer, would be Deer Snarer, patron of the deer hunt. Francisco, whose age was variously given as between 70 and 110, would be Our Great-Grandfather; Lupe, Ramón's wife, Our Mother Maize; Victoria, her niece, Our Mother of the Children; and Pablo, married to Carlos's daughter, Elder Brother Deer Tail. In a sense, this hunting god, Deer Tail, and the Sacred Deer Person, Kauyumari, are aspects of a single power: that represented as at once the hunter and the hunted in the dancing Animal Master of the Paleolithic cave, Les Trois Frères.[46] Barbara Myerhoff, finally, was identified with the deity Eyebrow of the Peyote (a fuzz in the center of each peyote which senses the ritual condition of the seeker), and Peter Furst, as driver of the camper, became the Arrow That Guard Us.

In conclusion, a sort of Last Supper was served of water and tortillas, before, during, and after which everyone prayed, offering water and bits of tortilla to the quarters and to Grandfather Fire; following this event a number of restrictions were in effect—among others, abstentions from salt, washing, full meals, sexual intercourse, and ample sleep.

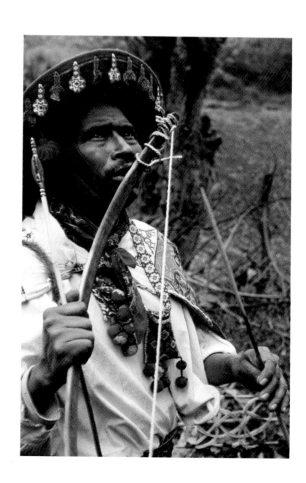

403. Ramón Medina Silva (c. 1926–71), Huichol *mara'akame*, artist, and, according to Peter T. Furst, a "superb reciter and singer of the sacred myths and songs,"[32] here plays the "bow drum."

404. *Nearika for the Deified Sun,* by Ramón Medina Silva, 1966; yarn and beeswax ("yarn painting") on plywood (24½" × 23¼") representation of a god disk (see 418) of Tayaupa (the Sun God), who, in Peter T. Furst's explication, is surrounded (clockwise from top) by: a double-headed eagle, the manifestation of the sky goddess Our Mother Young Eagle Girl; a sacred deer, representing Elder Brother, the stag that appears to the peyote pilgrims (*peyoteros*) and transforms, in death, into the sacred peyote cactus; a maize plant representing the young maize goddess; one of the terrestrial water goddesses (identified by a bottle gourd containing sacred water) who reside in the water holes that the *peyoteros* visit on their way to Wirikuta, the peyote's desert home in north-central Mexico; a branched cactus; a rain serpent with white-candle offering; the wild figwood box in which the old earth-mother goddess, Great-Grandmother Nakawe, saved one man, a black female dog, and seeds of beans, squash, and (above all) the five sacred colors of maize (see 419) from the flood that drowned the world and the previous races of human beings (when the land dried out, the dog transformed into a woman who became the mother of the Huichols and other humankind); and a blue deer, the manifestation of the Huichol culture hero, Kauyumari.

405. *Tatewari, Our Grandfather Fire,* yarn painting by Ramón Medina Silva.

The first act of the pilgrimage was to gather food for Grandfather Fire, who would be kept alive during the journey by four companions remaining behind. Ramón prayed over the wood, holding each piece aloft to the quarters, while all chanted and the mood became very solemn. From his house Ramón then brought out a stone disk—about two feet across and two inches deep—meant to cover the sacred opening that goes down to the center of the earth, from which Grandfather Fire was born. Scooping a hollow in the ashes and covering it with this stone, he recited prayers to the fire for success and then covered all with wood arranged to point east-west and north-south, after which everyone, in single file, made a ceremonial circuit around the flame.[47]

406. In a ceremony that for the Huichol is as ancient as time itself, the *peyoteros* contemplate Tatewari on the edge of Wirikuta.

Conversing with his apprentice Prem Das (see p. 302), Huichol *mara'akame* (Don Jose Matsuwa) (see **413**) spoke of Tatewari's power: "Anyone who really listens to great-grandfather fire will learn how alive he is, how alive the whole earth is, and the sun. These are our great-, great-, great-grandparents, and they can teach us and help us so much. But as our ancestors, who are living and seen as everything around us, they need one thing: our love. The ceremonies are hard. It's a sacrifice—to stay awake all night, sing from your heart for hours, dance with all your life upon the earth, to fast and pray for everyone. But look at me. I am an old man and I do it, and every time I do it I exhaust myself, yet Tatewari always restores me with *kupuri* [life force]."[33]

The next event was a ceremony of the restitution of innocence. Around the fire, each in turn arose, acknowledged the four directions, and in formalized speech named the names of all those with whom he had ever had illicit sexual relations. For each name Ramón tied a knot in a cord drawn from his quiver, and at the end of each revelation brushed the candidate down with his plumes and then shook them into the fire. Then the pilgrim shook and brushed himself, his clothing, and his gear into the fire, which he then circled back to his place. The knotted string was elevated, prayed over, and cast into the flames: and from this moment to the end of the course, the pilgrims knew each other as the Ancient Ones.

Ramón then placed one end of his deer-skin-strung bow in his mouth and, holding the other between his toes, with a ceremonial arrow beat on the string a rhythm which told Grandfather Fire that all was well and in readiness. From his quiver he took a cactus-fiber cord that he passed twice around the circle, first in front of, then behind, the pilgrims, after which he scorched it in the fire and returned it to his quiver. At last, he blew a horn and took up his violin, and the company danced and sang through the night. Anyone harboring resentment after this ceremony risked terrifying, even maddening, peyote visions in Wirikuta.[48]

The camper with its cargo of gods en route to the land of the knowledge of eternal life punctuated the adventure with stops at which Ramón recounted the related legends: tiny water holes, small caves, tree stumps, little clumps of rock, heaps of pebbles (compare pages I.2:135–137). On approaching a place called in Spanish La Puerta (but in Huichol, The Vagina), he required the curtains to be drawn, so that those on pilgrimage the first time (the *primeros*) should not see until properly instructed; and a short way beyond this portal he required the camper to stop. All descended and knelt in a semicircle, and with prayers for all and for each, he blindfolded the *primeros*. Here, in the Mythological Age, the First Pilgrims

wept: some of those now present did so, too. The company returned to the camper and drove on.

Proceeding, bumping over sunbaked cactus reaches, onward deeper into the natal zones of their lives, pausing here and there for little ceremonies, here and there to pass the night, at last the assembly arrived at the place called Where Our Mothers Dwell: a little cluster of water holes, from which a sacred water flowed that was to be drunk and sprinkled over each. In the First Peyote Hunt the female members met and joined the males at these springs, where even now they abide in the form of snakes.

Among those "Mothers" here to be brought to mind was old Nakawé, The One Who Came First, who, after the flood, remade the world. She is an old old woman with very long hair, who, leaning on her staff, walks alone in the Sierras. With her staff, she recreated the animals and plants and, while the earth was still soft, sent the

Macaw to scoop up mountains with its beak. In her canoe she had saved a single man, Watákame, and a little black she-dog, with which the man subsequently dwelt.

One day, on returning from clearing the fields, Watákame found his hut set in order. Next day, this happened again. To learn the secret, after next setting out he circled back to hide and to watch. Then he saw the little dog remove her animal skin and become a lovely young woman, who set to work about the house. The man stole the animal skin and burned it [as in the Eskimo version of the same old tale, see I.2:184], and the woman became his wife. Together they repopulated the earth, and the Huichol, as their descendants, know themselves as Sons of the Dog [see page 253].

At this very holy shrine, Where Our Mothers Dwell, Ramón removed the blindfolds from the *primeros*' eyes and, as they looked about in wonder, recounted legends of the Ancient Ones, pointing to places where they had stopped and rested go to Wirikuta. Because the old man, the tiny baby, they are the same."[50]

Driving north through San Luis Potosí, the company at last arrived at Real de Catorce, a former colonial mining town on the border of Wirikuta, which, as Myerhoff describes it, is "a flat stretch at the base of two sacred mountains...a featureless brush desert of creosote and cactus." The interior, where the cactus grows, can be reached only on foot, "for there are no roads or even paths into the center of the region."[51]

Here they would leave the camper. All got out and went to look for deer tracks, for, according to the legend, the first peyote appeared, in the beginning, in the tracks of the first deer. When they returned, a brush

fire was built; and after an interlude of praying, talking, and singing, Ramón drew from his quiver the scorched cactus-fiber cord for the ceremony of "knotting in." It was passed twice around the circle, first in front, then in back, of the *peyoteros*, while Ramón twanged his bowstring. Then he summoned each to his side, to kneel holding one end of the string, while he prayed and tied a knot in it. Carlos tied the knot for Ramón; then Furst and Myerhoff were knotted in. No one was to sleep that night. Remaining awake, all were to hold right thoughts, to be of one mind, and to ask Grandfather Fire and Our Father Sun for the strength they would be needing the next day in Wirikuta, whence they all had been born.

407. *The Shaman and the Sorcerer,* yarn painting by Eligio Carrillos Vicente, Huichol shaman of Nayarit, Mexico; yarn and beeswax on plywood, 23½" square.

The two paths, of the healing shaman (*mara'akame*, upper left) and the bewitching sorcerer (*tiyukewaya*, center right): Kauyumari, Elder Brother Deer Spirit, is perceived by the apprentice after eating peyote (below center) and peering into the passageway (*nierica*) that leads to the Realm of the Gods (*Tajeima*). Also perceived through this passageway is the cause of illness (central figure of the panel), whose destructive power can be seen rising from its head. The opposite, healing power of the life force (*kupuri*, upper left), descends to support the healing shaman, beneath whose winged spirit is the prayer bowl offered in the sacred land,

Wirikuta, to beg for healing powers strong as corn seeds—strong enough to cure illnesses of all kinds.

The two starlike lights above the deer to the left represent the wisdom bestowed by Kauyumari on the apprentice who has chosen to use his knowledge rather to help people than to harm them. This is a decision made by every apprentice when the powers are first revealed to him. Some decide to use their powers for healing, and these then become shamans. Others decide to use them to shift events to their own advantage, offering their special talents for hire or using them to inflict harm. These become sorcerers, like the figure (upper right) with poisons pouring from its mouth and destructive powers rising from its head (emanations visible only to the healing shaman).[34]

on the First Peyote Hunt and had eaten, sung, or talked with the animals. The mood of the company here changed to banter, and a language of "reversals" came into play. Ramón told Myerhoff that her hair was now cactus fiber; himself, the Pope; his wife, Lupe, an ugly boy; Victoria, a *gringa;* and Francisco, a *nunutsi* ("little child"). The camper was now a burro that would stop if it ran out of tequila; the miserable ruts that passed for roads were a paved highway. Someone sneezed, and the laughter was uproarious; for according to one of the conventional reversals, the nose had become the penis.[49]

"When the world ends," Myerhoff was told, "it will be as when the names of things are changed during the peyote hunt. All will be different, the opposite of what it is now....There will be no more difference. No more man and woman. No child and no adult. All will change places. Even the *mara'akame* will no longer be separate. That is why there is always a *nunutsi* when we his arrows into the peyote blood (which only he could see) and with this substance anointed the forehead, cheeks, eyes, and breasts of each god present.

One can understand why the Spaniards thought they saw in many of the Mexican rites satanic parodies of their own sacraments. Here is the deity incarnate actually sacrificed on a cross (of arrows), so that his flesh and blood should become his worshipers' spiritual food to eternal life.

With his knife Ramón next dug the peyote carefully from the ground, leaving some of the root, "so that the deer might grow again from his bones"; then slicing from the center outward, he placed a segment of the plant in each pilgrim's mouth, after touching it to the recipient's forehead, cheeks, and eyes.

The hole was then covered with gifts, and the company, still whispering, fanned, stalking out over the desert. After several hours, they returned, their baskets heavy with cactus. "Now," Ramón said, "we must leave as quickly as possible. It is dangerous to remain longer." And they left at a run, as though in peril, arriving at their camper to find the Old God, their fire, still aglow. The next day was spent searching for more peyote, then sorting, admiring, and packing the harvest; and that night, for the first time on the trip, much peyote was eaten, with laughter at first, but then a falling into silence, each alone, as Myerhoff tells, "engrossed in his private view of beauty and light."[52]

The final ceremony occurred only after the camper had rolled back into the yard of Ramón's rancho. The fire had been kept burning by the four who had remained and were now silently standing with lighted candles in their hands. All circled the fire, thanks were chanted to the gods, the bas-

Leaving their fire burning by the camper, at dawn they crossed the railroad tracks to a little stand of stunted trees that marked the perimeter of the sacred land, where they made again a fire, to which each brought a stick. Then the company fanned out, searching for tracks. Their manner was of stalking, stooping, whispering, and moving through the brush on tiptoe. Ramón, discovering signs of the passing of earlier Huichol searching parties, bade his company move on, and in single file they walked for three hours, until he gave the sign for all to fan out. After a time, he again gave a sign. He had seen the deer.

All gathered behind him as he drew his arrow and readied the bow. All prayed as he stalked carefully to within a few feet, aimed, and shot into the base of the plant an arrow aligned east-west, then quickly another, north-south. The peyote-deer was secured. Ramón, approaching, placed beside it, to the west, the horns of Kauyumari; he then cleaned the ground around the flat-topped plant, which was about two inches in diameter, and beckoned all to sit around it. With his plumes sweeping downward, he combed back into the plant the multicolored rays of energy (kupuri)— to most eyes invisible—which had spurted upward when the deer was struck. The company then presented their offerings: decorated gourds of sacred water, ceremonial arrows, yarn paintings, antlers, beads, miniature deer snares, and lighted candles. Then naming in a long chant the gods they represented, they knelt in a circle and wept, while Ramón dipped the tips of

According to Barbara G. Myerhoff's recounting of her experience, having at last arrived at Wirikuta, the party of *peyoteros* "begins to search for the peyote [**408**], which is tracked by following its deer tracks. When the tracks are sighted, the *mara'akame* stalks the peyote-deer, and cautiously, silently drawing near, slays it with bow and arrow. Blood gushes upward from it in the form of an arc of rays....The *peyoteros* weep with joy at having attained their goal and with grief at having slain their brother; his 'bones,' the roots of the peyote plant, will be cut away and saved, to be buried in the brush so that he may be reborn. The peyote is removed from the earth, and the resultant cavity surrounded with offerings [**409**]."[35]

Brother Deer and Mother Maize

There were two related ceremonies to follow the Peyote Hunt. The first, the Cleansing of the Spines, took place in the Sierra several weeks after the party had returned and involved, among other rituals, the clearing of small fields for planting of maize: one for Grandfather Fire, another for Our Father Sun, and so on, for all the deities represented on the trip. The second would then be a Deer Hunt, in which the deer was to be caught in a snare and neither bow and arrow nor gun might be used.[54]

"I will come up," said Ramón, "there beside him, there where the snare is. He is in the snare, he looks up at me, saying as he does so, 'Ah this is the death of me!' There he lies down, he stretches out before me of his own will. I speak to him. I ask that he understand. He calls to me, 'I am taking leave of my life, my life is darkening.' That is how it is. Here where my brother, the deer, roams, I have succeeded once again. I am able to place him on my shoulders. I have [his] blood to place on my ceremonial objects. Once more we have our life.

"And when I bring him back those others will say, 'Here you are with Our Brother. Now the earth will be able to bring forth once more, now it finally will.' I will say, 'That is what I am saying to him as I carry him here on my shoulders.' I will place him gently down on the ground. The women pick him up, they lay him gently down on their capes so that he will be well honored. They give him to eat, they give him to drink. They feed him the sacred grasses which he likes. He is in his place. I skin him. I extract his heart. I cut it through the center. I cut it into pieces. I take his blood, I paint it on Tatewari [Grandfather Fire]. I paint it on his house. I anoint the earth with it. I anoint the *útsa*, the arrows, all the ceremonial objects. That is how we obtain our life."[55]

The echo here of Väinämöinen's hunting of the bear in the *Kalevala* (see I.2:150–151) is too evident to be missed. As Myerhoff has remarked: "In the deer hunt, and the manner of his death, one detects evidence of the recency of the Huichols' past as hunters and their incomplete transition to agriculture. The concept that the animal is man's brother who sacrifices himself to the hunter willingly at the request of the

410. On the peyote pilgrimage in Wirikuta, Ramón, chanting, uses a blessed arrow to show the *peyoteros* a location with sacred significance.

kets were set down, and peyote was distributed to be eaten. Then Ramón removed from the coals the stone disk he had put there, and each male of the company dropped into the uncovered hole a small package of wild tobacco wrapped in maize husk and yarn; after this the stone was replaced and wood once more moved to cover it. Dipping some dried flowers into his gourd of sacred water, Ramón now touched with them the crown of the head, cheeks, and lips of each present, then took from his quiver the string of knots that represented their unity and passed it twice around, once before and once behind; then he summoned each to come and grasp the string to the right of the knot that represented himself while he slowly untied it from the other end. The string was then passed over the fire for the last time and returned to the basket of the *mara'akame*. A small bowl of salt was brought out, and Ramón, calling each before him, placed a pinch of salt in his mouth—which broke the fast, and with that the mystery play was ended.[53]

411. Cross-stitched embroidery, collected (1976–77) by Susan Eger in San Andres, depicting a deer in a field of peyote flowers. "For the Huichols," Myerhoff explains, "peyote as a sacred symbol is inseparable from deer and maize….The deer is associated with the Huichols' idealized historical past as nomadic hunters; the maize stands for the life of the present…; and peyote evokes the timeless, private, purposeless, aesthetic dimension of the spiritual life, mediating between former and present realities and providing a sense of being one people, despite dramatic changes in their recent history, society, and culture."[36]

Guardian of the Species, the fact that the deer does not die, for 'his bones are given to Tatewari, and in this manner, Tatewari, with his power, revives the deer and a new one is born'—these are ubiquitous features of hunting ideologies."[56]

Another sign of the incomplete transition is the character of the *mara'akame*, who is regarded by the Huichols and treated also in the anthropological literature as a shaman—yet a shaman of very different kind from the ecstatics of Siberia. In the estimation of two investigators: "More than two-thirds of Huichol males over the age of eighteen are either fully initiated, or well on their way to becoming *mara'akame*."[57] In fact, already in early childhood both the boys and the girls are introduced through the annual ceremonials to the structuring mythological symbols of Huichol culture, so that by the age of ten they can begin their training and by twenty become fully initiated *mara'akame*.

Two factors have contributed to the production of this spiritually supportive situation: one, the unbroken vitality of the native ceremonial heritage, and the other, the inward illuminations of peyote. "Through their observance of and participation in the ceremonies," state the observers, Susan Eger and Peter Collings, "children come to understand the sacredness of peyote and learn to esteem it at a very young age. Most children, although given peyote to taste and to play with when they become curious about it, do not actually consume it in doses large enough to produce visions until at least eight years of age. But...by the time they actually do partake of peyote, they are sufficiently clued in not only to experience prototypical, expected visions, but to interpret them with some degree of accuracy and to remember their significance."[58]

"Thus," they suggest, "Huichol culture in an abstract way can be thought of as a kind of school for high priests, since its entire belief system and way of life is directed toward providing motivation for becoming a *mara'akame*, instilling the self-discipline required, providing memory training, and making the individual worthy of this exalted profession....The knowledge does not simply come down from the elders; rather, each person must learn it anew through the use of the tools of the Huichol religion, the most important of which is peyote."[59]

Actually to press on to the attainment of the status of a recognized *mara'akame,* however, requires, first, the arrival at an explicit decision to do so, and then, unflagging labor. More generally, the ideal for the individual is the achievement of completion, "completing oneself," this being identical with what is understood as "being Huichol."[60] And this cannot be realized simply by participation in general ceremonies and attention to secular duties. There is an inward life to be developed as well, by way

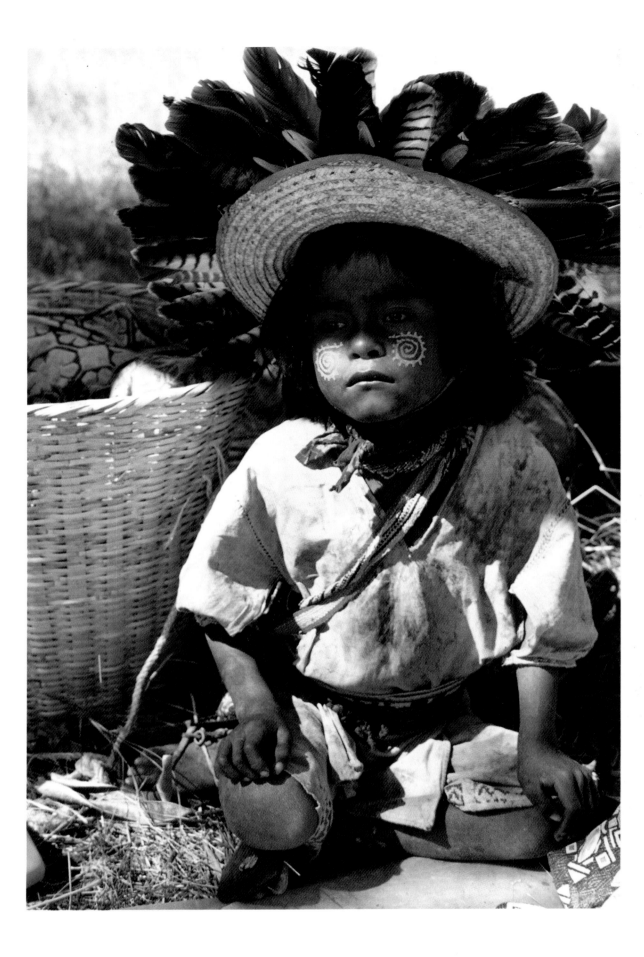

412. Huichol child, his cheek adorned with a sun-spiral of ground yellow root.

of the visions of peyote and translation of the beauty of those visions into works of art. Many have observed that most Huichols are excellent artists, and for the women this is the usual way to completion. Quoting Eger and Collings again:

"The religious path of the Huichol woman offers more than standing in her husband's shadow. If she desires, as a great many women do, she can set out to excel at various crafts, to become an expert at embroidery work, weaving and beadwork—a master artist. This is believed to be the destiny of every 'good woman,' as she will learn to bring the powers of the supernatural into her artwork and life. ...'Good women' are not at all hard to find among the Huichols....They excel in the arts, because they produce art not only for the sake of art and economics, but for the sake of preserving their collective cultural knowledge, thereby completing their destinies as Huichol women....The most dedicated do not sell any of their work from the time they begin until they have attained completion—a period of from five to ten years."[61]

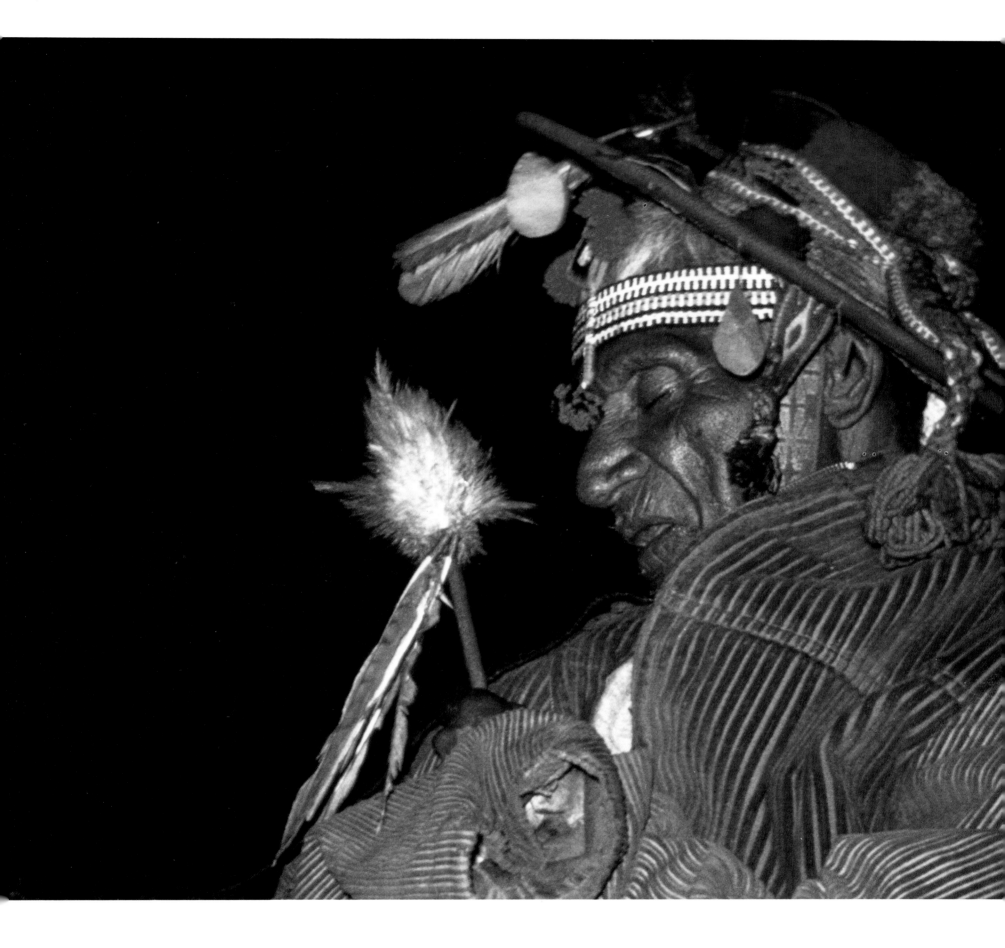

The decision to become a *mara'akame* involves, in contrast, an absolute and exclusive dedication. As described by a Huichol of about twenty-four:

"You must not think of anything but becoming a *mara'akame*, nothing else. and if you do this, then god will see you, look at you, hear you, and he knows all. He will test you to see if you can bear so many years dedicating yourself only to this, give you tests to see if you pass. He will tell you that every year you go to the peyote desert, from the time you leave to the time you return you may not eat salt, for five years you must do this.

"When you go to the peyote desert, thinking only of becoming a *mara'akame*, you will eat the peyote and speak to the deer, and say, 'I come here to learn how to be a *mara'akame*, I think only of this. I don't know anything, but what do you know?'…Speak to the peyote with your heart, with your thoughts. And the peyote sees your heart and then you can eat as much as you want, with total confidence you eat it, without fear you eat five, ten, fifteen, twenty, it doesn't matter. And you sit there thinking, what will I see, how will it be? But in a little while you lose all your thoughts, and then in a little while you

413. Entranced, shaman Don José Matsuwa, leading a ceremony, sings "the old songs."

begin to see and hear beautiful things, moving, beautiful things, *nearika*, and you don't move, you just sit there watching, as though at the movies. And if you have luck, you will hear things, and receive things that are invisible to others, but that god has given you to pursue your path.'"[62]

A second strain of endeavor essential to the apprentice is the accumulation of power objects through which to communicate with the Ancient Ones and inhabiting spirits of the Huichol world. This requires, as Eger and Collings point out, "years and years of traveling about the Huichol homeland, and a good deal of luck to locate the numerous power objects in the mountainous and precipitous terrain"—this being one of the main reasons, they note, why women rarely become shamans: "it is just too difficult a task for a woman with children."[63]

Alliances with animals are important in this training. Different animals have different powers. And as for the actual potency, finally, of the gathered power objects—crystals, snake tails, feather wands, cactus spines, and so on—all stored together in the *mara'akame*'s power basket (*takwatsi*), there is an anecdote told of old don José Matsuwa, a *mara'akame* on into his nineties, by Prem Das, a young American, who, after a season of studies in India, apprenticed himself to this master. They were driving back, one night, from Wirikuta to their rancho in the Sierra Madre, when, in Prem Das's words:

"Only a few miles outside San Luis Potosí I had to pull over to check my right front wheel, which was emitting a strange, whining sound. Lupe, the only one still awake, asked why I had stopped. I checked the wheel and told her that it was oozing grease; most likely a seal had broken, and the bearings were beginning to grind. She decided to wake up don José and inform him. She spoke to him in Huichol; finally he mumbled a reply, yawned, and asked to be let out of the car. I got out with him to show him the damaged wheel. Nodding his head, still half asleep, he asked for his *takwatsi*; Lupe handed it to him through the window. When I saw him take out a prayer plume and in all seriousness begin to 'feather off' or psychically 'dust off' the tire, rim, and then the whole car, I could barely keep from bursting out laughing.

"'It's O.K. now, let's go,' he said, getting back into the car. I stood there bewildered, wondering how I could drive the car in this condition over two hundred miles of rough roads, over steep, dangerous mountain passes, and at night.

"I thought I would at least give it a try for a few miles. I got in, turned to look at don José, only to see he had gone back to sleep, then started up. After driving about ten miles at 30 m.p.h., I pulled over again to doublecheck the wheel. It had quit making the whining sound, but I felt sure it was still leaking grease. A quick look assured me it was not, and as I got back in, don José said, 'What's wrong? Come on, let's go. Your car is fine. Now start passing those trucks again.'

"We drove all night and arrived in Tepic early next afternoon. After buying some candles, chocolate, and cigarettes, we headed out on an old, bumpy dirt road for some twenty-five miles, where it ended in a Mexican rancho community. I could not believe it. The car had made the whole trip with no problem."[64]

When and where the ancestors of the present-day Huichol passed from hunting to agriculture is unknown. Nor do we know when peyote became the sacrament of their spiritually inspired lives: not simply a hallucinogen for shamans, but the ultimate teacher and highest concern of the culture. The inspired mythologization of the landscape of the peyote hunt—all the way from the point known as La Puerta, past the freshwater springs called Where Our Mothers Dwell, on and on, beyond

414. *The Shaman's Dream*, 32" × 48", yarn painting; lower right, speech glyphs (dotted lines) link a dreaming shaman to a votive bowl (prayer) and to visions of the source of all life and every living thing, Great Grandmother Nakawe's fertile growth.

415. *Three Sacred Peyotes*, 24" × 24", yarn painting by Ramón Median Silva. A vision of three peyote cacti, rendered in x-ray style (to show both what appears above ground and the root stock below), emitting their fluorescent rays of power.

Real de Catorce, into the desert—suggests a long and intimate experience of the region. But experience of what kind? The associations are not simply historical, suggesting actual or imagined ancestral events or migrations, but in the profoundest sense mythological, representing accurately the universally known stages of an inward, *psychological* journey: a turning from the world and plane of common daylight consciousness, to pass through zones of increasing interest and danger, to reach, ultimately, in a desert beyond the bounds of reason—where pairs of opposites are reversed, time and eternity come together, each is all and all are one—the treasure of an actual experience of a blissful ground of unity, in which all temporal stress and strivings are at rest. The pattern is exactly that of the visionary journey which I have designated the "Monomyth" in *The Hero with a Thousand Faces*,[65] even to the last detail of the imperiled flight from the blessed land when the trophy of the quest has been obtained.

We have already referred (page 258) to a large trading outpost in the Sierra de Tamaulipas, at the edge of the peyote desert, dating from the Early Classic (c. A.D. 100 to 600). Were the Huichol at that time a desert tribe delivering peyote to the merchants of that frontier station?

They are agriculturalists today, in the western Sierra Madre, cultivating in their rugged highland retreat maize, beans, squash, and cucumbers, while dwelling in established ranchos—farmsteads ranging in size from the single patio of one family to clusters of related compounds. Moreover, the archaeology of the area reveals, as we have learned (page 258), all the signs of a significant commerce for centuries— south to north and north to south—by way of the two Sonoran corridors (see Map 26), passing directly over the present Huichol domain. What role, if any, did the ancestors of these people ever play in that trade?

Many have remarked the likeness of the Huichols' sacred architecture and religious paraphernalia to the ritual gear and kivas of the Pueblos. As Furst points out, the circular Huichol temple, which is known as a *tuki* or *tukipa* ("house for all"), is strikingly like the "great kivas" of the early Southwest. "The circular *tukipas*," he writes, "like the circular Great Kivas of Chaco Canyon with which they share many features, are really the former domestic architecture writ large—since the *tukipa* is the house of the gods (or the deified ancestors), who would not feel at home in unfamiliar surroundings.…As the mythology tells us," he continues, "the prototype of the circular *tuki* is the primordial council house of the gods, which Tatewari instructed the people to build after the transformation by fire of one of their number into the sun [an Aztec theme] and the sun's subsequent birth from the earth."[66] As Furst continues the myth:

416. *How We Contemplate Hikuri in Wirikuta*, yarn painting by Guadalupe, widow of Ramón Medina Silva. Of this interval in the *peyoteros'* ritual, as she experienced it, Barbara Myerhoff observes:

"On the evening following the ritual slaying and token consumption of the first peyote, the pilgrims seat themselves before the fire surrounded by their companions and eat several rounds of their best peyote. This generally quiet affair is the first release they have had from the earlier intense camaraderie and demanding conformity to ritual. Each one is now alone in his or her inner world, for it is not the custom, as the Huichols say, to talk of one's visions."

When later she discussed her observations with Ramón, he explained: "One eats peyote and sees many things, remembers many things. One remembers everything which one has seen and heard. But one must not talk about it. You keep it in your heart. Only one's self knows it. It is a perfect thing. A personal thing, a very private thing. It is like a secret because others have not heard the same thing, others have not seen the same thing. That is why it is not a good thing to tell it to others." Meyerhoff concludes, "All that is said is that ordinary people see beautiful lights, lovely vivid shooting colors, little animals, and peculiar creatures. These visions have no purpose, no message: they are themselves."[37]

Because the young sun had traveled far and faced many obstacles in his journey from west to east through the underworld, he was weak and, instead of rising to his proper height, fell back upon the earth, bringing the sky down with him. Tatewari raised the heavens by placing four giant trees in the four corners of the world—one to support the sky in the west, another in the east, a third in the south, and a fourth in the north. That done, he ordered the people to carve a large stone disk and make a shaman's chair exactly like his own, so that the Sun God might travel from east to west across the sky without tiring and again threatening the earth with a cosmic conflagration.

That done, Tatewari instructed the people to build the first *tukipa*, so that the gods might hold council in their proper house. He walked in a circle to mark off the walls and ordered four trees to be cut and set in the four corners as supports for the roof. In the center of the *tukipa* he dug a hole on which he placed a tepari [a "god disk"] with an opening in the middle, and next to it the people, under his direction, constructed a rectangular hearth, beneath which he made a place for himself [compare the Great Kiva plan of Figure 369].

When the gods assembled in council, the people carved for each his own *tepari*, which was also his *nearika*, his likeness. The "Little Old One," Greatgrandmother Nakawe, the old earth goddess who is sometimes conceived as both male and female, likewise was given her *tepari*, her seat of stone. And because the trees of the sacred directions were also gods, Tatewari gave them each a *tepari*.[67]

417. Above left, a disk of the Sun in the wall of a *shiriki*, the oratory or god house found on most Huichol *ranchos* and in front of *tukis*, larger circular district temples; above right, a sacred disk *(tepari)*, 12″ in diameter, incised and painted (two deer, three fish) for placement in a *shiriki* wall, where each successive offering of incense and candle sanctifies it more; collected (1934–35) by Robert Mowry Zingg, an early-twentieth-century student of Huichol ethnography.

418. Two *tepari* collected in Tuxpan, in the Sierra Madre Occidental, by Carl Lumholtz, who undertook in the 1890s three expeditions to Mexico and wrote the classic *Symbolism of the Huichol Indians,* in which he observed: "All sacred things are symbols to primitive man, and the Huichols have literally no end of them. Religion to them is a personal matter, not an institution, and therefore their life is religious — from the cradle to the grave wrapped up in symbolism."[38]

Below left, a *tepari* of volcanic stone, 16″ in diameter, with symbolic renderings of such deities and sacred animals as rain goddesses (snakes), Kauyumari (deer), and a peyote flower. Bottom right, a stone *tepari* (same size) with paintings of a double-headed—"all-seeing" — eagle (Our Mother Young Eagle Girl, the sky goddess) and a dove (the maize goddess), as well as an emergency hole, through which deities enter to participate in *tuki* ceremonies.

"In explaining the tradition," states Furst, "Ramón insisted that a fifth tree—'the tree that reaches from the earth to the sky'—had been placed in the center of the first *tukipa*. But that tree could be seen only by the shaman, he said, because it was the hole through the *tepari* in the center of the *tukipa* and the center of the world. Here Ramón spoke the universal language of shamanism, describing the world axis as the cosmic opening through which gods and shamans travel from one plane to another."[68]

Apparently, what we have here is a mythological fusion of at least two distinct traditions, facilitated by a third: one from the south, associated with agriculture, circular council chambers symbolic of the universe, an emergence legend, and a pantheon of ancestral male and female powers whose dwelling in the beginning was beneath the earth; another, from the north, associated with the hunt, shamanic individuals, a mythology of animal masters, and visionary journeys between planes of phenomenal and noumenal realities; and then a third, originating in the north-central Mexican peyote-desert itself, whereby the personal shamanic vision became translated into a communal event. The identification of peyote, not only with the deer, but also with maize (though less

emphatically), testifies to its service to both traditions, as well as to their amalgamation. The deer as the Animal Master of the hunters and maize as the Corn Mother of the planters are equivalent symbols of the mystery of the life-sustaining energy of that singular ground—transcendent of reason, yet identical in all—to which the mind is opened through the radiance and the beauty of peyote.

The hole, the "cosmic opening," in the center of the *tepari* is symbolic of this breakthrough into eternity. At Pueblo Bonito II, in Chaco Canyon, such a disk was discovered in Kiva Q at the bottom of the *sipapu* (see page 275). And during Ramón's con-

secration of the hearth of Grandfather Fire (see page 295), he placed such a *tepari* over a hollow among the coals and ashes. In the wall of every Huichol "god house" (*tuki*, or *tukipa*), there is such a "god disk" beneath the roof, as a kind of gable stone, "so that Father Sun may see in."[69] If a myth or mythic symbol be defined as a *metaphor transparent to transcendence*,[70] then every detail of the Huichol landscape, every ornamental motif of their culture and every ceremonial occasion of their lives is such an opening.

The Huichol legend of the origin of maize, like that of the Ojibwa (see I.2:207), represents the cultivated plant, not simply as the gift, but as the very body of a divinity. There the legend was of a divine youth; here, closer to the tropical source, it is of a maiden. Ramón called his version of the legend "The Story of Our Roots." "It is the story," he said, "of the maize we adore, that which we hold sacred, because it is our nourishment, it is our life. That is why we must know it well."[71]

419. *The Five Sacred Colors of Maize*, yarn painting, c. 23¾" square, by Guadalupe, after one by Ramón. For the Huichol, these sacred colors (yellow, white, speckled, red, and blue, the most sacred), are personified as young maize goddesses, each manifesting as a bundle of corn and together coalescing into Our Mother Kukuruku, the maize deity that appears as a wild dove.

The Story of Our Roots

A long time ago there was a woman who lived in a small rancho alone with her son, Growing Boy. They were very hungry, had nothing to eat, no maize, no squash. The boy, alone one day in the woods, heard the notes of a dove above him in the trees. Starving, he took aim. But it was Our Mother Dove Girl, the Mother of Maize. She warned him not to shoot, but to follow her to her house, where there would be maize. Growing Boy followed. In her house she gave him a gourd bowl of sour maize porridge and then a bowl of five small tortillas. As he ate, the bowls were replenished, and he found he could not finish it all. Our Mother Dove Girl had read his thoughts, and he realized with embarrassment that she knew he had been afraid there would not be enough to fill him up. When he thanked her she offered to give him some maize to take home to his mother. Then five maize girls came forward, one for each of the five colors. Very pretty little girls, all in their fine clothes! "Who will go with this boy?" she said to them. They sat there embarrassed, silent. Nobody? "But," said the Mother of Maize, "he should not be left to go hungry."

All continued to sit, silent, and Dove Girl, the Mother, scolded, until at last Purple Maize Girl came forward, very beautiful, with rosy cheeks, well-painted cheeks, with ear ornaments, bracelets, sandals—really beautiful. Our Mother Dove Girl, the Mother of Maize, told Growing Boy that he was to build the girl a house with a shelf in the center, a ceremonial shelf, on which Purple Maize Girl should be placed, as though on an altar. He agreed and arrived at home with the girl, whom he presented to his mother. She became angry, saying, "Oh, you have brought back a woman, another mouth to feed. You were to bring back maize." He explained that she *was* maize, and told how she was to be treated. And so, the house and shelf were constructed, and the maize girl remained. Growing Boy went out into the fields to plant, and then things began arriving, piling up in the house, all the colors of maize. "Ah!" he said to the girl, "Someone is giving us lots of maize." "You have found your life," she told him. "You are going to start to work now, seeing the way things are." That girl: she had all the virtues of maize.

The boy went out into the fields to plant, having told his mother not to make Purple Maize Girl work, not to let her grind, for she was delicate. She should remain where she was, on her shelf. But as the mother was grinding, she began to have bad thoughts about the girl. Working so hard, she felt sorry for herself, while the girl sat up there, a lazy person, beautifully dressed, while she was working. The poor girl became ashamed and came down to help the mother grind. She ground on the metate—that girl who was Purple Maize. As she ground, all that came out was blood—pure blood. That cornmeal was blood. Because the girl herself was maize. She was grinding herself, and every time she pulled back, what appeared was pure blood.

Growing Boy came running back, and when he saw what was happening, rebuked his mother. She denied any blame, but weeping, he said to her: "Ah! You let it slip from our grasp. That is what you have done. It all has come to nothing." He tried to stop the bleeding, the bleeding of Purple Maize girl, putting cornmeal where the blood was, where the poor arms had been. Then, during the night, she departed forever. "Here I cannot stay," she said to herself. "It is dangerous here. There are too many things I cannot control. I thought I might stay, but I see now, it is best to return to my mother. I am unhappy here: ill at ease."

Poor Growing Boy! In the morning he found her gone. He followed her trail to where he had received her and asked Our Mother Dove Girl to return her. But, although his heart was pure, he was refused. "No," the Mother of Maize replied to him, "she did not work out with you."

That is what Our Mother of Maize told Growing Boy. And that is why some of us have maize, others not. Those people did not properly care for it. They did not adore it. And just that was why the spirit preferred to leave their place, returning to its Mother, where there was no danger. Only the shell was left, a rotten shell.

That is why, among us, this is such a sacred story. It is very sad, very hard, this story. Maize is our nourishment. We have to work for it. We must gain it from the earth. We must treat it well, as a sacred thing, so that it may not leave us.[72]

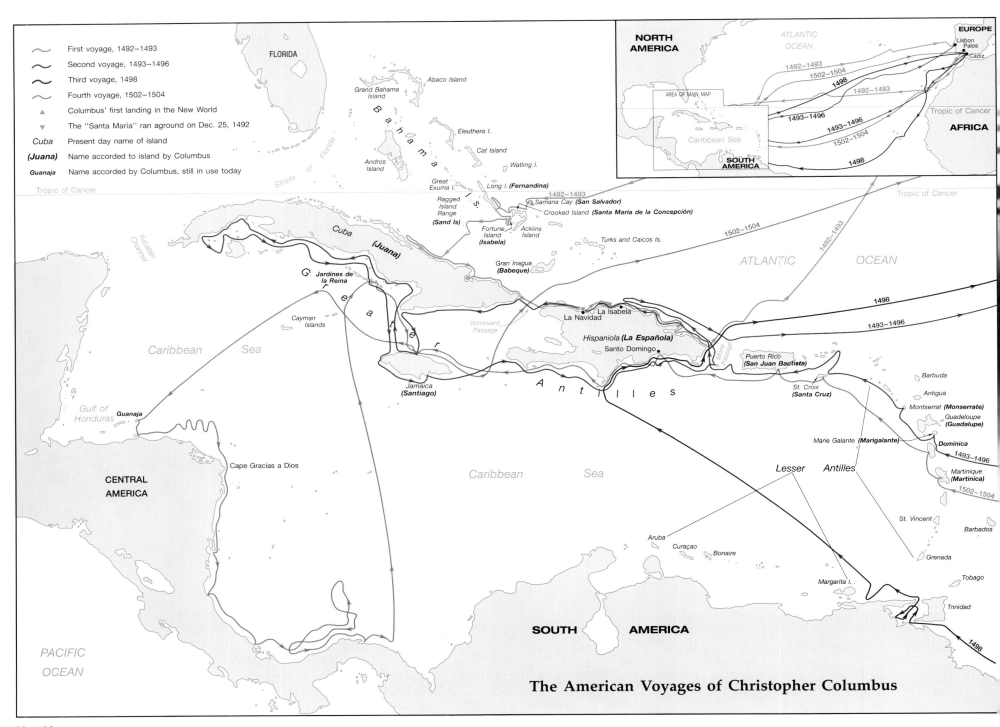

The American Voyages of Christopher Columbus

Legend:

~ First voyage, 1492–1493
~ Second voyage, 1493–1496
~ Third voyage, 1498
~ Fourth voyage, 1502–1504
▲ Columbus' first landing in the New World
▼ The "Santa María" ran aground on Dec. 25, 1492

Cuba Present day name of island
(Juana) Name accorded to island by Columbus
Guanaja Name accorded by Columbus, still in use today

Map 33.

The location of Columbus's first landing in the New World — fancifully depicted, left, in a fifteenth-century woodcut (**420**) — had always been a vexed question that, if unresolved, would have rendered approximate any such cartographic recapitulation of his American voyages as that presented here (**Map 33**). Various authorities, interpreting over the years in various ways the same data — namely, the Admiral's own log, the text of which is known only from a paraphrased transcription made by priest-historian Bartolomé de las Casas for his celebrated *Historia de las Indias* (see II.2:227–228) — have pronounced that historic site to be no fewer than nine different islands.

Now, without certain knowledge of which island is the one Columbus named San Salvador, it becomes impossible, of course, to chart his subsequent route or to ascertain with any confidence the identities of those islands that he later visited, naming them, in turn: Santa María de la Concepción, Ferdandina, Isabele, and so on (as pictured in the quaint 1493 woodcut [**421**] at right).

It was therefore an event of no small consequence when recently Joseph Judge reported in *National Geographic* that, after five years of painstaking interdisciplinary research, he was at last able to write with reasoned assurance: "Christopher Columbus first came to the New World at reef-girt, low, and leafy Samana Cay, a small outrider to the sea lying in haunting isolation in the far eastern Bahamas, at latitude 23°05′ north, longitude 73°45′ west."[39]

A NEW WORLD DISCOVERED AND DIVIDED

From the *Journal of the First Voyage of Christopher Columbus, Friday, October 12, 1492:*

Two hours after midnight, at a distance of two leagues, land appeared. They shortened all sail, remaining with the mainsail, which is the great sail without bonnets, and lay to, waiting for day, a Friday, on which they reached a small island of the Lucayos [Bahamas], which is called in the language of the Indians 'Guanahani' [now Samana Cay]. Immediately, they saw naked people, and the admiral [Columbus] went ashore in the armed boat, and Martin Alonso Pinzón and Vincente Yañez, his brother, who was captain of the Niña. The admiral brought out the royal standard, and the captains went with two banners of the green cross, which the admiral flew on all the ships as a flag, with an F [Ferdinand] and a Y [Ysabella], and over each letter their crown, one being on one side of the cross and the other on the other. When they had landed, they saw trees very green and much water and fruit of various kinds. The admiral called the two captains and the others who had landed, and Rodrigo de Escobedo, secretary of the whole fleet, and Rodrigo Sanchez de Segovia, and said that they should bear witness and testimony how he,

before them all, took possession, as in fact he took, of the said island for the king and queen, his sovereigns, making the declarations which are required, as is contained more at length in the testimonies which were then made in writing. Soon many people of the island gathered there. This which follows are the actual words of the admiral, in his book of his first voyage and discovery of these Indies.

"I," he says, "in order that they might feel great amity towards us, because I knew that they were a people to be delivered and to be converted to our holy faith rather by love than by force, gave to some among them some red caps and some glass beads, which they hung round their necks, and many other things of little value. At this they were greatly pleased and became so entirely our friends that it was a wonder to see. Afterwards they came swimming to the ships' boats, where we were, and brought us parrots and cotton thread in balls, and spears and many other things, and we exchanged for them other things, such as small glass beads and hawks' bells, which we gave to them. In fact, they took all and gave all, such as they had, with good will, but it seemed to me that they were a people very deficient in everything. They all go naked as their mothers bore

them, and the women also, although I saw only one very young girl. And all those whom I did see were youths, so that I did not see one who was over thirty years of age; they were all very well built, with very handsome bodies and very good faces. Their hair is coarse and short, almost like the hairs of a horse's tail; they wear their hair down over their eyebrows, except for a few strands behind, which they wear long and never cut. Some of them are painted black, and they are the color of the people of the Canaries, neither black nor white, and some of them are painted white and some red and some in any color that they find. Some of them paint their faces, some their whole bodies, some only the eyes, and some only the nose. They do not bear arms or know them, for I showed to them swords and they took them by the blade and cut themselves through ignorance. They have no iron. Their spears are certain reeds, without iron, and some of these have a fish tooth at the end, while others are pointed in various ways. They are all generally fairly tall, good looking and well proportioned. I saw some who bore marks of wounds on their bodies, and I made signs to them to ask how this came about, and they indicated to me that people had come from other islands, which are near, and wished to capture them, and they had defended themselves. And I believed and still believe that they came here from the mainland to take them for slaves. They should be good servants and of quick intelligence, since I see that they very soon say all that is said to them, and I believe that they would easily be made Christians, for it appeared to me that they had no creed. I, Our Lord willing, will carry away from here, at the time of my departure, six to your highnesses, that they may learn to talk. I saw no beast of any kind in this island, except parrots."[73]

And so it began, and so it continued, up and down the American coasts, in the various names of the various Christian kings and queens of Spain, Portugal, France, and England (always in the name of God, with intention to Christianize, regardless of any claims of natives to the regions they inhabited), until by October 12, 1892, four hundred years after that divinely witnessed landing, the native order of culture and life in the Western Hemisphere was extinct. There has never been anything like it in the history of the planet. Like a plague the virus of Christian love went across the continents, leaving in its wake museums where there had formerly been populations.

422. In a rare woodcut from 1493, King Ferdinand bestows his blessing on Christopher Columbus and crew, who, upon reaching Mundus Novus (the "New World"), encountered a native populace, now believed to be the Lucayan.

Circulus articus:

Mare germanicu

Terra del Rey de portugall

Has antilhas del Rey de castella:

da esta terca he descoberta p madado del Rey de castella

Linha equinoaialis:

Mare oceanus:

Tropicus capricorni:

Pollus antarticus:

In 1493 the Borgia Pope Alexander VI issued two bulls apportioning all parts of the world yet to be discovered to the two Iberian thrones: Spain to possess those lands westward of an imaginary longitudinal line to be drawn one hundred leagues (345 miles) west of the Cape Verde Islands; Portugal to possess and govern those eastward. On June 7, 1494, at a meeting in Tordesillas (Spain), the two Catholic powers proposed to move the line westward another 270 leagues (to longitude 49° west of Greenwich), and in 1506 Pope Julius II conferred on this revision God's sanction. Hence, in Brazil, to this day, the language spoken is not Spanish, but Portuguese.

423. Following Pope Alexander VI's *ex cathedra* division of New World lands, Spain and Portugal, in the Treaty of Tordesillas (1494), repositioned the boundary, moving it westward to approximately the position indicated by the demarcation line drawn, 1502, on the *Anno Nimo*, this hand-colored parchment from *Portugaliae Monumenta Cartographica*.

Inter Cetera

Alexander, bishop, the servant of the servants of God: To our most dear beloved son in Christ, King Ferdinand, And to our dear beloved daughter in Christ, Elizabeth Queen of Castile, Legion, Aragon, Sicily and Granada, most noble Princes, Greeting and Apostolic Benediction.

AMONG OTHER WORKS acceptable to the divine majesty and according to our heart's desire, this certainly is the chief, that the Catholic faith and Christian religion, especially in this our time may in all places be exalted, amplified, and enlarged, whereby the health of souls may be procured, and the barbarous nations subdued and brought to the faith.... For which, as we think you worthy, so ought we of our own free will favorably grant all things whereby you may daily with more fervent minds to the honor of God and to the enlarging of the Christian empire, prosecute your devout and laudable purpose most acceptable to the immortal God. We are credibly informed that whereas of late you were determined to seek and find certain islands and firm lands far remote and unknown (and not heretofore found by any other) to the intent to bring the inhabitants of the same to honor our redeemer and to profess the Catholic faith...you have, not without great labor, perils and charges, appointed our well-beloved son Christopher Colonus (a man surely well commended as most worthy and able for so great a matter) well furnished with men and ships and other necessities, to seek (by the sea where hitherto no man has sailed) such firm lands and islands, far remote and hitherto unknown, Who (by God's help) making diligent search in the Ocean, has found certain remote islands and firm lands which were not heretofore found by any other. In which (as is said) many nations dwell, living peaceably and going naked, not accustomed to eat flesh. And as far as your messengers can conjecture, the nations inhabiting the aforesaid lands and islands believe that there is one God Creator in heaven: and seem apt to be brought to the embracing of the Catholic faith and to be imbued with good manners: by reason whereof, we may hope that if they be well instructed, they may easily be induced to receive the name of our savior Jesus Christ. We are further advised that the aforenamed Christopher has now built and erected a fortress with good munition in one of the aforesaid principal islands in which he has placed a garrison of certain of the Christian men that went thither with him: as well to the intent to defend the same, as also to search other islands and firm lands far remote and as yet unknown. We also understand that in these lands and islands lately found, is great plenty of gold and spices, with diverse and many other precious things of sundry kinds and qualities. Therefore all things diligently considered (especially the amplifying and enlarging of the Catholic faith, as behooves Catholic princes following the examples of your noble progenitors of famous memory) you are determined by the favor of Almighty God to subdue and bring to the Catholic faith the inhabitants of the aforesaid lands and islands.

We, greatly commending this your godly and laudable purpose in Our Lord, and desirous to have the same brought to a due end and the name of Our Savior to be known in those parts, do exhort you in Our Lord and by the receiving of your holy baptism, whereby you are bound to Apostolical obedience, and earnestly require you by the bowels of mercy of Our Lord Jesus Christ, that when you intend for the zeal of the Catholic faith to prosecute the said expedition to reduce the people of the aforesaid lands and islands to the Christian religion, you shall spare no labors at any time, or be deterred by any perils, conceiving firm hope and confidence that the Omnipotent God will give good success to your godly attempts. And that being authorized by the privilege of the Apostolical grace, you may the more freely and boldly take upon yourself the enterprise of so great a matter, we of our own motion, and not either at your request or at the instant petition of any other person, but of our own mere liberality and certain science, and by the fulness of Apostolical power, do give, grant, and assign to you, your heirs and successors, all the firm lands and islands found or to be found, discovered or to be discovered toward the West and South, drawing a line from the pole Arctic to the pole Antarctic (that is to say) from the North to the South: Containing in this donation whatsoever firm lands or islands are found or to be found toward India, or toward any other part whatsoever it be, being distant from, or without the aforesaid line drawn a hundred leagues toward the West and South from any of the islands which are commonly called De los Azores and Capo Verde.

All the islands, therefore, and firm lands, found and to be found, discovered and to be discovered from the said line toward the West and South, such as have not actually been heretofore possessed by any other Christian king or prince until the day of the nativity of Our Lord Jesus Christ last past, from which begins this present year being the year of our Lord 1493, when so ever any such shall be found by your messengers and captains, We, by the authority of Almighty God granted unto us in Saint Peter, and by the office which we bear on earth in the place of Jesus Christ, do for ever by the tenor of these presents, give, grant, assign, unto you, your heirs, and successors (the kings of Castile and Legion) all those lands and islands, with their dominions, territories, cities, castles, towers, places, and villages, with all the right, and jurisdictions thereunto pertaining: constituting, assigning, and deputing, you, your heirs, and successors the lords thereof, with full and free power, authority, and jurisdiction....

Furthermore, We command you in the virtue of holy obedience (as you have promised, and as We doubt not you will do in mere devotion and princely magnanimity) to send to the said firm lands and islands, honest, virtuous, and learned men, such as fear God, and are able to instruct the inhabitants in the Catholic faith and good manners, applying all their possible diligence to the premises....

It shall therefore be lawful for no man to infringe or rashly to contrary this letter of our commendation, exhortation, request, donation, grant, assignation, constitution, deputation, decree, commandment, prohibition, and determination. And if any shall presume to attempt the same, he ought to know that he shall thereby incur the indignation of Almighty God and his holy Apostles Peter and Paul.

Given in Rome at Saint Peters: In the year of the incarnation of Our Lord 1493. The fourth day of the nones of Mary, the first year of our Pontificate.[74]

THE ANTILLES

In 1515, Bartolomé de Las Casas, the first Catholic priest ordained in the New World, returned to Spain to protest before the emperor the enslavement and inhuman abuse of natives by *conquistadores* zealous only for gold and enrichment. His *Historia de las Indias*[75] and *Brevísima relación de la Destrucción de las Indias*[76] are lurid documents of the holocaust; and in 1517, in desperation, he proposed the importation of African slaves, who would be better able than the Indians to endure and survive the forced labors. So it is that today the Caribbean population is not red but black, with little remaining of either evidence or knowledge of the earlier population.

Columbus's reported recognition of two distinct peoples in the isles of his discovery is the earliest recorded anthropological observation in the New World. Those of his first meeting were the comparatively gentle Arawakan Taino; the others, the invaders, were the Caribs, after whom the Caribbean has its name, and from whose

The Early Inhabitants of the Antilles: Languages and Distribution

Arawakan
Cariban
Ciboney group (unclassified)
} Ethnolinguistic culture areas

Ethnolinguistic boundary

Yekuhaná Tribes of the Makiritare (Yekuana) tradition

Map 34.

custom of eating their enemies the word "cannibal" comes. An early account of the character of these Caribs can be found in *Historia de los reyes católicos, Don Fernando y Doña Isobel,* a work based on the words and letters of Columbus and composed c. 1510 by Andrés Bernáldes, an acquaintance of the great Admiral of the Ocean Sea and the parish pastor of a town, Los Palacios, near Seville:

"There are there, at the entrance of the Indies, certain islands, which the Indians of the islands already mentioned call Caribs, which are inhabited by certain people whom they regard as very ferocious, and of whom they are much afraid, because they eat human flesh. They have many canoes with which they go about all the neighboring islands and steal whatever they can, and take and carry away captive such men and women as they can, and kill them and eat them, a matter for great wonder and amazement. They are more ill formed than the others only in the fact that they have this evil custom; they are a very powerful race and have many arms, for they use arrows and bows of cane, and they set a sharp flint in the arrow head, or fish bones, in place of iron, which they do not possess. They wear their hair long like women, and are dreaded as ferocious by the people of the islands already mentioned, and this is because the other people are very cowardly and very domesticated and without malice, and not because the Caribs are strong or because our men have to take more account of them than of the others. And in the islands of the Caribs, and in the other islands mentioned, there is gold beyond measure, and an infinite amount of cotton; there are especially spices, such as pepper, which burns more and has four times as much strength as that which we use in Spain, and is regarded by all the people of these islands as very useful and very medicinal. There are bushes of flax, aloe, gum-mastic and rhubarb, and many other things, as it seemed to the said Columbus. There are no four-footed beasts, or any animals such as there are with us to be seen in such of the islands as were discovered, except some small curs, and in the fields some very large mice, which they call hutias and which they eat and which are very savoury; and they eat them as rabbits are eaten here and they regard them as of the same value. There are many birds, all different from those here, and especially many parrots."[77]

424. Seated figure of wood with inlays of conch shell, from Jamaica, c. 26¾" high. Atop the figure's head is a bowl, part of a platform extending from its back, that apparently once held a powder used for ceremonial purposes. Visible from the rear are skeletized ribs.

The Taino

a

b

c

The native Americans first confronted by Columbus and his landing party were the Taino, a tribe whose language was a dialect of the largest and most widely spread linguistic stock of South Ameica, the Arawakan, which at that time was spoken by resident tribes from Florida to Paraguay and from the Andes to the Atlantic (see Map 43). And since some fifty Arawakan languages survive in South America as spoken tongues to this day (in Colombia, Venezuela, Guyana, French Guiana, Surinam, Bolivia, and Peru), it has been possible for the distinguished linguist and historian, José Juan Arrom, of the Cuban Academy of Arts and Letters, to reconstruct by a controlled comparative method, from certain documents of the period—most notably, the Catalonian friar Ramón Pané's *Relación acerca de las antigüedades de los indios*[78] (completed c. 1498)—an abstract of the mythological foundation of the ritual life of the Taino at the moment of the Conquest.

The Taino were extinct 100 years (three generations) after that first landing of Columbus. Pané, however, who arrived on the second voyage (1493–94), was directed by Columbus himself to live with the natives, to learn their language, and to make note of their beliefs. His manuscript has disappeared, but three redactions have come down to us: an abstract in Latin by Pedro Martir de Anglería, quotations by Las Casas in his *Apologética historia de las Indias*,[79] and a full translation into Italian by Alfonso de Ulloa, printed in Venice in 1571. Through all this, of course, as Arrom remarks, ''the Taino words have suffered considerable alteration…not infrequently the same term appears in differing forms in the versions of Ulloa, Anglería, and Las Casas.''[80] By means, however, of a scrupulous translation of Ulloa back into Spanish, with attention not only to Las Casas and Anglería, but also to the known Arawakan counterparts of the *distorted* Taino terms, Arrom has succeeded in restoring the mythic vision of the primary race of the American Aegean.

''They believe,'' states Pané, ''in a Great Lord who dwells in the sky and is immortal, whom no one can see and who has a mother but no beginning, and they call him *Yócahu Bagua Maórocoti*.''[81] *Yócahu* is a proper noun composed of *yoca* (meaning ''yuca'') and *hu*, an intensifying suffix. Yuca—not to be confused with Yucca—is a flowering plant, *Manihot esculanta* (known also as cassava, manioc, and mandicot),

425. Differing in subject depicted, in medium, and in quality of execution, a diverse array of carved, tri-cornered, enigmatic zemis have been recovered from sites scattered throughout the Antilles. Here arranged are several specimens from Puerto Rico: (**a**) dated c. A.D. 1000–1500, c. 7½″ long, a head of gray stone dominated by an elongated nose; (**b**) 4″ long, a fish-mouthed personage with flexed legs; (**c**) a gaping figure of white marble, 3″ in length, evidencing a distinctive headdress and perforated earlobes; and, from Santo Domingo, (**d**) a conical head of stone, 7″ high. While acknowledging that some others consider these strange Antillean artifacts and their like to be merely "decorative mortars," the noted scholar of Mesoamerica Frederick J. Dockstader nonetheless concludes: "From whatever side we approach the subject, we come back to the conclusion that they were idols, or zemis. If they were not actually worshipped, they assumed forms which were duplications of idols that were worshipped."[40]

d

426. Also from Santo Domingo, this ingenious prehispanic nose-pipe, 3⅜″ high and 2⅛″ wide, was clearly intended for ritual use, realistically depicting Maquetaurie Guayaba (*guayaba*, "guava"), the mythic figure described by Pané as being the Lord of Coaybay, the Land of the Dead.

that is cultivated throughout the American tropics for its tuberous roots (see page 342), from which a bread-flour and an alcoholic beverage are prepared and, today, in North America, tapioca and a laundry starch. *Bagua* was the word for ''ocean.'' *Maórocoti* is composed of the privative prefix *ma-* plus the noun *órocoti*, ''grandfather.'' Hence, *Yócahu Bagua Maórocoti* yields the meaning ''spirit, without male ancestor, of the yuca and the sea.'' Another title recorded by Pané is *Yucahuguamá*, composed of *yucahu*, ''spirit of the yuca,'' plus *guamá* or *wamá*, ''lord.''[82]

Dance festival of the Haitian Taino in honor of their image of the Mother of God, after an eighteenth-century engraving in Picart's *The Religious Ceremonies and Customs of the Several Nations of the Known World* (London, 1731–37).

The image of the goddess here shown (Figure **428**, at right) is an invention not of the native American, but of the European, imagination, even to the trident in the idol's right hand. Its counterparts exist only in sixteenth- and seventeenth-century woodcuts and engravings of imagined scenes of occultism, diabolism, and sorcery (see Figure **427**, above), the obvious present implication being that since the gods of the heathens are devils (2 Kings 5:15: "There is no god in all the earth but in Israel"), the religious festivals of the New World were invocations of Satanic forces, comparable to the rites of the Witches' Sabbath.

The five, instead of three, heads of the idol must have been inspired by the friar Ramón Pané's mistaken five names of the Taino goddess: Atabey, Yermao, Guacar, Apito, and Zuimaco (see p. 314). The two seated idols to the left are Gothic devils, even to the trident in the raised left hand of the one to our right. The form of the temple itself is an invention of the artist. And the drums are of a British fife-and-drum corps: Taino drums were not properly drums but hollow-log gongs (see the example illustrated in the upper right corner of Figure **435a**). Yet through all these distortions, the engraving reflects two eyewitness accounts of an actual Haitian Taino festival in honor of the Mother of God, one by the Spaniard Francisco López de Gómara,[41] and the other by the Italian Girolamo Benzoni[42] (herein translated, in part, on page 318).

"Their stone zemis [images]," states Pané, "are of various shapes. There are…[among others] those with three points, which they believe give rise to the yuca."[83] Arrom sees this as an evident reference to the numerous three-pointed stone images (see Figures 425a–d) that have been known to scholarship—though uninterpreted—for some time.[84] These are almost certainly representations of Yuca-huguamá and, as Arrom suggests, "were used in agricultural rites…whereby they were buried in the *conucos* [garden plots], so that their magic might fertilize the sewn

ground and so, increase the harvest."[85] As he points out, "it was a fundamental idea of the peoples of America, with respect to their agricultural gods, that the plants bequeathed by those gods to mankind were manifestations of the very bodies of the gods themselves, perennially renewed in their immortal substance."[86] The idea of a "great spirit," a "high god" (in Andrew Lang's and Father Schmidt's sense, see

I.2:139), as a personificaton of the living ground of all being, is likewise a shared theme of all of the major Amerindian mythologies. (Compare Letacost-Lesa on Tirawa, I.1:8; the Winnebago tale of the visionary who desired to see Ma-o-na, I.2:204–205; and the words of Chief Seattle, I.2:251.)

The second divinity recognized by Pané was the mother of that supreme being who had a mother but no beginning. "They called her by five names," he wrote: "*Atabey, Yermao, Guacar, Apito* and *Zuimaco*."[87] Las Casas, however, rejected this list with the observation that "since Pané was by birth a Catalán, he did not speak quite well our Castilian tongue."[88] *Yermao*, he observed, was a misconstruction of the Castilian noun *hermano*, meaning "brother," and *Guacar* was the name, therefore, not of Atabey, but of her brother. Las Casas simply ignored both *Apito* and *Zuimaco*, which leaves but two of Pané's five names to be interpreted: *Atabey*, or *Attabeira* (Anglería's version of the same) and *Guacar*.

Atabey and *Attabeira* were apparently derived from the noun *itaba* ("lake," or "lagoon") plus *era* ("water"), *itabo* being a term still in use in the Antilles in the sense of a "pool or reservoir of fresh pure water...with springs rising from the bottom." *Atté*, the vocative form of an Arawak word for "mother," is another element which, Arrom suggests, may have entered into the shaping of this water-goddess's name.[89] For the Water Mother is a well-known figure in a number of South American (Carib as well as Arawak) origin myths, and this Water Mother's brother, typically, is the Moon. *Guacar*, which is here his name, is composed of the pronominal prefix *wa-* ("our") and *katti*, or *kairi* ("moon," or "month") *kairi* itself being compounded of the noun *ka* ("force") and *iri* ("menstruation").[90] There is a Cariban legend (reviewed on page 330) in which the Moon Brother of the Water Mother is the cause of his sister's menstruation.

"Most of the chieftains [caciques]," Columbus wrote, "have three stones which they and their people hold in great reverence. One, the say, is good for the grain and vegetables that they sow, another to help women bear without pain, and the third to bring water and sun, when these are lacking."[91] Arrom suggests that stones of the first kind must have been the three-pointed zemis symbolic of Yócahu (Figures 425a–d, 429). Stones of the second kind would have been little images of the Water Mother herself, as patroness of childbirth. The stones of the kind to bring rain and sun were undoubtedly images of the mythological twins Boinayel and Márohu, as represented in the zemi of Figure 430.

"And they say," Pané reported, "that the Sun and Moon rise from a cave in the country of a cacique named *Mautiatihuel*, and that the cave is called *Iguanaboina*, and they hold it in high regard. And they say it is all painted, not with any figures, but with foliages and the like. And there are said to be in that cave two small zemis of stone, about half the length of an arm; and they appear to perspire. Which zemis, they greatly revered. And when there was no rain, they would enter that cave to visit them, whereafter it would rain. And those zemis were

429. This head of polished stone, c. 8³/₁₆" high and 5¼" deep, from Puerto Rico, is almost certainly yet another representation of the master of Coaybay, the Antillian realm of the dead (see **426**). When viewed from the side, this zemi exhibits a radically inclined forehead, suggesting that its creators were practitioners of artificial cranial deformation.

430. Stone amulet, c. 2" tall, of two conjoined anthropomorphic figures with incised teeth, hands, and toes; Taino, c. A.D. 1000–1500.

named, one, *Boinayel*, and the other *Márohu*."[92]

The name *Mautialtihuel*, however, means Son of the Dawn, or Lord of the Region of the Break of Day. "It would therefore," as Arrom remarks, "not have been the country of any actual, historical cacique, but of some mythical being corresponding to the god whom the Aztecs call *Tlahuizcalpantecuhtli*, 'Lord of the House of Dawn.'. . . The reported cave in the country of that cacique, consequently, could not have been anywhere on the island of Española, but the cosmic opening through which the sun rises to illuminate the earth, and into which it descends and disappears, when from it the moon rises."[93] *Iguanaboina*, according to Arrom, would not have been *that* cave, since the two stone zemis, *Boinayel* and *Márohu*, belonged to a very different story from that of the rising and setting of the spheres of the day and night. *Iguana* is the lizard iguana, whose serrated dorsal crest suggests the solar rays of a beautiful day, while *boina* is a word related to *boíuna* (*mboi*, "serpent"; *una*, "dark"), the dark serpent that in many American mythologies connotes rain-laden clouds. The name of the first twin, *Boinayel*, therefore, means Son (*-el*) of the Dark Cloud-Serpent (*boina*), while that of the second, *Márohu*, is a compound of *ma-* ("without"), *aro* ("clouds"), and the intensifying suffix *-hu*. In short, the mythological twins of the Cave of the Radiant Iguana and Dark Serpent were the Lord of Good Weather and his twin, the Lord of the Rain.[94]

The detail of the sweating stone zemis is readily explained, Arrom suggests, since they were kept in a cave whose temperature would have been a great deal lower than that of the humid tropical air outside, and the entrance of a group of worshipers would have brought in enough of the moist warmth to cause a condensation, such as can appear on a glass of cold water. In any case the long eyes and axial nose of each of the twins were designed, as Arrom perceived, to channel the drops of such a condensation; so that the twins of this zemi would have seemed not only to be sweating, but also to be crying.[95] And Frazer, in *The Golden Bough*, has shown that a shedding of tears has at times been employed as a magical means to bring rain.[96]

Mythologies of the Hero Twins are prominent throughout the world, but emphatically in the Americas, where the two appear under many guises; in cosmogonic myths as the Sun and Moon or, as in the Navaho legend Where the Two Came to Their Father (see I.2:244–248), as the twins sons of the celestial lights. In that Navaho tale, the two, when fully empowered, become four, representing the four quarters of the earth and sky. In the following Taino legend, the Exploits of the Four Twins of One Birth, recorded by Pané c. 1494, the mythological twins are four throughout.

The Exploits of the Four Twins of One Birth

There was a man called Yaya, whose name we do not know. He had a son called Yaya-el, who wanted to kill him, and so, was exiled. For four months he was exiled, after which his father slew him, packed the bones in a mortuary urn, and hung the urn from the roof, where for some time it remained.

Then Yaya one day said to his wife, "I would like to see our son, Yaya-el." She was pleased. So, taking down the urn, he turned it upside down to have a look at the bones, but what fell out were fishes, large and small. And seeing that the bones had turned into fish, the couple ate them.

Evidently, as thus recorded by Pané, what had been related to him as a folktale was actually the deformed fragment of a cosmogonic myth. For the syllable *ia* means "life energy," the informing *élan vital* that distinguishes animals, plants, and man from inert matter. *Ia-ia* is the superlative, suggesting that originally the man Yaya must have been a god personifying the energy of life, the source of which is beyond knowledge. Hence, his true name is unknown. And the suffix *-el* means "son," so that Yaya-el is simply "Yaya's Son."[97]

The mythological theme of a god's or king's son sacrificed either by or to his father could not have been unfamiliar to the padres, who, in their own ritual of the mass, daily celebrated something of the kind as the highest mystery of their faith. The association of the sacrificed Son with a fish meal must also have been familiar, both from the Gospel episode of the miracle of the loaves and fishes,[98] and from the fish meal of Friday (Good Friday), not to mention the early Christian symbolization of Christ himself as a fish, Greek *ichthys*, through an acrostic reading of the letters of this Greek noun as initials of the five words, Iēsous CHristos, THeou Yios, Sōtēr, "Jesus Christ, Son of God, Savior."

The bizarre Taino myth continues:

When one day Yaya had left his house to go to inspect his gardens, the four sons arrived of a woman who had died in giving birth to them. Itaba Cahubaba, she was called, The Blood-bathed Old [Earth] Mother.[99] She had been cut open and the four taken out. The first was called Deminán Caracaracol; the other three were nameless. And when Yaya had departed from his house, these four entered to get the mortuary urn. Only Deminán dared to take it down, but all were gorging themselves on the fishes it contained when Yaya was heard returning. In haste to hang the urn up, they hung it badly. The urn fell, broke, and out poured so much water that it flooded the earth. Many fish came too. The origin of the sea was from that urn. And the Brothers, terrified, fled.

They came to Bayamanaco's door and perceived that the old man had been cultivating cassava. "Bayamanaco," they said, "is our grandfather." And determining to learn from him the art of preparing food from that plant, Deminán decided to go in.

For cassava (manioc, yuca), when improperly prepared, is painfully and deadly poisonous. The proper preparation requires the use of fire to volatilize the toxic prussic acid. The implication, therefore, of Deminán's confrontation with his grandfather was that he had come to ask for the release to mankind of two essential secrets: (1) the art of preparing cassava and (2) the means of producing fire.

But who, then, was this grandfather Bayamanaco? The name of the Aztec firegod, Huehueteotl, means The Old God. Bayamanaco was evidently his Taino counterpart,[100] even as Tatewari, Grandfather Fire, is today his counterpart among the Huichol (see page 295).

Now when Deminán entered Bayamanaco's house and presented his request, the old man put a finger to his nose and blew at him a charge that struck his back between the shoulders. It was full of the powdered tobacco that he had been using that day as snuff, and when Deminán returned to his brothers, his back was in great pain. He told them what had happened. They looked and saw that a tumor had appeared. It was swelling to such a size that Deminán was on the point of death. The brothers were unable to open it, until they gave it a blow with a stone axe, and out came a living female tortoise. So in that place the four built their home and reared the tortoise.[101]

Pané's account concludes at this point with the baffled words: "Of this tale I could learn no more; and of little help, what has here been writ." Anglería in his Latin version states that what was born from the tumor was the woman through whom the four brothers engendered the human race. Figure 432 demonstrates, however, that the creature was indeed a tortoise. Moreover, there is an Amazonian Cariban tribe, the Waiwai, dwelling at the juncture of the Esequibo and Mapuera (1°N, 59°W), whose creation myth opens with a female tortoise.[102]

"The brothers," Arrom suggests, "having ended their cosmic escapades, settled down at last in a definite place, built a durable house, and set themselves to the task of engendering mankind.... They had acquired fire, cassava, and tobacco, and had passed from the primitive stages of a wandering foraging band to the position of a settled agricultural community with a situated population, liberated living conditions, and customs relatively advanced. They had passed, as Lévi-Strauss would say, 'from the raw to the cooked,' from the natural to the civilized state. As the four children of Mother Earth and as personifications of the winds of the quarters, they were now to become the patriarchs and civilizers of mankind—the ancestral founders of the Taino culture."[103]

431. From Santo Domingo, melancholic crouched figure of black stone, c. 12⅞″ × 2⅞″, one of the many "crying idols" that have been found.

432. Ceramic effigy figurine—arguably Deminan Caracaracol, the named first son of Itaba Cahubaba, the Blood-bathed Old (Earth) Mother—with a tortoise growing on his back (see text), c. 15⅞″ tall. Found, 1916, on an altar in a cavern in Santo Domingo by Theodoor de Booy, this thin-walled statue has been called by Frederick J. Dockstader "a tour de force in the ceramic arts."[43]

The Arawak

Writing of the native cultures of Map 34, Julian H. Steward, general editor of the six-volume *Handbook of South American Indians*,[104] remarks on the shattered condition of the evidences remaining in these first areas entered by the Europeans as well as on the reduced condition of the surviving natives. "A comparison of data from the modern tribes with those from the early chroniclers and from archaeology," he writes, "shows that all but the very backward and isolated tribes have suffered drastic changes. Gone are the intensive horticulture, the dense population, the large villages, the class-structured society, the mounds, temples, idols and priests, the warfare, cannibalism and human trophies, the elaborate death rites, and even the technological and esthetic refinements evidenced in the early metallurgy, weaving, ceramics, and stone sculpture. The modern tribes who retain a predominantly aboriginal culture have come to resemble the Tropical Forest tribes [of Map 37] rather than their own ancestors. They carry on small-scale slash-and-burn farming, and many of them now hunt and fish more than they till the soil. They live in small villages, weave simple cloth, and make only plain pots. Their society is unstratified, their religious cults are scarcely remembered, and the principal survival of former days is the shaman."[105]

With respect specifically to the Antilles (Map 34), he names three distinct waves of occupation that had populated the islands before the landing of Columbus. The first was of a primitive hunting-and-gathering people, the Ciboney, from the north, evidently Florida. The second was of the Arawak, a people from South America of an advanced Formative Culture stage typical of the Circum-Caribbean cultures (Map 35). The third was of the Carib, who were also from South America, but from the interior, the tropical forest (Map 37). Though relatively recent arrivals, these last had already occupied the Lesser Antilles (Grenada, Martinique, Guadeloupe, and the rest), but had been stopped at Puerto Rico. The Ciboney had been reduced to parts of Cuba and the southwest peninsula of Haiti. The Arawak were in possession of the rest of the Greater Antilles and the Bahamas.[106]

Of the Ciboney, next to nothing is known but that they occupied at one time the greater part of Cuba and a large part of Haiti. Very primitive hunters and gatherers, living in caves and temporary shelters, they subsisted primarily on sea foods,[107] and their disappearance has been complete. Not even of their language do we have a clue.

433. *Arawak Village*, c. 1850 painting by George Catlin, oil on cardboard, 19⅜″ × 24⅞.″

Of the Antillean Arawak, the Taino, however, sufficient evidence remains to demonstrate that Columbus in his judgment of the poverty of the culture was deceived. The culture level, as just remarked, was of an advanced Formative grade, supported by intensive farming. Moreover, it was of a kind with—though less developed than—the mainland civilizations of Mexico and Peru. Steward describes these tribes as follows:

"The Circum-Caribbean tribes differed from the civilized peoples of the Andes and Mexico in the elaboration of the basic sociopolitical and religious patterns. Among the latter, social classes were more complicated, more fixed by heredity, and more strongly and endogamous. In the Circum-Caribbean area status was somewhat mobile and, though hereditary rank was not absent, status often could be obtained by warfare. The civilized peoples had achieved political states, with rulers of dominions and even empires, and their warfare was directed toward conquest and tribute. The Circum-Caribbean tribes had

434. *Four Arawak Indians*, oil on cardboard by George Catlin, 18⅜″ × 24⅜″, c. 1850.

One of the few extant historical accounts of the pre-hispanic inhabitants of the Antilles is that provided by Gonzalo Fernández de Oviedo y Valdés in his *Historia general y natural de las Indias islas y tierra firme del mar oceano*, first published in 1535 and reissued in 1851. Redrawn from this original source are the various artifacts shown below (435): (1) Christopher Columbus's coat of arms; (2) the Southern Cross, used by the conquistadors for navigation; (3–6) various types of Taino drums; (7) the tube used by Taino for sniffing *cohoba* snuff; (8) a Taino hammock, as set up when they are traveling; (9) the circular house (*caney*) used by Taino commoners; (10) the rectangular house (*bohio*) used by Taino chiefs; (11) the genital covering worn by Taino men before the arrival of the Spanish; and (12) the kind of stone ax used by the Taino to hollow out canoes. At right (436) is a facsimile reproduction of a page of the original publication.

only incipient states, and warfare furthered personal ambition rather than political ends. Its purpose was cannibalism, display of human trophies, capture of female slaves, and, in some cases, taking of sacrificial victims. In religion, Mexico and the Andes had succeeded in separating shamanism from temple worship, and they had a special class of priests dedicated to community worship in temples. The Circum-Caribbean peoples also had temples, but their shamans performed not only as priests but also as medicine men. [Compare the Huichol *mara'akame*.]

''In their material arts the civilized peoples of Mexico and Peru excelled mainly in the elaboration of the processes which they shared with the Circum-Caribbean tribes. The greater variety of crops and better

llaman Canoas: las quales son d'vna pieça o vn solo

Hablando plinio en las cosas de la india oriental dize lib. vj. cap. veynte y tres / que Modusa abbada esta en vna region lla conocionada : desde la q'l region se lleua la Pimienta al puerto llama do Becarecon manezillas de vn leño. Estas tales nauetas creo yo que deuen ser como las que aca van los Indios : que son desta manera. En esta Ysla Española y en las otras partes todas destas indias que hasta el presente se saben / en todas las costas de la mar y en los ríos que los christianos han visto hasta agora / ay vna manera de varcas / que los indios llaman Canoa/con que ellos nauegan por los ríos grandes / y assi mismo por estas mares de aca. de las quales vsan para sus guerras y saltos: y para sus contrataciones de vna Ysla a otra/o para sus pesquerías y lo que les comiene. E assi mesmo los christianos que por aca biuimos no podemos seruir nos delas credades que están en las costas dela mar y de los ríos grandes sin estas Canoas. Cada Canoa es de vna sola pieça o solo vn arbol. El qual los indios vazian con golpes de hachas de piedras enastadas / como aqui se vee la figura dellas y con estas corta o muelen el palo aocándolo: y van quemando lo que esta golpeado

y cortado poco a poco : y matando el fuego toman a cortar y golpear como primero / y continuando lo assi hazen vna barca / quasi de talle de Artesa o dornajo: pero honda y luenga y estrecha: tan grande y gruessa como lo sufre la longitud y latitud del arbol de que la hazen: y por debaxo es llana / y no le dexan quilla como a nuestras varcas y nauios. Estas he visto de porte de quarenta y cinquenta hombres: y tan anchas que podria estar de traues vna pipa holgadamente: entre los indios caribes flecheros. Porque estos las vsan tan grandes o mayores como he dicho y llaman las los caribes Piraguas: y nauegan con velas de algodon, y al remo assi mismo con sus Nahes (que assi llaman alos remos.) Y van algunas vezes bogando de pies y a vezes sentados: y quando quieren de rodillas. Son estos Nahes como palas luengas: y las cabeças como vna muleta de vn coxo: segun aqui está pintados los nahes o remos: y canoa. Ay algunas destas canoas tan pequeñas q' no caben sino dos

317

methods of cultivation made their farming more productive. Their pottery was better made and esthetically far superior, especially in painted decoration; their weaving involved many special techniques; and their handling of stones, whether in construction or in sculpture, outranked that of the Circum-Caribbean peoples. The Andes also had metallurgy, which became part of the Circum-Caribbean culture, and domesticated animals, which did not. The Circum-Caribbean cultures are distinguished from the civilized peoples not only by their lack of the latter's elaborations but also by their possession of certain material items probably derived from the Tropical Forest....

"That the Andean and Mexican civilizations differ from the Circum-Caribbean culture more in elaboration than in essential form or content means that they grew out of something generally similar to it and that each acquired its own emphasis. It must be postulated, therefore, that a Formative Period culture once existed from Mexico to the Andes, and perhaps farther."[108]

Among the known features testifying to a common ground are large villages of up to 3000 persons, carefully planned and enclosing ball courts. That such a game should have been developed independently among the Maya of Guatemala, Taino of Puerto Rico, and Hohokam of Arizona, is hardly likely, even though the rules of the game did differ from region to region (as do those of British rugby and American football or, indeed, of American football as played in 1912 and in 1981). The Puerto Rican version of the game is described by Irving Rouse as follows from contemporary Spanish accounts: "As many as 20 persons participated on a side. They used a rubberlike ball made from the gum of a tree. The players had to keep it in the air without crossing a line, knocking it out of the court, or touching it with their hands and feet. Each time one of the sides failed to do this, its opponents scored a point. The spectators sat around the court on slabs of stone, the chiefs on their carved wooden stools.

"Both men and women played this ball game, but never together (except that the young men of the village occasionally opposed the young women). Often village played village, using the large courts outside the villages. The chiefs sometimes offered prizes.

"The ball games and other contests were accompanied by dancing, which also took place upon ceremonial occasions, such as the marriage or death of a chief, before and after victory in battle, and during the autumnal festival in honor of the chief's zemis. The more solemn dances were organized by the chiefs, who sent messengers to inform the people; the more jocular ones, however, took place without authority; sometimes the men and women danced

437. *Five Carib Indians*, painting done by George Catlin c. 1850, oil on cardboard, 18⅜″ × 24⅜″.

together; sometimes they had separate dances....

"Three kinds of musical instruments were used to accompany the songs and dances: drums, rattles, and a kind of castanet. The drums were actually gongs hollowed out of logs. Like modern matracas, the rattles consisted of gourds filled with stones; those of shamans had split handles. For castanets the Taino used little plates of metal attached to the fingers. Only the chiefs and principal men were accustomed to play these instruments, but the ordinary people wore strings of small shells on their arms and legs when dancing, to give a rattling sound."[109]

Birth, marriage, death, going to war, curing the sick, initiation and puberty rites all seem to have had their ceremonies (called by the Spaniards *areitos*) in which song and dance played a part. "The Spaniards lived for some time in Hispaniola," states Anglería, "without suspecting that the islanders worshiped anything but the stars, or had any kind or religion...but after mingling with them for some time...many began to notice among them divers ceremonies and rites."[110] Apparently the most important of these—or at least the most conspicuous—was a festival in honor of the Mother of God celebrated by the Haitians and described by two observers, an Italian, Girolamo Benzoni,[111] who traveled in the New World from 1541 to 1556, and a Spaniard, Francisco López de Gómara, of whose account the following is a translation:[112]

"When the cacique celebrated the festival in honor of the principal idol, all the people attended the function. They decorated the idol very elaborately; the priests arranged themselves as a choir about the king, and the cacique sat at the entrance of the temple with a drum at his side. The

men came painted black, red, blue, and other colors or covered with branches and garlands of flowers, or feathers and shells, wearing shell bracelets and little shells on their arms and rattles on their feet. The women also came with similar rattles, but naked if they were maids, and not painted; if married, wearing only breechcloths. They approached dancing and singing to the sound of the shells, and as they approached the cacique he saluted them with a drum.

"Having entered the temple, putting a small stick into their throat, they vomited in order to show the idol that they had nothing evil in their stomach. They seated themselves like tailors and prayed with a low voice. Then there approached many women bearing baskets and cakes on their heads and many roses, flowers, and fragrant herbs. These formed a circle as they prayed and began to chant something like an old ballad in praise of the god. All rose to respond at the close of the ballad. They changed their tone and sang another song in praise of the cacique, after which they offered the bread to the idol, kneeling. The priests took the gift, blessed, and divided it; and so the feast ended. But the recipients of the bread preserved it all the year and held that house unfortunate that was without it."[113]

As Hartley Burr Alexander has remarked of the pitiful scraps of information that have come to us from the Caribbean: "As in the case of myths, so in the case of rites, it is chiefly those of [the Arawak of] Haiti which are described for us; but there is little reason to doubt that these are typical of all the Greater Antilles."[114]

The Carib

The whole interest of the Caribs of the Lesser Antilles was in war—specifically, war in conquest of the Arawak. "The youths," states Irving Rouse, "were taught to value courage and endurance and were periodically rubbed with the fat of slaughtered Arawak to make them brave. When they had reached the age of becoming warriors they were tested in these qualities. The youth having been seated on a stool in the center of the carbet [the men's house], his father crushed a bird over his head, scarified his body, and rubbed the cuts with pepper sauce. Then the boy ate the heart of the bird, to give himself courage, and his father beat him. He had to endure the entire ceremony without flinching. When it was over he lay in a hammock and fasted for three days. Then he demonstrated his skill in wielding a club and was accepted into the company of the warriors, being given a new name. His father gave a feast in celebration.[115]

"Each warrior kept his female captives and her children as slaves, incorporating them in his family. The male captives were tortured, killed, and eaten at a feast celebrating each victory. For five days beforehand each prisoner was kept without food in the house of his captor, bound onto one of his hammocks. Then he was brought into the carbet, where the villagers had assembled. They thrust burning brands into his sides, cut his flesh and rubbed in pepper, and shot his body full of arrows, trying (usually without success) to make him cringe. Then one of the old men of the village dispatched him with a club. The Carib cut up his body, washed the flesh, and roasted it, catching the fat in gourd containers. This fat was kept by the chiefs, who used it to season the food during later feasts. Some of the flesh also was kept until later, but most was eaten then with many signs of enjoyment. The most courageous warriors received the heart, the women arms and legs, and the other men the rest of the body.

"At this time the chiefs recounted the exploits of the warriors, and they took the names of the enemies they had killed. A sponsor was chosen to present the new name, and he received gifts of ornaments in return. At this time, too, the fathers gave their daughters to the successful warriors to be their brides."[116] "The men with the most wives were considered the most prominent.... The wives were treated as servants; they dressed and fed their husbands, cleaned and thatched the houses, tilled the fields, and carried all burdens. Their husbands could abandon them without ceremony, in which case the younger children remained with the mother and the older children were divided according to sex.[117]

"The Carib sometimes killed the old and infirm. They feared the dead and never mentioned their names. When a man died all the relatives examined his body to satisfy themselves that he had not been killed by sorcery. The body was washed, painted, oiled as in life, flexed, and wrapped in a new hammock. It was placed upon a stool in a grave dug in the carbet, near the wall in the case of an ordinary person but in the center if the man were prominent, its eyes were weighted shut, and mats were added to protect it from the soil. The grave was not filled for ten days, during which the relatives brought food and water to the corpse twice a day and lamented over it. A fire was built around the grave to purify it and to prevent the deceased from catching cold. The deceased's possessions were either cast into the fire or placed in the grave; sometimes the house was burned too. In prehistoric times a slave or a dog was killed and put in the grave to care for the dead person. If the deceased were a warrior, the chief delivered a funeral oration, extolling his exploits. There was also a feast over the grave, accompanied by dancing. The close relatives fasted and cut their hair in mourning; some time afterward they held a second feast over the grave. In the case of a chief the Carib sometimes burned the corpse and mixed its ashes into a drink."[118] According to some accounts, all brave Caribs at death entered a paradise where they waged successful war forever against the Arawak, while cowards were enslaved in the future world to Arawak masters.[119]

438. Picart engraving of the manner in which the Carib increase their courage before battle: ceremonially attired chieftains, using long tubes, blow an unidentified powder into the faces of the dancing warriors. Even today, various Amazonian tribes ingest hallucinogenic snuff in a similar way.

Of the myths and legends of the island Caribs no more than fragments are preserved. Their reputation for ferocity was such that the Spaniards made no attempt to occupy and settle the Lesser Antilles. As Rouse remarks, "There was no gold there, and the agricultural potentialities did not compensate for the difficulty of subduing the Carib."[120] In 1623, however, the British and the French moved in. First driving the

Carib from St. Kitts, the British went on to colonize Nevis, St. Lucia, Barbados, Montserrat, and Antigua, while the French settled Guadeloupe, Martinique, Désirade, Marie-Galante, St. Lucia, and Grenada. Meanwhile the Dutch came along for a share of the kill and occupied Montserrat and Antigua. After 1650 missionaries arrived to reside among the quelled Indians. They learned to speak the native language, and what we know of the culture is from their reports.[121]

Besides the lurid accounts of their cannibalism, undoubtedly the most striking of the Carib's reported traits is the custom of the couvade, whereby, at the birth of a child, the father is put to bed to participate in his own way in the birthing. The ritual is based on the idea of a mystical relation between father and child. When reported of the Caribs, it was first received as extraordinary, or even absurd. It is an institution, however, that is found throughout the forest culture and among many peoples of tropical Asia. It has also been reported of the Basques. Diodorus Siculus reports it of the ancient Corsicans;[122] Strabo, among the Thracians, Scythians, and Celts. "The women themselves after giving birth," Strabo tells, "go on with agriculture and also tend their husbands, putting them to bed in their own steads."[123] The nineteenth-century anthropological theorists Edward B. Tylor, Ling Roth, and E. Sidney Hartland, among others, believed the couvade to be in the greatest force among tribes in which matrilineal kinship was in process of transition to patrilineal, the frequency and elaboration of the custom diminishing with the gathering strength and prevalence of paternal kinship.[124] Yet, even where kinship is reckoned through both parents, observances linger which are based upon what E. Sidney Hartland called "mystical sympathy."[125] One offered explanation is that a part of the father's being is, in these societies, supposed to have been separated from him and born in the child, so that both the father and the child require attention. Another view is that under conditions which exalt the privilege of motherhood, as is the case in a matrilineal context, these rites bear witness to the concurrent responsibilities of fatherhood: the father thereby demonstrating his spiritual connection with the child, whose physical connection with the mother admits of no argument. But actually, in most aboriginal societies rites such as those that have been called the couvade are observed by both parents: food taboos, avoidances of contact with others, and abstention from work of all kinds. Recognized as a moment of deep wonder, involving grave dangers—both physical and psychological—the birth of a child is an occasion set apart for both of those responsible.

Among the Carib, as related by Irving Rouse: "Sexual intercourse was forbidden during pregnancy. The birth often took place by a fire. If it caused trouble, the woman drank a juice made from a certain root. Afterward she washed the child in a stream and placed it in a tiny hammock or on a couch of leaves. If the birth had taken place at night, the men of the house bathed themselves so that the child would not catch cold.

"For several days after the birth the mother fasted, eating only dried cassava

439. *Watchdog of the House of the Dead*, c. 3′3″ tall, from the Dominican Republic. "Named Opiyelguobirán [*opiye*, 'spirit of those absent'], this idol has four legs, like a dog; is of wood; and at night often leaves its place to run through the forest. They go to find and lead him back, tied up; but he again escapes. And when the Christians came to Española, he fled, they say, to a lagoon, to which they traced him by his tracks. But he has never again been seen; nor is anything more

known of him."[44] One might ask (it has been suggested) whether the night forays of this Antillean Cerberus might have been meant to guide the recently deceased on the uncertain journey to Coaybay. Or was it to warn shades at large on nocturnal adventure—with a barking inaudible to the living—to return to their underworld dwellings before the break of day, when by the light of the sun they would be transformed into wandering ghosts?[45]

and drinking warm water. The father, on the other hand, practiced the couvade. Immediately after the birth he complained of pains, went to a separate hut, and lay in a hammock. He remained there for at least forty days after the birth of his first child, and for four or five days after the birth of other children. During this time he went out only at night and avoided meeting anyone for fear that they might tempt him to break his fast, thereby making the mother sick and the child cowardly. At first he took no food. After five days he was permitted to drink corn beer and after ten days to eat manioc bread in increasing quantities. He ate only the insides of the bread, the crusts being hung up in the hut until the end of the forty-day period, when they served as the basis for a feast in the village carbet. Preceding the feast the father was brought into the carbet, was stood on two large flat cakes of cassava, and was scarified by two men chosen by the carbet chief. A mixture of urucú, pepper seeds, and tobacco juice was rubbed into the cuts, and the blood which fell from them was daubed on the face of the child, so that he would have the courage shown by the father in undergoing scarification. The man was then fed the two cassava cakes upon which he stood and also fish, which he had to spit out. He went back to bed for several days and had to abstain from the flesh of animals for a period of six months or a year, lest the child become deformed."[126]

There is little doubt that these people entered the Caribbean from the mouth of the Orinoco, as had (probably) the ancestors of the Taino before them. Whereas the Taino were of a Circum-Caribbean background, however, the Carib (as already remarked) were from the deep rain forest area, very much farther up the river, and so skilled were they in the management of boats that some authorities have called them river nomads. According to Rouse they had vessels of four kinds: pirogues, large canoes, small canoes, and rafts. "Both the pirogues and the canoes," states Rouse, "were dugouts, but the sides of the former were built up with planks, sewn together and pitched with bitumen. The average length of the pirogue was 40 feet (12 m.); some were large enough to carry 50 persons. Each one had a keel, a raised and pointed bow, a series of plank seats, and a flat-topped stern carved with an animal's head (maboya) to frighten the enemy and often decorated with a barbecued human arm. The larger variety of canoe was 20 feet (6 m.) long. It, too, had a series of seats and also thwarts against which the paddlers leaned their backs. Both the stem and the stern were high and pointed; there were holes in the gunwales to which the travelers could attach their belongings. The smaller type of canoe was just large enough for one person; it had a flat stern and served mainly for fishing. The rafts consisted of a series of logs, lashed to two transverse bars.

"The pirogues and canoes seem to have been better finished than the Arawak canoes. Their sides were smoothed, polished, and often painted to represent Indians or maboya spirits. In historic times (and perhaps earlier) the pirogues had three masts and the canoes two, each supporting a sail made from cotton or from palm leaf matting. (Some sources say the pirogues had topsails as well as the usual square mainsails.) The paddles were spade-shaped, like those of the Arawak; that of the steersman was one-third longer than the rest."[127]

Of the myths and legends of these aggressive people only summaries and fragments survive; yet these suffice to make known the burden of the tradition. And by good chance there has been lately brought from the upper reaches of the Orinoco (the region from which the Caribs sprang) the whole length of a cycle of tales that matches and clarifies the mythology of these vestigial fragments.

440. *A Fight with the Peccaries—Carib*, 17 3/16" × 24 1/16", an oil-on-cardboard view of early Antillean life, painted by George Catlin, c. 1850.

441. The Yekuana, aptly dubbed "river nomads," still navigate the Orinoco River and its tributaries, exactly as their Carib ancestors once did.

SOUTH AMERICAN

AGRICULTURAL
RITES AND MYTHS

Culture Areas in South America

CENTRAL
AMERICA

Caribbean Sea

ATLANTIC OCEAN

PACIFIC OCEAN

Equator

Tropic of Capricorn

Strait of Magellan

Goajiro
Calamari
Caquetío
Caraca
Chayma
Carib
Uarau
Tolú
Carate
Bubure
Timote
Guamo
Palenque
Guamontey
Chocó
Patangora
Chibcha
Achagua
Yaruro
Tamanaco
Caliña
Baudo
Guahibo
Sáliva
Mapoyo
Camaracotó
Acawi
Caliña
Pijao
Piapoco
Makiritare
Casapare
Macusi
Trio
Galibi
Barbacoa
Achagua
Manapai
Baté
Mauaco
Pauxiana
Ararau
Oayana
Oyampi
Carijona
Cubeo
Waiwai
Apalai
Tucujú
Aruan
Colorado
Bora
Macú
Aruagui
Moheyana
Teremembé
Quitu
Cofán
Jumana
Manáo
Apanto
Manabí
Quijo
Zápato
Yagua
Marawa
Ibanoma
Mura
Aráta
Pacajá
Tembé
Gamela
Teremembé
Cañari
Shapra
Catauishi
Yúma
Maué
Cayapó
Manayé
Guanare
Potyguara
Jívaro
Cutinana
Catuquina
Mura
Maué
Curuaya
Yuruna
Crahó
Timbira
Geicó
Cariri
Mayna
Uaraicú
Paumari
Tupiocón
Munducurú
Cradahó
Caeté
Chachapoya
Curina
Parintintin
Xavante
Amoipira
Hivito
Canamaré
Caritiana
Urupa
Tapanhuna
Tapirapé
Aricobé
Tupiná
Amahuaca
Ipuriná
Araona
Campa
Toromona
Caviña
Movima
Apiaca
Bakairí
Acroa
Camacán
Rimac
Machiganga
Paicone
Paresí
Cayapó
Cherente
Chicriabá
Patacho
Quechua
Mosetene
Guarayo
Orari
Nazca
Cana
Yurácare
Bororó
Goyá
Nacnanuc
Cavana
Aymará
Chiquito
Guató
Cayapó
Guarayo
Zamuco
Tereno
Opaie
Otí
Tupí
Purí
Chiriguano
Moro
Kaingáng
Chicha
Mataco
Sanapaná
Tupí
Tupinambá
Lipe
Humahuaca
Pilagó
Guaraní
Chiripa
Guaraní
Atacamans
Mocoví
Toba
Caringuá
Pinaré
Jurí
Abipón
Carijó
Kaingáng
Comechingón
Tapé
Minuane
Huarpe
Allentiac
Querandí
Charrúa
Mapuche
Millcayac
Puelche
Divihet
Chechehet
Puelche
Gennaken
Huilliche
Poya
Tehuelche
Chono
Téuesh
Tsoneca
Ona
Yahgan

Culture Areas in South America

Circum-Antilles
Tropical Forest
Tropical Aquatic
The Andes
Marginal Forest
Pampas-Patagonia-Pacific Archipelago
Present-day International boundary
Cubeo Tribe

324

Map 35.

Watunna: A Cariban Creation Cycle from the Upper Orinoco

The Rain-Forest tribe in the interior of Venezuela from whom—during a season of fifteen years, from the late 1940s to early 1960s—the French ethnographer Marc de Civrieux collected the material of this cycle are the Makiritare, a people of the same Cariban linguistic stock as the boat-warriors of the fifteenth-century Caribbean. Their first experience of the Spanish took place only in 1759, after which the usual attempt to subdue and missionize was followed by a succession of revolts, withdrawals of the Spanish, and returns. These ugly episodes are reflected in the later portions of the cycle in a way that illustrates—with an ironic turn at the end—the ability of myth to assimilate alien matter. The earlier episodes, however, are of ancient heritage, and the evidence of their counterparts in the reports from the Caribbean testifies to the ability of a living mythology to maintain its fundamental sense and structure even through enormous transformations of the historical environment.

Hartley Burr Alexander has summarized the main themes in the recorded origin myths of the Caribbean Caribs:

1. The sky is eternal.
2. The earth, at first soft, was hardened by the sun's rays.
3. Louguo, the first man, came down from the sky.
4. Other men were born from his body.
5. After his death he ascended to heaven.
6. The First Race of men were nearly exterminated by a deluge, from which the lucky few escaped in a canoe.

442. Yaribaru, one of three traditional weapons of the Yekuana—"tree" (*ye*), "water" (*ku*), "people" (*ana*): that is, "Canoe People"—of the Upper Orinoco and its tributaries. In Yekuana origin myths, the yaribaru belonged to Vulture.

7. After death the soul of the valiant Carib ascends to heaven.
8. The stars are Carib souls.[1]

In addition, Alexander points out that Maboya, or Mapoia, the Great Snake, was the god who sent the hurricane, and that there were many other Maboyas—dangerous spirits to be feared (projections by the Caribs, one might say, of the ferocity of their own natures). Good spirits were also recognized, however, so that a rudimentary dualism of beneficent and malignant spirits motivated their universe.

In the following creation cycle of the Cariban Makiritare at the headwaters of the Orinoco (whence the Caribbean Caribs sprang), the dominant character throughout is an unrelenting creature of evil, Odosha, who frustrates at every turn the creative projects of the earthly incarnations of the light of the highest sky. The dualism here is even stronger than in what has been learned of the Cariban myths from the sixteenth century. Indeed, such a dualism of good and evil, with evil everywhere triumphant, is something quite exceptional, even alien, to the spirit of other native American mythologies. It is almost Zoroastrian and may have been influenced by the idea of the Christian devil and his host, who everywhere "wander through the world seeking the ruin of souls."[2] Indeed, I know of only one other aboriginal tradition in which anything comparable can be found, namely, the Melanesian (across the Pacific) of two opposed creator brothers: To-Kabinana, the creator of good things, and To-Karvuvu, who produces the bad or spoiled, but is stupid, not deliberately evil. According to that mythology, however, although the course of creation has involved accidents and misfortunes, there is in the cosmogonic process nothing of intrinsic evil—unlike the Zoroastrian, Christian, and Makiritare mythologies of Angra Mainyu, Satan, and Odosha. Ironically, at the conclusion of the Makiritare myth, the satanic figure, Odosha, is identified as the god of the Spanish priests and musketeers, while their own, native American incarnation of the light of the highest sky, Wanadi, assumes the role of the crucified Redeemer.

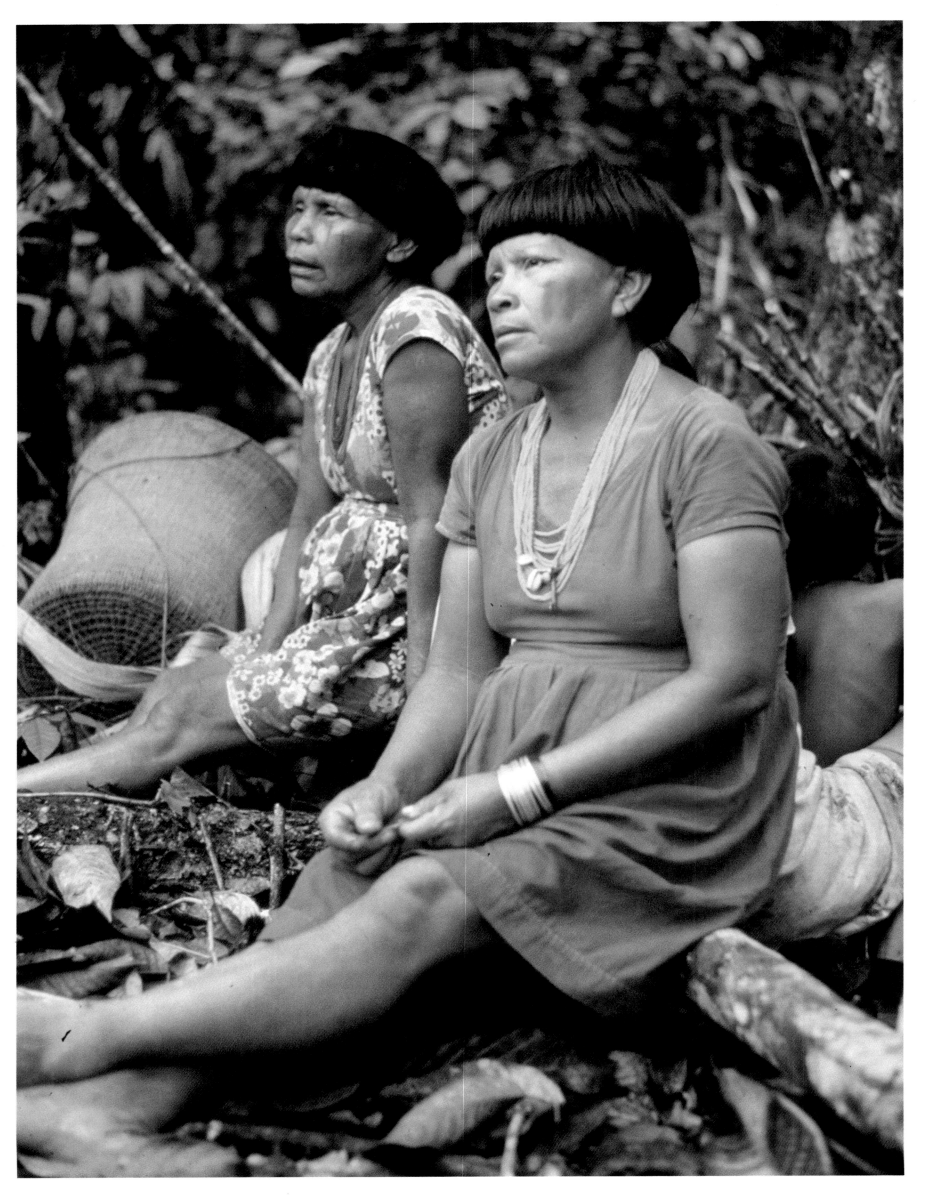

The following, then, is an abstract of some of the leading episodes of this long, rich, and now, at last, fully published Cariban recitation of the epic of creation.[3]

443. Women singing *avanso catajo*, the type of Watunna sung (by women only) before planting a new garden. David M. Guss, author of *To Weave and Sing* (a seminal study of Yekuana art, symbol, and narrative), points out that "listening to stories among the Yekuana turned out to be an entirely different proposition than I had originally imagined. There were no neatly framed 'storytelling events' into which the foreign observer could easily slip, no circles of attentive youths breathing in the words of an elder as he regaled them with the deeds of their ancestors. Rather," Guss explains, "*Watunna* was everywhere, like an invisible sleeve holding the entire culture in place. Derived from the verb *adeu*, 'to tell,' it existed in every evocation of the mythic tradition, no matter how fragmentary or allusive."[46] The only distinction made in the singing of Watunna is between individual (*achiudi*) and collective (*ademi*) singing. *Achiudi Watunna* is sung for widely varied occasions, including: while making a canoe, before using a new child's sling or hammock, over menstruating women, when fasting, or before the first eating of a new food; *ademi Watunna*, on the other hand, is sung only on three occasions: (1) as shown here, before the annual planting of a new garden, (2) when building a new house, and (3) when someone returns home after a long departure.

Cycle of the First Emanation

All was sky and light, and the highest sky, Wanadi—created by the Invisible Sun—gave life and light to the Sky People. Thinking to make people on earth, he sent down his Emanation, Seruhe Sanadi, who shook his rattle, chanted, smoked, and through the power of his quartz crystals created the Old People. When born, however, he had cut his own navel cord and buried the placenta, which rotted, producing Odosha, an evil, hairy creature wishing to master the earth. Odosha saw a man fishing. "If you kill that man," he told the Old People, "you will have fish." They did so and became animals. Then Seruhe Sanadi returned, defeated, to heaven.[4]

Cycle of the Second Emanation

Wanadi sent down Nadeiumadi, a second Emanation, who, when he saw the people who had become animals dying, said: "But now I am here. They will live again. Death is unreal. It is one of Odosha's tricks." Nadeiumadi had brought down with him Huehanna, a beautiful stonelike egg that was full of unborn people. You could hear them inside, laughing, singing, dancing. With his head in hands, sitting, smoking, thinking, he shook his rattle, sang, and dreamed that a woman was born: Kumairiawa, his mother. "You will die," he thought. And she died. But he knew that death was unreal.

Summoning the Orange-winged Parrot to help bury Kumairiawa, he next called the Capuchin Monkey to watch over Huehanna. "You guard the grave," he told the Parrot. "When Kumairiawa comes out, that will be a sign for the unborn to leave Huehanna." Then he left to go hunting, but forgot his medicine bag full of herbs, tobacco, quartz crystals, and Night. (For there was then no night in the world.) The Monkey had been warned not to open that bag.

The earth moved, a hand stuck out, the grave opened, and the Parrot screeched. Nadeiumadi came running, but as he ran everything went dark, for Odosha had spoken to the Monkey. "Open!" the Monkey heard, as though in a dream. "Open, and learn a secret!" He opened and, when Night burst out, fled in terror.

Now, Odosha had sent a hairy dwarf to watch the grave, and when this fellow called, "She's coming out!" Odosha pissed into a gourd, which he gave to the Lizard to fling at Kumairiawa the moment she appeared. The poisonous urine covered her, her flesh roasted, and the bones fell apart, so that when Nadeiumadi arrived in the night, there was nothing he could do. Gathering his mother's remains into a basket, he picked up Huehanna and carried it to Mount Waruma, where he hid it; then he went on to Ahuena, the heavenly lake of eternal life, into which he threw the bones. Kumairiawa there returned to life, and there she is living still. And so the earth was left a second time to Odosha.[5]

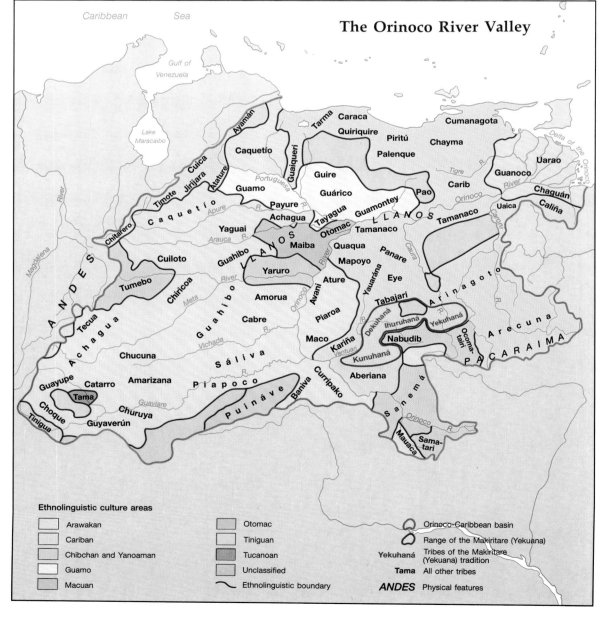

The Orinoco River Valley

Ethnolinguistic culture areas

- Arawakan
- Cariban
- Chibchan and Yanoaman
- Guamo
- Macuan
- Otomac
- Tiniguan
- Tucanoan
- Unclassified

Yekuhaná — Orinoco-Caribbean basin
— Range of the Makiritare (Yekuana)
— Tribes of the Makiritare (Yekuana) tradition
Tama — All other tribes
ANDES — Physical features
— Ethnolinguistic boundary

Map 36. The Makiritare (known to scholarship also as Mayonkong, Yekuana, or Dekuana; to themselves, however, as So'to) are a people of Cariban linguistic stock inhabiting a mountainous region of rain forest and riverways on the uppermost Orinoco, in Venezuela. Their legendary place of origin is the area eastward of Mount Paru, whence stream tributaries to the Amazon and to the Orinoco. A single group originally, they split, as they grew, into four: the Dekuhana, Yekuhana, Kunuhana, and Ihuruhana; the last, whose name means "Headwater People," dwelling still in their legendary place of the beginnings.

Now the name So'to means "twenty," which is the number of toes and fingers of the human body. The name therefore signifies "human being," and is thus a term reserved for speakers of the So'to tongue. All speakers of languages unintelligible to the So'to are regarded as animals to be feared. And indeed, the neighboring Kariña, to the east—whose tongue, though also of Cariban stock, is alien to the Makiritare—are greatly feared by them. In their myths the Makiritare portray the Kariña shamans as jaguars out hunting for people to eat. Their own shamans are also envisioned as being jaguars, of course, but at least they are not hungry for Makiritare.

The long and complex origin legend common to all four of the Makiritare subgroups, as recently made known to the world by Marc de Civrieux,[47] is the best reported single cycle of myths yet collected from any quarter of the South American forest. Its recitation is an essential feature of the *Wanwanna* festivals, whereby the young men are initiated and new communal houses and fresh gardens are inaugurated. As observed by David M. Guss—de Civrieux's translator and, for a time, collaborator—its rituals "include dancing, singing, drinking, and a trance-like communion leading to a total collective frenzy."[48] The festival is introduced by the deep mooing sound of long horns (made of a certain bark) approaching along a jungle path. The sound "is identified," states David M. Guss, "with that of the jungle spirits and calls the supernatural beings to the village to participate in the *Wanwanna*."[49] Such horns are known to nearly all of the South American Tropical Forest tribes (see **487**).

Cycle of the Third Emanation

Creation of the Celestial Ceiling

Wanadi blew on his quartz crystals, and there appeard a third Emanation, Attawanadi, who immediately created the visible sky, sun, moon, and stars, whereupon, the people, in their animal bodies, began emerging from caves. They had neither houses, nor hammocks, nor food.[6]

House-making

Attawanadi's first act was to go to the food mistress, Iamankave, and ask for food for the earth. "Fine," she said, and she sent a messenger down with cassava. Odosha, however, while Wanadi was away, disguised himself as Wanadi and, choosing two children, taught them to copulate. The Old People never had done that. Now they started, and got sick and died. The cassava messenger left them, and again there was no food. "What am I going to do now?" thought Wanadi. "These people hear only Odosha. I must make new people."

Going to Wanahidi, a mountain on the Kuntinama, he built for himself the first house. Odosha, however, on seeing this, built right in front of it a house of his own. "I see," thought Wanadi, "I am going to have to work fast." He brought down into his house twelve people, Wanadi's People. They were strong and wise. But Odosha then brought into his own house many people, evil and destructive. Wanadi sat down, elbows on knees, head in hands, dreaming food. But no food came, for Odosha was

dreaming hunger right in front of him. "We can do nothing here," Attawanadi said to the twelve and departed with them to where Wade lived. Wade was the grandfather of all sloths. He was good, the most powerful of the Old People's shamans. He lived in a cave, and whenever he wished to, could appear in his sloth form. "We're fleeing from Odosha," Attawanadi said. "Very well," said Wade, "stay here." So there they stayed, and from there Wanadi would go out to hunt, to fish, and to make houses.[7]

444. Men completing the infrastructure for the roof of an *atta*, a Yekuana roundhouse designed, built, and envisioned as a replica of the cosmos; it will be used as a communal dwelling, housing between forty and one hundred people.

445. A critical part of the process of house-building is the playing of *wana*, the twin flutes that are an integral part of Yekuana ceremonies. The *wana*, although similar to Yurupari sacred flutes (see Figure **487**), are not considered secret.

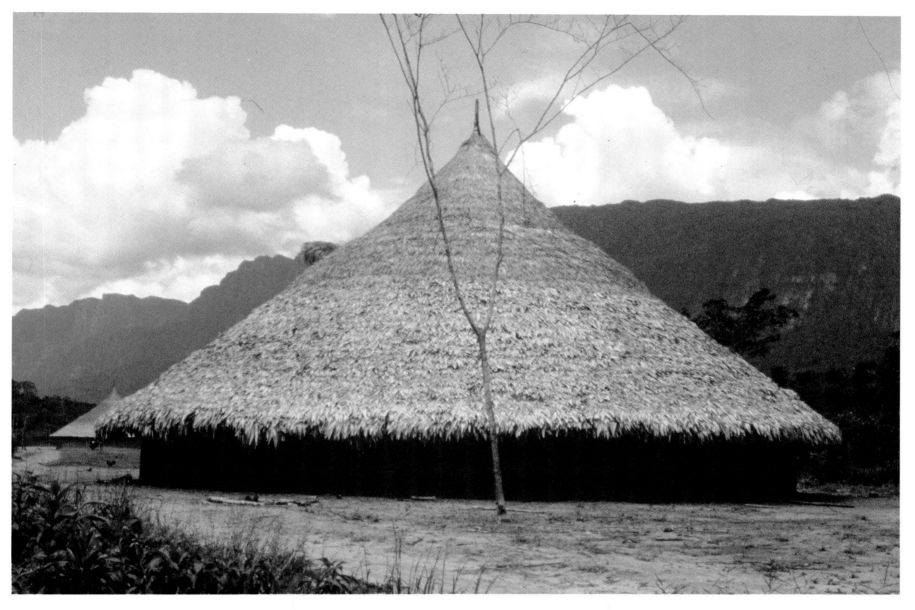

Felling of the World Tree

One day one of the starving people said, "I know the cassasva road. I'll go and bring back food." He was the Kinkajou. Climbing, he reached heaven and came to the house of the Yuca Mistress, Iamankave. There, in a fenced-off garden, grew the great Food Tree, and the Kinkajou, assisted by Iamankave's son, contrived to hide a splinter of its wood beneath his tail. Caught and nearly killed by Iamankave, he nevertheless escaped and returned to the earth, where he drew out the splinter and planted it.

Overnight a great tree grew. However, it had been planted very far from the people. A woman was sent to obtain from it a sprout, which again took root, and again overnight an immense tree grew, so vast that, like a roof, it covered the earth, every branch budding and bearing fruit. Marahuaca was its name. But it was so tall that no one could reach the fruit. Then branches began falling, killing people; and, crying for help, they ran to Attawanadi and surrounded him.

Attawanadi then made a new people, the Birds, to fly and harvest the fruit; but when they did so, much of it fell, and things were no better than before. Then said Semenia, the chief of the Birds: "Let us stop this gathering. Let us fell the tree and plant gardens." (It was thus he who taught us to cultivate.) But the felling of Marahuaca was not easy.

Four toucans began; then more toucans arrived, and woodpeckers. They chopped all day and rested at night, but in the morning Marahuaca was whole again. So then they labored in turns day and night; but the tree, when cut through, did not fall. Squirrel was sent to the top to investigate. The branches, he found, were caught like roots in the sky. It was an upside down tree. Semenia sent him back with an ax, and when Marahuaca fell, the earth shook. The people had taken refuge in caves, and when they came out, it was raining: the first rain. "Now," Semenia said, "we can plant." From the rain the rivers were born and ran like snakes across the earth.[8]

446. Designed, built, and envisioned as a replica of the cosmos, after some four to five months of intermittent labor, the *atta*, with its newly thatched roof in place, is at last completely finished.

447. Home to about one hundred and twenty-five people, the village of Canaracuni, near a tributary of the Upper Caura River, Estado Bolivar, Venezula. Approximately thirty traditional Yekuana settlements are scattered throughout the upper Orinoco; each village is viewed as being an *atta*.[50]

Attawanadi now decided to bring the unborn people forth from Huehanna. He told this to Nuna, the moon, who was a cannibal, hungry for people to eat, and immediately Nuna rose to the highest sky, where the door (which is never opened) to the house of Wanadi (who is never seen) is watched by guardians. "I am Attawanadi," Nuna said to the guardians. "I have come for Huehanna, to bring forth people on earth." Deceived, the guardians reported to Wanadi. "Very well!" said he. "Let him have it." So when Attawanadi himself arrived and asked to be given Huehanna, the guardians said, "We just gave it to you." And he returned, perplexed, to the earth.

Now the moon had a sister, Frimene. "What's that?" she asked, when she saw him with Huehanna. She knew that he had stolen it. "It is full of unborn people," she thought. "I cannot let him eat them. I'll hatch them and be their mother." So when he left the house, she hid the beautiful egg-shaped thing in her vagina. Returning, he looked for it. "Did Wanadi come?" he asked. "Did he come and take Hue-

hanna?" But he saw his sister's stomach and knew what she had done.

That night, lying in her hammock, listening happily to the songs and laughter, drums and horns of the unborn people in her stomach, Frimene heard approaching footsteps. Something fell into her hammock, and hands began feeling and searching all over her. She pressed her legs together; the hands tried to separate them, and at dawn the presence had left. "What was that?" she thought. "Was it Odosha? Nuna? Wanadi, looking for his children? Was it a dream?"

Next night she covered her face and body with the black *caruta* oil that our women use for body paint, and when again those steps approached and something fell into her hammock, one of the hands, feeling, forced its way between her thighs, reached into the cave, and touched and tried to grasp Huehanna. She began to bleed (which is why our women bleed when the moon passes), and again, when day dawned, she was alone. Going out, she met her brother in a field. His face and body were stained black. "I've found him out!" she thought, and fled. We can still see those stains on the moon's face.[9]

448

Among the Yekuana, David M. Guss observes, "all economic activities are strictly divided along sexual lines, and even when both sexes participate in a single activity some form of gender differentiation will be employed....But most activities demand no such collaboration, and the daily working lives of tribal members are spent almost exclusively in the company of their own sex."[51] Above, an elderly Yakuana woman (**448**); at right, a young girl cares for a younger sibling (**449**), one of her primary responsibilities; a two-year-old girl (**450**) wearing jewelry having protective qualities; this girl of marriageable age (**451**), adorned with face paint, recently menstruated for the first time.

449

450

451

452

453

456

454

The principal responsibilities of Yekuana women are the maintenance of the gardens, the growing of food, and the processing of their main staple crop, bitter yuca (*Manihot utilissima*), which is such a labor-intensive activity (see **462–468**) that, as David M. Guss points out, "it is no exaggeration to say that a Yekuana woman, working in necessary collaboration with all other adult females in her extended family, spends a full ninety percent of her working time involved in some aspect of yuca production....In addition to this lengthy preparation process, the women are also responsible for all domestic maintenance: the drawing of water, the gathering of firewood, the serving of food, and the collection of game left out on the trails by the men who have shot it. When there is no game to collect, the women may supplement the village diet by gathering grubs, ants, or sacred worms called *motto*. Even when uninvolved in the physically demanding daily regime of food preparation, women relax by making the two principal artifacts used in it—yuca graters and carrying baskets."[52] Herewith a sampling of women's activities, clockwise from above left: (**452**) weaving a hammock on a simple loom, an activity little pursued of late, since most hammocks are now obtained by trade with neighboring tribes; (**453**) weaving a *wuwa*, the all-purpose carrying basket (**454**) used to transport firewood, game, fish, and household possessions, as well as to carry yuca from the gardens to the village; (**455**) preparing fermented *iarake* from yuca; and (**456**) weaving a woman's *muaho*, the bead apron that is the most intricate item of a woman's wardrobe.

The Great Water Mother

When Frimene, running, came to the Orinoco, she splashed into it and turned into an enormous anaconda. "I am the River Mother, Huiio," she said, and, diving to the bottom of the rapids, there built her house. The rainbow that we see where the rapids foam is her feathered headdress.

Presently Attawanadi, searching for Huehanna, came to Nuna's house and asked if anyone there knew where it might be. "My sister hid it in her stomach and ran off," Nuna replied. Turning, Attawanadi dashed into the forest, shouting for everybody to help find her. All night there was hooting and hallooing, until at dawn Huiio lifted her immense serpent form from the water, cried, "Here I am!" and then dove, and the rainbow marked her way as she swam downriver.

Arrows flew and so filled the Water Mother's body that she looked like a porcupine. Over she fell, and Huehanna shot into the air. Falling on a rock in the rapids, it burst, and the unborn people, in the form of fish eggs, flew all about. So were born the fish, crocodiles, anacondas, and other water dwellers. And Huiio, leaving as reminders to us her body covered with arrows and the rainbow, departed to the lake of eternal life, where she lives today in the center of the highest sky.

Then Manuwa, the Jaguar, approached and took a bite of the serpent flesh. That was the first eating of meat. When the others saw the red blood flow, they all pressed in for a mouthful. All the rivers, however, began to rise, and flooded the earth, and the people fled to high cliffs and caves. Then the Great Water went down, and they returned to gorge themselves on the body of the Water Mother.[10]

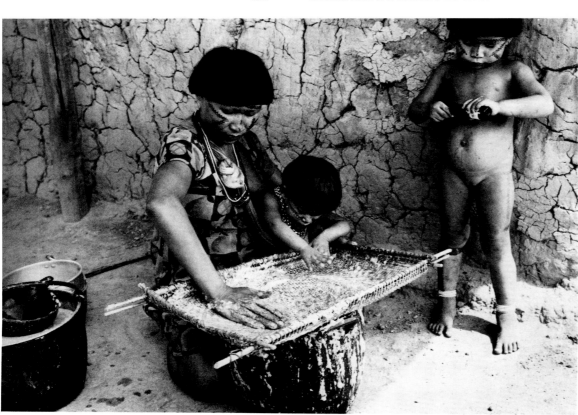

455

Cycle of the Twin Heros

The Fire Theft

The people had no fire at that time, but the Jaguar's wife, Kawao, the Toad-woman, had fire in her stomach. That was her secret. When alone, she would open her mouth, pull the fire out, cook dinner, then pull it back with her tongue, and when her husband returned, "How do you do it?" he would ask. "By the heat of the sun," she would answer. He was not very bright, and so she had him fooled.

Now the day they killed the Water Mother, Toad-woman found on the shore two fish eggs, which she took home to hatch. The warmth of her fire opened them, and two boys were born: Shikiemona, the elder, and Iureke. Right away they walked, talked, and were not infants any more, but unruly pests, playing pranks on people, now as boys, now as fish, cockroaches or crickets. "I am your mother," Toad-woman told them, and they knew nothing of their Water Mother's death.

"How do you do it?" they asked, one day, when she had ordered them out of the house, in order to be alone to cook. "By the heat of the sun," she answered. "No," they said, "that wouldn't do it." Angry, she beat them and threw them out, and they went directly to the river, dove, and turning into fish, swam to the bottom of the rapids, where they came to an enormous house. They called. No one answered. They went in. "Nice house," Shikie-mona said. "I feel I've been here before," Iureke said. They found two hammocks, got in, fell asleep, and in dream saw their mother, Huiio, the Great Serpent. "This is my house, your house. I am your mother," she told them. "Wanadi is your father: not the Toad and the Jaguar. They killed and ate me. I live now in the sky. The Jaguar plans to kill and eat you. You must kill him first." They woke, found a gourd of black *caruta* oil, then slept and dreamed again. "That was my gourd for painting myself," they heard. "If you throw it away, the rivers will rise, and their waters will cover the earth. Those who ate me were many, down to the smallest."

They woke and, returning to the Jaguar's house, asked the Toad-woman for dinner. In order to cook, she ordered them out, but only Shikiemona left. Iureke hid in the roof to spy. "Good," she thought, "they're gone." But in her pan she saw the younger brother's reflection. "What are you doing up there?" she called; "Get out!" "I can't," he answered. "I've lost an eye and can't move. But I won't look. I'll look at the ceiling." He had fixed one eye in the back of his neck, and this watched as she opened her mouth, blew fire under the pan, then shot out her tongue, and took the fire back. "Dinner's ready," she called. Iureke, replacing the eye, came down; Shikiemona entered, and with a large scissors the woman approached the two to kill them. "Boys! Let me cut your hair," she was saying. But they sprang upon her. "Throw it up!" they yelled. "Bring that thing out of your stomach!" She tried, terrified, but choked. They slit her mouth, and out gushed the fire. (That is why toads have wide mouths today and a lump in their throat that goes up and down.) Iureke pounced upon the fire, and cutting up the Toad, they made a stew of her with chili peppers. When they heard the jaguar coming home for his meal, they quickly went out and hid the fire in two trees. Iureke hid half of it in the wishu tree, Shikiemona half in the kumnuatte. When we want fire we remember this. We take wood of the wishu and wood of the kumnuatte and rub the two together. Right away, the fire jumps out. Those two boys, in the beginning, hid it for us in two trees. Because of that, people now eat well.[11]

457. Men making sieves (*manade*), a type of *waja*, the twill-plated flat baskets used as plateware.

458. Below, four examples of "painted" *waja* that feature bichromatic twill plating.

The Eye-juggling Game

Sitting facing each other, the boys were playing their eye game. "Catch!" said one, tossing an eye to his brother. "Catch!" said the other, tossing it back. Jaguar, hunting to kill them, arrived, but on seeing the game, became curious. "What's this?" he asked. "We're airing our eyes," they said. "They were covered with dreams this morning. Now they're clean and dry." "I also dreamed last night," said Jaguar, "and I'd like to see better, too." "Well then, give us your eyes. We'll wash them for you." And he gave them both his eyes.

"Are they ready yet?" he presently asked. "They're really dirty," the boys answered. "They're covered with dreams. Just hang on a little." Laughing, they tossed the eyes back and forth. "Here, catch!" they teased. "No, please!" he cried. "We'll put them out on this rock to dry. They're really beautiful!" the boys told him. Then Wadakane, the Crab, came by. "Give those eyes a turn," the boys called to him. He turned them; they continued to roll; they hit the water: "Plump!" The Jaguar screamed, "They've fallen in!" and striking out a paw to find them, hit the Crab and split his skull. (So crabs now have split skulls.) The boys were just laughing. "Let's go fishing!" they said, and swam away.

The Vulture flew down, expecting a meal. "Here I am!" he said. The Jaguar whined, "I can't see. I've lost my eyes. Who are you?" "I'm Vulture. I'll find you a new pair." Flying off, he returned with two wonderful eyes. They were a bit too large, but he shoved them in. So now jaguars have big beautiful eyes, and are good hunters.[12]

The Great Water

The People were all together, feasting, many of them drunk. "Let's punish them now," Shikiemona said. Iureke agreed, and diving, they swam to their mother's house, recovered the gourd and threw it away. Then the rivers, rising, covered the earth. Only two tall palms were left standing, reaching all the way to heaven. These the boys climbed and, making a platform between them, looked down, day after day, until the flood withdrew to the Caribbean. When they then came down, the palms turned into Mount Moriche, and the brothers looked around. "Everybody's dead," they said, and together ascended to the sky.[13]

459.

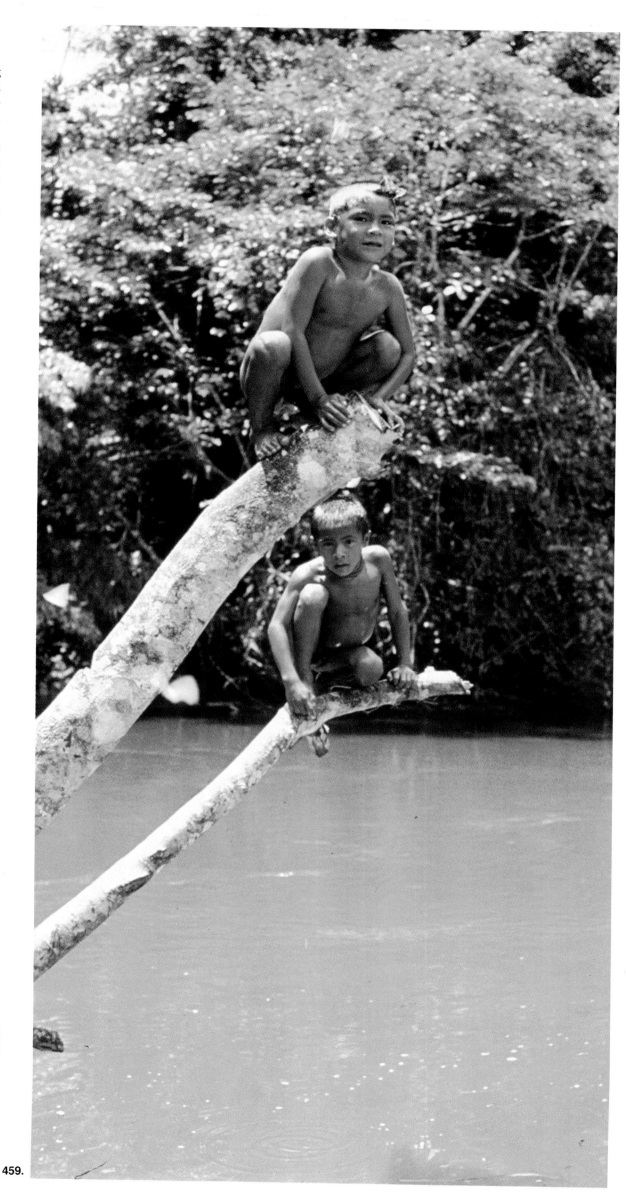

333

The End of the Mythological Age

Wahnatu and Wetashi, Our First Parents

The Old People had departed to the sky, leaving their animal bodies on earth, along with their food plants. "How can I keep these plants from getting lost?" thought Attawanadi. "The animals can't take care of them." He went to Mount Dekuhana, took clay, shaped it and with fire dried it, shook his rattle, lit his cigar, sang, blew smoke, and so made Wahnatu, the first man. "You are a So'to," Wanadi told him. "You will make slash-and-burn gardens." [So'to—True People—is the name by which the Makiritare know themselves.] Then Attawanadi made Wetashi, the first woman, to plant the gardens her man was to prepare. And Attawanadi then made for these two a house.

At Mount Marahuaka, where the great tree had once stood, Wahnatu cleared a garden plot. "The conuco's ready," he told his wife. "Now we'll celebrate. You make the yuca beer; I'll make the bark horn." He climbed the mountain to find bark, made the horn, and then blew it: "Wooo-wooo-wooo." Down came the Bird and Animal Masters, all of them, dancing and singing. "Did you call?" they asked. "We'll help you celebrate." They made a dance stick to beat the earth and summon Food Spirits from below; they cut bamboo and made clarinets and flutes, then played them. "This," they said, "is our voice. Listen and learn the story of how we felled the great tree." They gave him feathers to wear; made dance pendants, hats, and palm-leaf dance skirts; then painted themselves while he watched to learn the patterns. And when they had taught him all, they left, promising to return when his gardens were ready and he blew his horn.

"My, you are beautiful!" exclaimed Wetashi when she saw her husband returning. When everything was ready, he blew the bark horn. "Your beer is ready," said the horn, but all the woman heard was "Woooo-wooo-woooo!" Singing, the Masters arrived, and Wahnatu, listening, repeated their song of the felling of Marahuaca. Wetashi, however, neither heard nor saw the visitors, but only her husband's repetitions of their teachings.[14]

Attawandi, Odosha, and the Soldiers of the Cross

Having fashioned Wahnatu and Wetashi, Attawanadi left to find places to make other people. At Maipures Rapids he made the first Spaniards, but before he could give them a house, Odosha arrived, and he had to leave. Downstream he then made the Puinave tribe and gave them a fine big house. "Wanadi is bad," Odosha told the Spaniards. "He left you with nothing, yet has made a fine house for those new people downstream. Make war on them and take their house." Immediately, they marched, beat and killed the Puinave with clubs, took their house, and went on to get Wanadi. That is how war, injustice, and theft began.

At Angostura [now Ciudad Bolívar] Attawanadi made another white man to replace the Spaniards ruined by Odosha. He made a merchant, wise and rich, with a beautiful house and goods of every kind. "You are a merchant," Attawanadi told him. Forever traveling around,

460

461

462

463

464

465

The Yekuana, like other residents of the Tropical Forest, grow yuca in slash-and-burn gardens and use age-old techniques to process the plant. After a plot of jungle has been clear-cut, the vegetation is left in place to dry out. Later, the plot is burned off (**460**) and planted with yuca. While the yuca is growing, the garden is regularly tended and carefully weeded (**461**). When the yuca is ready for harvesting, the women dig up and peel the large tubers (**462**), fill their *wuwa* baskets, and carry them back to the village (**463**). In the workhuts shared by each extended family (**464**), the tubers are grated, and the wet pulp is stuffed into long mesh yuca presses (*tingkui* or *sebucans*) that are carried (**465**) to an elaborately constructed device known as *tingkui-yedi* ("the *sebucan* teeth"), where they are hung and stretched (**466**) to squeeze out the prussic acid. When dried, the chalky yuca pulp is forced through *manade* baskets that act as sieves. The resulting flour, spread on hot grills (once made of stone, but now of iron), is transformed into cassava (**467**), which, if not eaten at once, is dried (**468**) and stored for future use.[53]

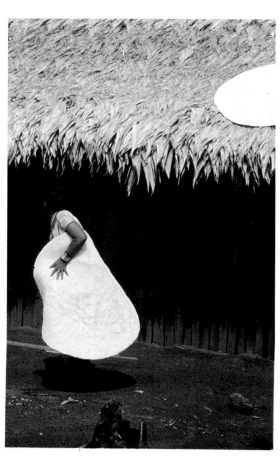

466

467

468

he became Wanadi's friend to the poor. Our grandfathers would go to his village for his wares.

Then at the mouth of the Essequibo, on the shores of the Caribbean Sea, Attawanadi made another white man, Hurunko, the Dutchman, rich, strong, and very wise. But while he was making still another fine house at Caracas, Odosha's Spaniards arrived.

"We're here!" they said. "Whose village is this?" "Mine," said Attawanadi. "No, ours!" they said. "Everything on earth is ours." "I am Wanadi. I made you," Attawanadi said. "You are not Odosha's. Now give up this robbing and killing of people. Go back to your own place. I'll give you everything you need."

They grabbed him, tied him to a pole, took him to a mountain top, and left him there with a guard, who was to watch and to shout when he died; then they went to plunder Caracas. But Attawanadi—by dreaming "I am free!"—got loose and turned the guard into a rooster. "Wanadi's gone!" the rooster crowed. Returning, the soldiers couldn't figure it out.

They searched and found Attawanadi at his home on Kushamakari. They now had gunpowder, mountains of it, but he blew on it, and it turned into a cloud. Though surrounded, by dreaming he turned the soldiers into pigs, cattle, and horses. That is where all those began. A few, however, escaped and caught him by surprise. Then their priests arrived, the padres.

"Who are you?" the padres asked. "Where do you come from? Who is your father?" "I am Wanadi," Attawanadi replied. "My father is Wanadi, and I come from the highest sky." "You lie," they said. "You are Odosha." They began whipping him with vines. "Whose village is this? Whose house? Whose earth?" "All mine," Attawanadi said. "I made it all. I made you!"

So they sent for a post in the form of a cross. A cross: that is what they called it. They nailed him to it with iron spikes, and again set the rooster to watch. At dawn he crowed, "Wanadi's gone!" They arrived and saw the body hanging. "Here he is!" they cried. But the rooster continued to crow, "He's gone! Wanadi's gone!" Three times he crowed. "Shut up!" the soldiers yelled. "He's here! You're a worthless watch."

The body was like a corpse. It was, however, a trick. He had withdrawn his Emanation. The rooster knew that, the padres and the soldiers didn't. "We killed him," they said. "He was Odosha, not Wanadi." And they kept the cross as a reminder. They like to make crosses to show people. "On this post," they say, "he died." They didn't know, and they still don't know. They were tricked. Attawanadi got away.[15]

Wanadi's Farewell

When Wanadi, at the rapids of Kunukunuma, said goodbye to the So'to, he first spoke, then made a feast. They danced, drank, and sang for three days. "I am going," he said, "going back to the sky. Odosha has made himself master of the earth. There is war, sickness, death, every kind of evil. But I shall come back, Odosha will die, and this present earth will no longer exist. The sun, moon, stars, and all are going to fall to the earth, and you will then see the True Sky, as it was in the beginning. Wanadi's light will again be seen, and I shall return as a new Emanation, the new Wanadi of the new earth, myself again, with another body.

"You are all now going to die, as I did in Caracas. But it will not be real, only a trick for Odosha. In my Sky Place your food and houses are awaiting you. It will be only your bodies that die. Your eternal spirit-doubles will depart through the Heaven-door. They will ask its Keeper—the Scissors Master—for allowance to pass, and the good he will let go by. These will climb by many ladders to their houses in the Sky. But the bad will be sliced to bits in the door and, falling back down to earth, will remain forever with Odosha—to die with him when the world ends.

"In my Sky Place there are no wars, only peace, food, and happiness; no sickness or disease; life never ends and there is no night."

Then he turned and spoke separately to the twelve who had been living with him at the place of Wade, the sloth. "I can't take you all to Heaven," he said. "You will remain on earth for now. But I have made for you another house, the New Kushamakari, in which to wait for me. The light from Heaven shines there, Odosha can't get in. I shall come for you when I return."

The twelve went off to hide in Kushamakari at the Duida, there to wait for the end of the world. We can see the mountain, but not their house. There are guards hidden along the way, and a giant bat that lives in a cave. Shamans, yes, they can see the house. They go right up to the door, and speaking through it to its people, tell them all about us and ask for power, health, food, and wisdom.[16]

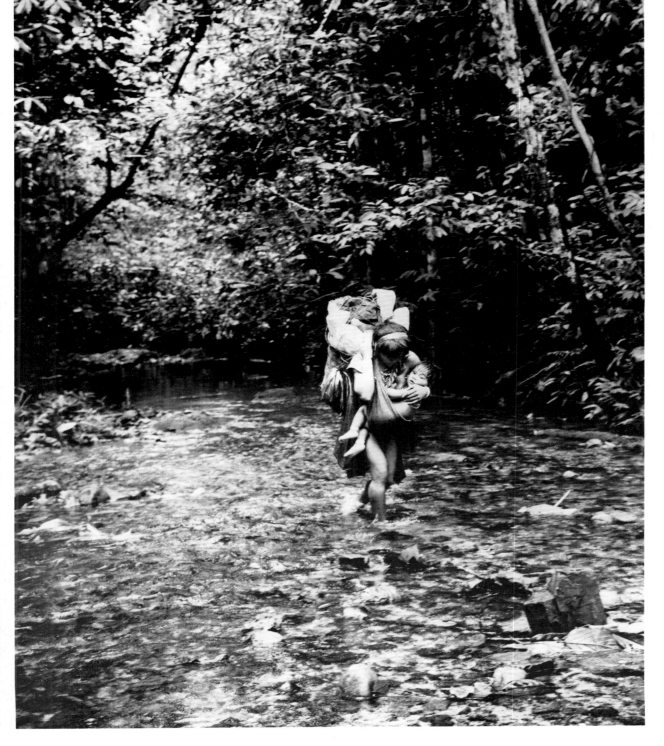

469. A Yekuana woman, carrying in her arms a child and bearing a *wuwa* filled with yuca grown in the Conuco, returns to her village.

470. Yekuana dancers, wearing skirts made of cokerite palm, sing *Wasai yadi ademi hidi,* the Watunna (taking two to three days to sing) that welcomes back a group of travelers gone from the village for a long period of time.[54]

South American Rain Forest Tribes

Amazonia

Caribbean
Sea

Orinoco River

Chaguán
Caliña
Caribisi
Arinagoto
Eye
Acawai
Arecuna
Caliña
Piaroa
Guinau
Taurepán
Macusi
Galibi
Piapoco
Waica
Mersiu
Yavitero
Casapare
Wapishana
Oayana
Puináve
Sanemá
Parawiyana
Shikiana
Oyampi
Tinigua
Guyaverún
Mapanai
Samatari
Araraú
Taruma
Mapidian
Marawan
Paracotó
Taiguana
Tariana
Anauyá
Parukoto
Apalai
ATLANTIC
OCEAN
Tama
Saha
Umáua
Barasana
Araraibo
Manáo
Yuauapery
Warikyana
Apama
Aruan
Tetete
Garú
Barè
Bonari
Tapuisú
Tucujú
Amaguaje
Bora
Macú
Caburichena
Pariquí
Aratú
Jacunda
Mapua
Tupinamba
Teremembé
Piole
Yuri
Yufina
Alarua
Bahuana
Aruaqui
Arará
Cayapó
Pacajá
Tembé
Mehin
Záparo
Cóto
Yagua
Jumana
Zuana
Maué
Arará
Paracana
Guajá
Manayé
Jívaro
Tucuna
Yúma
Bohurá
Arará
Tacunapé
Purucaru
Tacayuna
Meitajé
Shuara
Shapra
Uauarate
Marawá
Burué
Arará
Cradahó
Shaguaruna
Simacu
Cutuquina
Yamamadí
Cayapó
Iraamráire
Cahuapana
Morique
Uaraicú
Burué
Mamori
Mundurucú
Yuruna
Cruatire
Lama
Sensi
Maruba
Curina
Mura
Cayabí
Cutinana
Remo
Canamari
Parintintin
Tupiocón
Cognomona
Cushichineri
Ipuriná
Matanawi
Apiaca
Yuruna
Maspo
Catuquinarú
Caritiana
Ariquem
Arará
Tapanhuna
Cabixi
Chontaquiro
Canamaré
Caxarari
Caripuna
Yarú
Erikbaktsa
Apiaca
Bakairí
Amahuaca
Araona
Chacobo
Laconde
Coeozú
Mashco
Abitana
Huari
Toyeri
Inapar
Itene
Arazaire
Arasa
Baure
Pauserna
Borôro

PACIFIC
OCEAN

Macú Tribes
Tropical Rain Forest region
Ethnolinguistic boundaries

Arawakan
Cariban
Catuquina

Chapacura
Chibchan
Ge (Žé)
Jívaro-Yagua-Záparo
Macuan
Nambicuara
Pano-Tacanan
Tucanoan
Tupian
Unclassified and/or isolated groups

— Ethnolinguistic culture areas —

Map 37.

337

471. A sequence of sketches, first reproduced (1557) in *Warhaftige Historia und beschreibung eyner lantschaff der Wilnen / Nacketen / Grimmigen Menschen fresser Leuthen / in der Newenwelt America Gelegen....Da sie Hans Staden von Homberg aus Hessen durch sein eygne erfarung erkant....,* depicting an island settlement (**a**) of Tupinambá, who, engaging in constant intertribal warfare, attack a neighboring palisaded village (**b**) to gather the captives—one such newly-captured prisoner is here pictured (**c**), dancing, surrounded by celebrating women—that they needed for their elaborate ceremonials, during which the hapless victims were clubbed to death and eaten (**d–e**) amidst much frenzied drinking, singing, and dancing.

Possessed of religious and social values centered upon such continuous internecine fighting and ritualistic cannibalism, the Tupinambá—the collective name of all Tupian-speaking South American Indians, including those groups of slash-and-burn farmers, river people, and coastal navigators known individually as the Potiguara, Caeté, Tupinikin, Tupinambá, and Guarani—were the sixteenth-century masters of a domain that included the entire Brazilian seacoast, from the mouth of the Amazon River in the north all the way south to Porto Alegre, as well as a substantial portion of the adjacent interior.

472. Employing a hunting technique common to many of the protohistorical peoples inhabiting the various tropical forests ranged throughout the equatorial belt, a Hoti Indian in the Guana Highlands (Venezuela) uses an enormous blowgun and a tiny poisoned dart to fell his treetop prey.

b

c

d

e

338

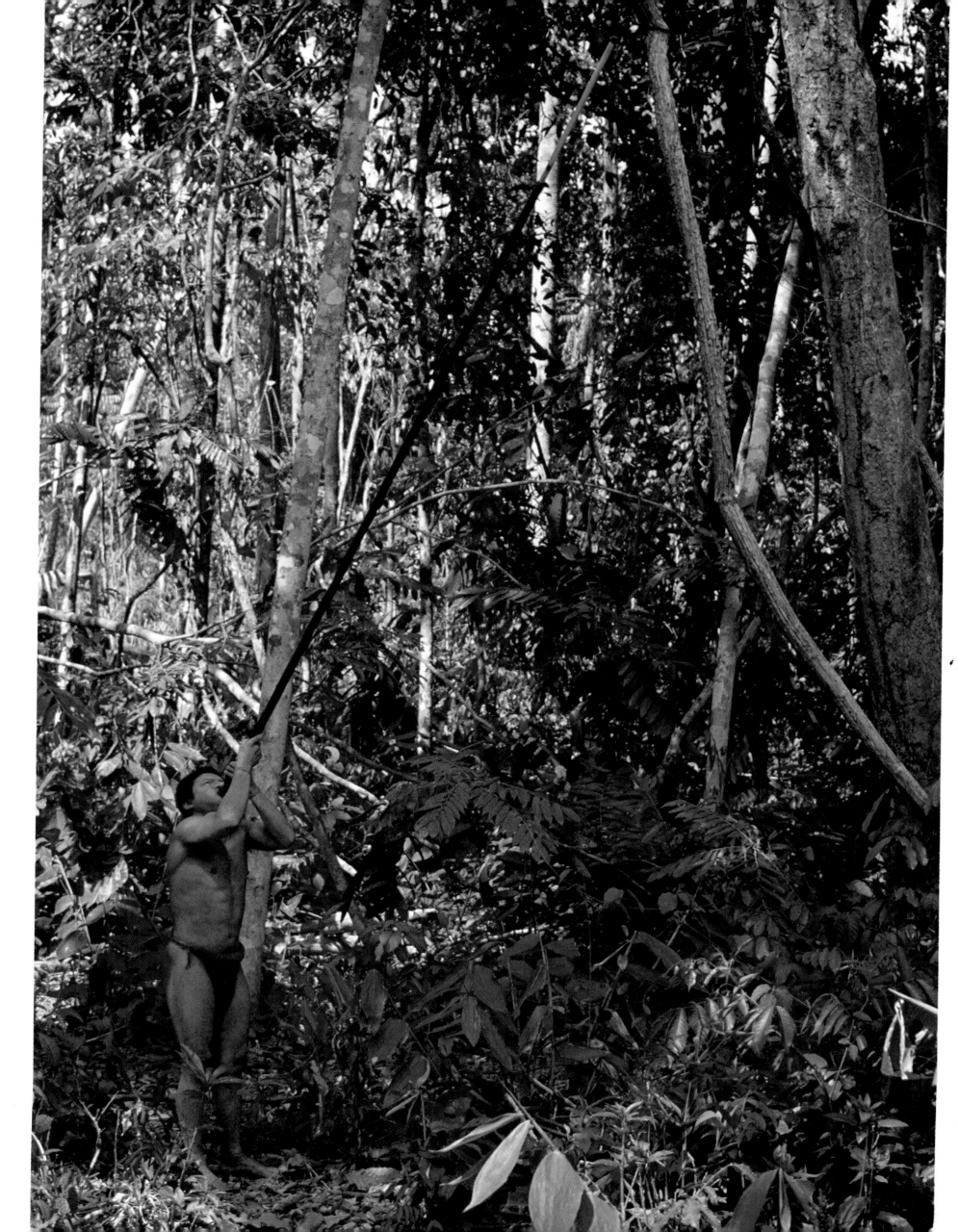

The Desana Creation Myth

The Sun Father's Intention

In the beginning, the Sun Father, Creator of all things—who is not the daily sun that is seen passing overhead, but an eternal yellow light, invisible to physical eyes—produced the universe, not by any act or word, but by mere purpose or intention; and the rays of this "yellow purpose" or "intention" now penetrate and sustain all things, both visible and invisible, in a universe of three levels. The middle level is of this earth and of the color red. Below is a "River of Milk," bathed in a pale green light, the color of coca leaves, while above is a level of two distinct zones: one white, yellow, and orange, of the visible sun and moon; the other blue, of the Milky Way.

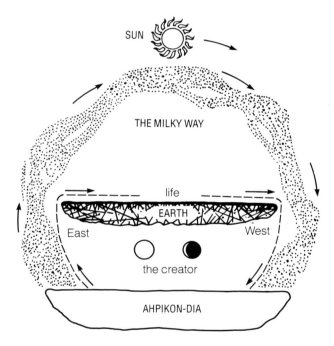

473. Graphic representation of the structure of the Desana cosmos.

This Milky Way is described as an immense and dangerous river, seething with the seeds of life, but also with putrefaction, vomit, and disease. It takes its rise from the River of Milk and arches overhead, flowing from east to west, tossed by the winds of the high heavens. Known as "Wind Current," this high zone is that to which people are carried in vision by hallucinogenic drugs, the most important of which is a powder, sniffed through the nose, prepared from a vine known as *vihó* (from the verb *vihíri*, "to inhale, to absorb"). Vihó Man is its guardian, himself in a state of perpetual trance. His dwelling is the Milky Way. And it is to him that shamans address themselves, to be brought through him, in his meditation, into visionary touch with the other great invisibles. For the Milky Way is the place of meeting and communication between supernatural and earthly beings.[17]

Map 38.

The Maternal Snake Canoe

The coming of mankind to inhabit the middle level of the universe was a paramount feature of the Sun Father's first intention. He produced in the River of Milk an ancestral male of each of the many tribes of the Vaupés region and appointed for them a spiritual guide named "Fermentation Man" or "Flowing Forth [Ejaculating] Man" to conduct them to this earth. They were brought in a live Snake Canoe, named "Fermentation Placenta," painted yellow on the outside with a long black strip along its back and black diamonds along the sides, but inside, red, where the people sat. And whenever they came to rapids (there were many on the long journey), the waters rose and they passed over. At Ipanoré, on the Vaupés River, however, the Snake Canoe struck a rock and the people scattered forth through an opening at the prow.

All human beings are connected in their lives by an invisible umbilical cord that runs back through the rivers to the cosmic womb in the River of Milk, and the Snake Canoe that traced the journey is the sign of that connection.

When the people had dispersed, each went to the place to which Fermentation Man had assigned him, and to each there had been given, also, the token of an assigned manner of life: a bow and arrow to the Desana; fishing gear to the Tukano, Pira-Tapuya, Vaiyára, and Neéroa; a manioc grater to the Kuripáko; and to the primitive Makú, a blowgun and a basket.[18]

The peoples of this northwest Amazonian rain forest are of greatly differing culture stages intermixed: foragers, hunters, fishers, and horticulturalists, with significant influences, also, from the civilizations of the Andes. And the mythologies, accordingly, are composite as well. The Desana, for example, take pride in themselves as hunters; yet fishing and horticulture contribute greatly more than the hunt to their economy; and although the Old Stone Age mythic figure of the Animal Master looms large in their rites and thinking, the structuring energies of their universe are mixed of female and male aspects, with their only culture heroes, two females: (1) a Melusine-like water spirit and ancestress, known as The Daughter of the Aracú fish (an important species of food fish in the riverine economies of the Amazon), and (2) The Daughter of the Sun.

474. This tree lizard (*Plica plica L.*), although rare, is the principal manifestation of *Vaí-mahsë* (*vaí*, "fish"), the Desana "Master of Animals," who, when he thus appears, "tries to bite menstruating or pregnant women or to whip them with his long tail that, like the arm of payé, contains magical splinters and thorns that he can shoot out to cause sickness. For the men, however," Gerardo Reichel-Dolmatoff continues, "his manifestation as a lizard represents no danger but is rather a sign of friendship and protection."[55]

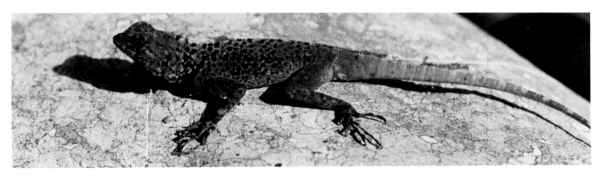

The Daughter of the Sun

The Daughter of the Sun [vaguely, of the Sun Father, as well as of the visible sun] had not reached puberty when her father lay with her at Wainambí Rapids, violating thus, his own first law, against incest. Then the Moon, his twin brother, becoming jealous, tried to seduce her, and the Sun, in revenge, removed from him his feather crown, thus reducing his light. All of which so upset the Moon that for the next three nights he hid his light entirely; and this he continues to do, every month. He is obsessed, furthermore, with sex and at night descends in the form of a man to cohabit with women in their sleep. It is said that he even opens graves to violate and to eat the dead. The stain of the menstrual blood of the Daughter of the Sun remains marked upon his features.

But the Moon also has beneficent powers. Dew, which is called the "saliva of the moon," influences the growth of plants and the gestation of pregnant women. Magical herbs are under his influence, and since many are used in love potions, his fascination with sex is evident even here. His cycle coincides with the cycle of women, whose loss every month of menstrual blood is in memory of the blood lost by the Daughter of the Sun when she lay with her father at Wainambí Rapids.

It is said that she remained with him thereafter as his wife, but thought so much about sex that she became thin, ugly, and lifeless. During her next menstruation, the sex act hurt, and she no longer wanted even to eat. Where she lay dying on a boulder at Wainambí rapids, her imprint can still be seen. But then the Sun, her father, performed for her the invocation to be used when girls attain puberty. Chanting and puffing tobacco, he thus revived her.[19]

475. Standing at the approximate spot where the Pirapiraná river crosses the Equator, this petroglyph illustrates an episode in Tukano mythology.

476.

The Coming of Night

In the beginning there was no night, only the yellow light of the Sun Father's intention. When the people set forth in their Snake Canoe, however, the Sun gave to each something to carry, and to one, a small black purse, tightly closed. The journey being long, this keeper of the purse became curious. He opened it, and out swarmed such a multitude of black ants that their number obscured the Sun Father's light, and that was the First Night. Fermentation Man tried to correct things by giving to each a firefly; but this light was weak and the ants continued to pour forth. The people implored them to go back into their purse, but in vain. Then the Sun Father himself came down with a stick with which to beat the purse, and this compelled them to return—but not all. Those refusing remained in the forest, and from that time there have been ants and anthills.

The First Night is known as the "Night of the Ant," and the man who opened the purse, as "Man of the Night."[20]

Supernaturals

Among the supernaturals put forth in the beginning as intermediaries between the Sun Father and this earth were, first, in the sky, the Beings of Day, in charge of the spiritual development of mankind; next, in the rivers, the Beings of Blood, representing the rules of physical health and the good life; in the Milky Way, Vihó Man, who, is mixed of negatives and positives, being a master of disease and witchcraft, no less than of visionary inspirations; and in the dark region beyond the most distant west, the Night People of sorcery and witchcraft, there established to be the punishers of all who disregard tribal custom. An Owner of Thatch is in charge of palm leaves for the roofing of malocas, and in the wilderness are two Animal Masters: one for the forest beasts, the other for the fish, the first residing in a large maloca within certain forested rocky hills, the other in such a maloca beneath the waters of the rapids. And then finally, there is the Jaguar, whose color is the very yellow of the Sun Father's intention, whose roar is as the voice of the Sun Father, heard in thunder, and whose presence on earth is as the Father's security watch.[21]

The visible sun and moon, meanwhile, rotating in their courses, far above the Milky Way, are brothers (whether twins or not is unclear), representing in our visible world two aspects of the original "yellow intention." "The moon," states Reichel-Dolmatoff, in interpretation of this brother pair, "is called *nyamí abé*, or 'nocturnal sun,' a name that clearly suggests that, basically two aspects of the same thing are involved. The moon is part of the Sun, a negative, evil part."[22]

But there is mention, also, in this mythology of an invisible Moon, of which the visible one is representative; and this can only mean that, although the "yellow purpose" or "intention," of which this world is a reflex, is in its origin transcendent of duality, in its effects and operation in space and time—whether visibly or invisibly—it is dual: not only evil and good, but also dark and light, creative and destructive, female and male (compare II.1:**81**).

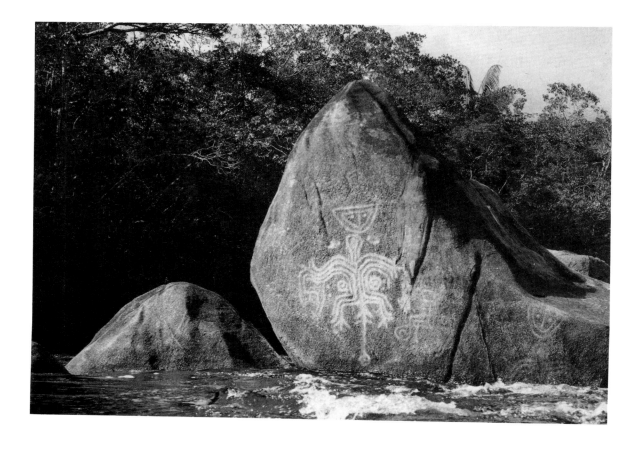

341

The First Maloca

The Sun caused the first maloca to be built at the place now called Wainambí, ordering the Beings of Day, the Beings of Blood, and Vihó Man to instruct the people in the art of building homes. Vihó Man, however, brought sorcery and sickness, which hid in the cracks and crannies of the houseposts. He also persuaded the eagles that were sitting in the trees about the big maloca, chewing coca (so that their beaks were flecked with white), to set nets to entrap the people. The Beings of Blood, however, contrived to entrap the eagles themselves, wrapped them in their own nets and threw them into the Milky Way, where they became transformed into the beneficent protectors of malocas that they are today. Moreover, the people at the time were taught protective invocations; also, the art of setting up invisible protective enclosures around their malocas, and invisible nets at their doors.[23]

The Daughter of the Aracú Fish

At that time there were only men. The animals and the fish had wives; so too, the Master of Fish. But none of the company of the Snake Canoe had yet a wife to beget descendants.

The men, one night, were feasting and dancing, when the daughter of one of the wives of the Master of Fish, an aracú fish, saw the yellow light of their fire and, coming out of the river to watch them all, fell in love with the Desana. He gave her honey to eat and she remained with him. One can still see the imprint on the rock of her buttocks where she lay with him. Sons and daughters were then born to them, and these were the first sib of the Desana tribe.

But at that time the invocations to be recited when a woman gives birth were unknown. As a consequence, when the Daughter of Aracú bore her first child, the scorpion and a large black ant, who were watching, licked the blood, and their sting now makes one vomit and feel pain like the pains of childbirth. The stingray ate the placenta, and its sting, too, produces pain. The centipede and a large black spider licked the blood, and they now look like the umbilical cord and vagina. The bat, formerly a bird, became as now, a thing of filth. While the woman herself, who had been afraid to go to the river to bathe because of all the animals that were there, became covered with lice. A bird who noticed her in this condition sang: "This lazy woman! She perhaps doesn't know about invocations." Hearing that, the Daughter of Aracú invented, then and there, the invocations for the ritual bath following childbirth.

Moreover, it was this Daughter of Aracú who planted the first garden. She planted manioc, which she had brought from the underwater malocas of the Aracú; and when these people saw her washing their manioc tubers in the river, they tried to carry them off, but failed. She not only washed the roots, but also invented the long tube through which the manioc has to be squeezed to remove its poison.

Others declare that when the Daughter of the Aracú Fish gave birth to her first child, she took it to the river to bathe, and that the fish, recognizing the babe as one of their kin, came and rubbed themselves against it. The mother then

went to work in her garden, and the infant's father, noticing the congregation of fish at the place of his child's bathing, took his bow and arrow and killed them. When the mother returned and saw all her relatives dead, weeping she carried them back to the water, went into it herself, and never again was seen.[24]

478. A *tipití* (see **464**) is used to extract prussic acid from bitter manioc (*dëhkë*), the staple crop of the Desana, who, Reichel-Dolmatoff notes, distinguish "*boréka dëhkë*—according to myth, it is related to the sib *boréka*; starchy manioc, *bo'o dëhkë*, also having a mythological origin; white manioc (*boréri dëhkë*); yellow manioc (*diári dëhkë*); and one kind called *nopára*, said to have been introduced from the territory of the Karihóna Indians."[56]

The Great Flood

When everything had been created, the world began to be filled with plagues and monsters. No one knows why. Kidnappers and ravishers appeared in the guise of friends along the trails, carried off women and raped them. Others, like large horseflies, brought terror and disease, the hum of their wings being like the sound of a bull-roarer, whose voice is the sound of the radiance of the Sun.

The Sun took note of this situation and, deciding to assume charge, ordered, first, a great flood, and the monsters drowned; then a great drought, and everything caught fire. The armadillo's once fluffy tail was burned off and only one little bird was saved. That was 250 years ago. But in time, life returned, renewed.[25]

477. Derived from yagé-induced hallucinations, the design painted on the front of this maloca, situated on the Pirá-piraná river, depicts the Master of Animals amid a series of abstract symbols.

The First Death

The Sun then sent his Daughter to the earth to teach the people how to live. And what she taught them was, to make pottery, to use baskets, to eat fish and certain wild fruits, and to make fire with fire sticks. The first death in the world was of one of her sons, of which there were two, both apprenticed to become shamans. One was doing very well, but the other, because he was always thinking of women, declined in health and died. His copper earrings had turned, so that their concave parts faced inward, and that was an ominous sign. When he died, the Daughter of the Sun taught the people proper burial rites, after which she departed, returning to the River of Milk, out of which she had appeared. The grave in which the body is buried is the womb to which the corporeal part returns, while the womb to which the part that is spiritual goes is the womb of the River of Milk.[26]

Origin of the Yagé Vine and Coca Plant

When one of the daughters of the Animal Master was pregnant with the pain of childbirth she went to the river shore and lay twisting in anguish. An old Desana woman, wishing to help her, took her hand, but with the writhing, one of her fingers broke off. The old woman kept it in her household, but a young man stole it, buried it, and there grew from it the hallucinogenic yagé vine [*Banisteriopsis caapi*].

A second daughter of the same Animal Master, writhing on the shore in the same condition, was likewise helped by an old woman. Again a finger broke off, which the woman buried, and from this there grew the coca plant.[27]

479. A Tukano woman mixes coarse manioc flour (*pogá*). Other by-products of manioc production are starch (*verá*), tapioca (*bo'óru*), the squeezed-off liquid (*nyohká*), and the leftover scraps (*pulí*).

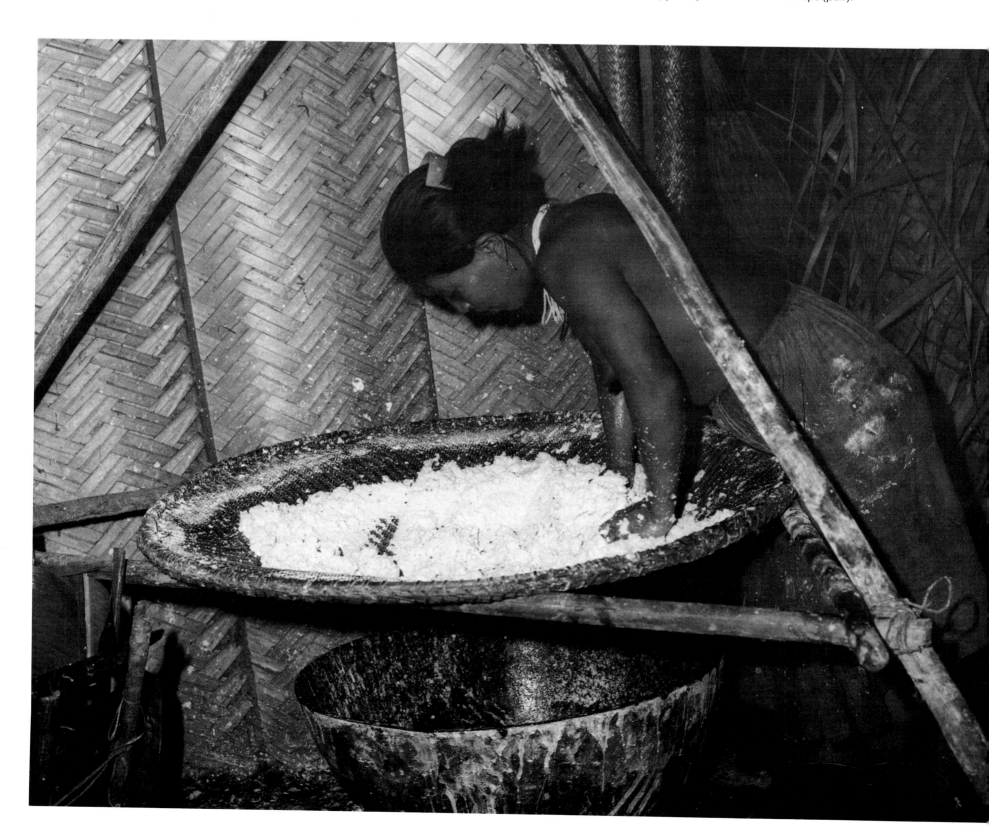

The Hallucinogenic Voyage

The ceremonial imbibing of an infusion of yagé (Desana, *gahpí*) is known as *gahpí irí-inyári*, from *irí*, "to drink," and *inyári*, "to see." It is experienced as a visionary journey, back along the riverway of the original maternal Snake Canoe to the River of Milk, whence all have come. The participants in the rite, sitting in the center of the maloca, are adult males exclusively, being guided on their visionary way by the voice of a holy man, or Sun priest (*kumú*), who interprets to them the shared vision as it unfolds its revelation. At the rear of the building are the women, who are not allowed to drink yagé, yet play an important part in the ceremony. "Drink, drink!" they sing. "This is why we were born. Drink, drink! For this is our task. By drinking they will come to know the traditions of their fathers. By drinking, they will be brave. We are to help them."

The hallucinogenic liquid is kept in a special pottery vessel (see Figure 481) manufactured by an old woman, who, before firing it, polishes the surface with a very hard and smooth yellowish stone. The vessel is of three parts: a yellow base, red body, and blue top, with the globular red body bearing white and yellow designs, such as adorned the Snake Canoe. As Reichel-Dol-

480. A Tatuyo Indian displays the hollow dancing staffs used during ceremonial gatherings.

matoff was told by Antonio Guzmán, his Desana Indian interpreter and informant:

As mankind arrived in this world in the Snake Canoe, so will it now undertake the journey of the return.[28] One of the men dips from the vessel a small cupful of the liquid and, repeating rapidly, "*Ma, ma, ma!*" [Take, take, take!], carries it to the others, who, while in silence drinking, smoke tobacco to enhance the hallucinations. The kumú, in a loud voice, then declares: "I am the central person, the only one left. Therefore, I am to teach you." And in a hypnotic tone, with great precision, he begins explaining and directing the voyage.[29]

During the first moments, there is talking, a general questioning of the kumú, with him in turn inquiring of each concerning the clarity of his visions. Some may see only lights and, feeling nauseated, withdraw, to the deprecating laughter of the women, who continue with their insistent chant: "Drink, drink, drink!" Those remaining are experiencing a violent current of air, as though of a strong wind bearing them away. That—as the kumú explains—is the Wind Current of the Milky Way, mixed of vomit and disease, together with the seeds of life. They begin descending toward the River of Milk. Walls of fluttering, floating cloth enfold them. Lights appear, growing stronger, which become a moving, luminous mass. When the plunge occurs into the River of Milk, shapes of differing colors, moving, changing in size, come into view. These—the kumú's voice is telling—are the forms of the Beings of Blood, the Beings of Day, Vihó Man, the Daughter of the Aracú Fish and Daughter of the Sun. The sound of the kumú's stick-rattle is heard as the voice of the Sun. The light is seen of the Yellow Intention. A distant music is heard, and the buzz of a hummingbird's wings, as it moves from flower to flower, sucking honey. All the figures of myth and the mysteries of nature appear: the Animal Master in his house within the rocky hills; the Yellow Squirrel, representative of the Sun's generative power, its rodent teeth a magical force that gnaws and penetrates; the Cock-of-the-Rock, who stands watch before the dancing grounds of the forest herds....

For a blessed time—perhaps half an hour—the canoe company, in silent rapture, floating in the River of Milk, participates in the experience of the first things of the universe. The earth plane, viewed from below in this way, is transparent, like a large, extended cobweb with the light of the sun shining through. Its threads are the rules men live by. Toward the sunrise there is a vast lake, into which are pouring all the rivers of the earth, and in the west, where the sun sets, is the dark place of the Night People of sorcery and disease. The River of Milk itself is "Paradise" [*ahpikondiá*]. And as the canoe company rests there, at the Alpha and Omega, the beginning and the goal, they are at peace.

But then the images fade. A music can still be heard in the distance, but the forms, the colors, and the movements are no more. The trance dissolves, and the men are sitting around, conversing and drinking chicha. They have beheld the web of the laws of life, the light of the Sun Father's Intention; the chanting of the women has ceased; they have voyaged far and well.[30]

481. One of the special tripartite pottery vessels in which the Desana keep yagé, the hallucinogenic infusion that induces their visionary revelations.

Sun Priest (Kumú) and Shaman (Payé)

The character of the holy man, or Sun-priest (*kumú*)—whose role as conductor of this spiritual voyage to Ahpikondiá corresponds precisely to that of the Huichol *mara'akame* on the geographically simulated voyage to Wirikuta (above, pages 294–299)—is of the greatest importance to the spiritually grounded architecture of Desana life. Figure 482 shows the manner of organization of the inhabitants of a Desana communal dwelling. The roof-beam (*gumú*) is likened both to the Sun-priest (*kumú*) in the structure of the society and to the Sun Father himself and his light in the structure of the cosmos. For, as Reichel-Dolmatoff learned, "the maloca is the uterus of the sib and as such its structure corresponds to that of the Cosmos."[31] By analogy, the cosmos, then, is the uterus of all things, and as the Sun Father's Yellow Intention is the supporting principle of the cosmos, so is the roof beam, of the house. Its name, *gumú*, is recognized as equivalent to *kumú*. Moreover: "Although it is laid horizontally, it has the meaning of a 'ladder' that penetrates the cosmic levels and forms an axis."[32] Compare the archetype of the pole, or ladder, up which the Siberian shaman ascends (I.2:172).

"According to tradition," states Reichel-Dolmatoff, "the office of the kumú was created by the Sun Father who determined that these men should be called upon to perpetuate moral teachings in the highest ethical sense."[33] The kumú identifies himself with the function of the roof beam, gumú, and through his identification with the role of the Sun and transmission of tradition gives stability to his society. It seems that the office is hereditary, transmitted from father to son. The apprenticeship lasts several years, and in it are emphasized the interpretation of images produced by the drug, yagé, the giving of constructive advice, and the power of conviction in the settling of social conflicts. The kumú's province is of wisdom and meditation.

"Generally speaking," Reichel-Dolmatoff reports, "a kumú does not live in the maloca of his group but occupies an isolated dwelling with his nuclear family. There he receives visits from people who resort to him; he may also take part in certain collective rituals, celebrated in the malocas of the different sibs of the neighborhood. On these occasions the kumú occupies an important and highly respected position. When officiating the kumú puts on a red skirt-like garment of barkcloth decorated with short feathers. On his head he wears a feather crown different from those used in dances; the feathers are short and white, rising horizontally from their ring-shaped base. On his arms he wears several wide bands woven of very fine fibers, adorned with feathers and with

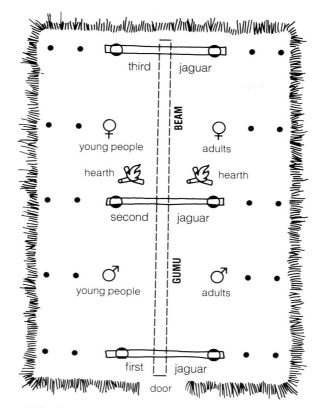

482. Sketch of the ritual distribution of a maloca.

483. This Tukano man proudly wears a necklace of jaguar teeth and a polished quartz cylinder.

interwoven diamond motifs. Hanging from his left elbow he wears a large black palm seed in which he keeps some little red and white feathers as well as a red pigment to paint his face. This adornment is the exclusive privilege of the kumú and publicly represents his authority; a cylinder of quartz hung from his neck complements this costume.

"Although the kumú occasionally intervenes in some rites of the life cycle, his main function consists of pronouncing the *go'a-mëë bayari*, the 'songs of god,' that are sometimes sung on the occasion of large gatherings when gifts of food are distributed between phratries. During these ceremonies, which may last for two or three days, people bring quantities of smoked fish or wild fruits that the kumú receives and keeps in his house.

"After having recited invocations to the

Sun, offering him these foods, he distributes them among the participants in the gathering. This ceremonial distribution is called *abé kóa*/sun-gourd bowl, and the food is interpreted as consecrated, coming directly from the divinity. This ceremony generally takes place at the end of the first rainy season, between May and June, and begins at dawn. The kumú faces east to greet the rising sun. Because at this time of the year the fish begin to run, and it is also the time in which the new planting is begun in the fields, the main objective of this ceremony is to ask the Sun for abundance and the fostering of growth.

"On the occasion of these rites the kumú sometimes uses a small altar-like object that consists of a woven box of the leaves of a certain palm. The box is called *go'á-mëë komóro*/god's chest, and in it the kumú keeps his ritual objects. Among these objects there are several anthropomorphic figurines of wood some twenty centimeters in height that represent the Sun, the Daughter of the Sun, and *Emë kóri-mahsë* [the Being of Day]. These figurines are made by the kumú himself or by some youth who is still unmarried and has not yet had sexual relations. It is also said that in the past these figurines were made of stone and were carved with sandstone tools of a white color that were extracted from a lagoon located near a rapids on the Mihpinya, a tributary of the Macú-paraná. For the invocation of the Sun, the kumú places his little figurines on the box and then dances in a circle around them. During this dance he marks the beat with a stomping tube decorated with two black stripes and a series of triangles, representing the designs of the Snake-Canoe.

"On a much higher level than the payé [the shaman, see below], the kumú is a luminous personage who has an interior light, a brilliant flame that shines and unveils the intimate thoughts of all people who speak to him. His power and his wisdom are always compared to an intense light that is invisible but perceptible through its effects. The manifestation of this luminous energy is the 'penetrating glance' that is attributed to the kumú, his capacity of fathoming the psyche of a person and of thus knowing his intimate motivations. From time to time the kumú summons a person who has not lived according to the traditional norms, and on other occasions he is approached spontaneously to discuss some personal problem. The dialogue which then develops has the character of a confession. It is here that a concept called *penyóri* enters. This word is derived from *peri*/to hear, and *nyóri* that designates the effect of the 'penetrating glance.' *Nyóri* is the impact that the words of the kumú make, the sudden insight that then leads to comprehension." As explained by Antonio Guzmán, Reichel-Dolmatoff's interpreter and informant:

"The entire conversation is directed to *Ahpikondiá*. When concentrating (*pepiri*) in this manner, one sees, one is there." And again: "After conversing in this way with the kumú, one goes away relieved."[34]

I have quoted this passage at length for the clarity of its exposition of the role and character of the Desana Sun-priest (*kumú*), as distinguished from the shaman (*payé*). Between the two, according to Guzmán, the relations generally are of mutual respect, since they represent distinct structuring functions in the architecture of Desana life, much as, in the structure of the maloca, the function of the roof beam (*gumú*) is distinct from that of the cross beams, known as "jaguars," which is a term that is applied, also, to the payé.

"The most important part of the structure," states our author in discussion of the maloca, "is formed by the 'three red jaguars,' represented by three pairs of large forked posts and their respective beams, located at the two extremes and in the center of the building. These three 'jaguars,' which are sometimes painted red and adorned with black spots, are interpreted as the guardians and the most important fecundating forces of the dwelling; they 'cover' (*bëári*) the occupants."[35]

The jaguars are grounded, we observe, on the earth, whereas the roof beam (*gumú*), which rests upon them, hangs, as its were, in space. Comparably, the efforts of the shaman, the payé, are dedicated to the earthly, economic concerns of the inhabitants of the maloca, while the Sun-priest, the kumú, is concerned chiefly with their spiritual well-being. And although the latter does, indeed, officiate in the fertility ceremony of food distribution, just described, its form, as Reichel-Dolmatoff points out, "is far removed from the crude sexual symbolism that characterizes other ritual activities, and it is evident that what is involved is a true cult in which the problem of mere earthly existence has been sublimated."[36]

In that author's view, the historic background of the Sun-priest tradition is to be sought in the "sub-Andean priest-temple-idol complex"[37] of the South American Formative Culture Stage; whereas the role, in contrast, of the shaman is of an old, hunting and gathering, Paleolithic tradition, modified and adapted to the circumstances of a settled, village style of existence. According to our author:

"In order to become a payé an individual must have demonstrated since childhood a profound interest in the religious traditions of his culture besides having a good knowledge of myths, genealogies, and invocations. He must know how 'to sit on his bench' and reflect; he must practice sexual abstinence, and he must also be a good drinker of chicha, a good dancer and singer, and he must be able to give sound advice to others. He should not be too fond of women, and he must channel his sexual

484. This remarkable photograph, taken (1928) at an unspecified location in the Brazilian Amazon, records an interval in a Yurupari initiation rite. The identity of the celebrants is no longer known.

energy toward other goals; however, he should be a family man. The most necessary quality is that he have the capacity to achieve well-defined hallucinations when he takes a concoction, and to be able to interpret them. Also, in the learning of myths and traditions what is involved is not so much a good memory but a capacity for interpreting their symbolism, and of 'hearing the echo' of the tales told by tradition.

"It is at about twenty-five years of age that a person begins to show these qualities, and it is then that formal training is begun. The office of the payé is not hereditary but depends on personality type, recognized early in childhood by other members of the group, observed and evaluated in detail, and, from that time on, fostered by the older men."[38]

"In Desana the payé is called *ye'e*, a word that also means jaguar and, in effect, the payé is said to be able to change himself into this feline. The word is derived from *ye'éri*/to cohabit, *ye'éru*/penis, and the payé is thus a phallic instrument that intervenes with its power (*ye'e tulári*) directly in the process of biocosmic procreation. His characteristic attributes are also phallic; in the first place we have the stick-rattle (*ye'egë*), the payé's staff of command and his 'voice.' The payé also possesses the phallic weapon, the ceremonial hoe. The cylinder of quartz that every payé carries is called *abé ye'éru*/penis of the Sun Father, and represents semen. Lightning, besides its luminous aspect, is produced when a payé casts his quartz and is in itself a symbol of fertilization. When lightning strikes nearby, the payé goes to the spot to collect from the ground fragments of quartz because these particles are a very dangerous seminal matter and have to be neutralized. The gourd rattle that the payé uses in his rituals is called *nyahsáru*, a word derived from *nyahsá*/a white ant that stings; allusion is

made to the swiftness with which these insects disperse when their nests are touched, the same swiftness with which the noise of the rattle spreads. The rattle is a prolongation of the payé's arm, and the dry seeds that produce the sound represent the movement of the splinters [or thorns of the *macana* palm that the payé is supposed to carry] locked up in his arm. When he shakes the gourd rattle these splinters are shaken toward the victim. The splinters or thorns are always imagined to be carried in the left forearm because otherwise any blow the payé might strike with his right hand, perhaps during an unimportant quarrel, would be fatal. The left side is always associated with death and the forces of evil.

"In order to establish contact with supernatural beings, the payé uses the hallucinogenic powder of *vihó*....The ability to have visions by means of *vihó* and the power of establishing this contact determine the potential capacity of a payé. A payé ought to view the Milky Way as a road, the hills and pools as malocas, and animals as persons. Those who do not react in this manner to the hallucinogenic drug see only clouds and stones, and 'the birds laugh at them.' In their trance they tear off their loincloths and walk around naked, without shame; they even urinate or defecate in public. But others, the truly experienced payés, control these impulses; they are transported to the Milky Way or to the 'houses' of the hills or the waters, and there they talk and negotiate with the beings occupying these places. Then they return and rejoin their bodies that meanwhile have remained in their hammocks as if asleep."[39]

The Animal Master: His Malocas in the Hills

The principal task of the payé is to visit the abode of the Animal Master (*Vaí-mahsë*), there to negotiate for a certain number of game animals to be killed in exchange for the deaths of an equivalent number of human beings, whose souls would be then reincarnated, not in the usual way, as hummingbirds, but as game animals in replenishment of those the hunters would have killed.[40] The Animal Master is a mercurial figure, described generally as a dwarf with body painted red and covered with the juices of magical plants, by whose strong odor his presence can be known. He appears also in the form of a small lizard that is quite rare and lives in dry clearings at the foot of large rocks. In this aspect he likes to bite menstruating or pregnant women, or to whip them with his long tail, which, like the left arm of a payé, contains splinters and thorns that shoot out and cause sickness. *Vaí-mahsë*, his name, is derived from *vaí*, meaning "fish," but is applied to the Master of Animals as well as to the Master of Fish, who fundamentally are of one being, though in two functions, each dwelling with his charges. As described in Reichel-Dolmatoff's *Amazonian Cosmos*:

"In the rain forests of the Vaupés there exist, here and there, rock formations that stand out like dark islands on the horizon. These isolated hills or ridges often have steep walls and flat, mesa-like plateaus and are full of caverns and dark recesses. These uncanny places are the dwellings of *Vaí-mahsë*, where, surrounded by his animals, he dominates the forest. The rapids of the rivers, where the torrents pass between huge rocks and form deep whirlpools, are the dwelling places of *Vaí-mahsë* as protector of fish. Both places are imagined as large malocas regardless of whether they are in the hills or under the water; there the creatures live and thence they go forth to the forest or to the river.

"These 'houses of the hills' or 'houses of the waters' are sacred and dangerous places. The rapids are, of course, unavoidable passes for the traveler and are navigated in silence, but the hills of the forest are avoided at all times. Besides being the places where the animals live, the houses of the hills also contain illness, and their dark and inhospitable aspect indicates this danger. The cracks, caverns, and tunnels are the entrances to the interior of the hills, to the great malocas of the animals. There, within their dark interior, the gigantic prototypes of each species exist, and thousands of animals are kept—deer, tapirs, peccaries, monkeys, rodents, and many more, in a great community similar to that of human beings."[41]

The Animal Master is not only the guardian of the animals of his maloca, but also their procreator, a personification of their sexual life. And yet, at the same time, he is the patron of hunters and a hunter himself. His weapon is a short red wand, highly polished, which he carries with him when he goes into the forest, and when he points this at an animal, it falls down dead. It is said that hunters have seen this occur. He is interested, also, in women, especially those who have not yet reached puberty, for whom he lies in wait. Or he follows women who walk in the forest or on river-banks alone. He may appear, then, as a fish, a squirrel, or a lizard, and, causing them to fall asleep, cohabit with them, as in a dream. But after a short time, then, they die, and at the place where the act occurred there will be an abundance of animal or aquatic life.[42]

When the shaman, the payé, on his hallucinogenic quest, arrives in the Animal Master's house, either in the hills or in the waters, *Vaí-mahsë* receives him willingly and shows him his animals hanging in bunches from the rafters. The payé indicates those that the hunters have asked him to release, and when the price in souls has been agreed upon, *Vaí-mahsë* shakes the relevant rafters to wake the animals selected, which then go out into the jungle to be killed. "The price," it is said, "is charged 'per shake' and sometimes more are awakened than had been agreed upon and the payé must reopen negotiations."[43]

"But sometimes," Reichel-Dolmatoff found, "the payés go to the hills, not in their hallucinations but in reality, to affirm their requests and to foster the fertility of the animals. On many of the hills the rock walls are covered with pictographs representing various animals and fertility symbols, where generations of payés have drawn, in red, yellow, or black, the forms of game animals. The drawings show deer, tapirs, monkeys, rodents, turtles, and birds, together with phallic and uterine symbols; the stripes and diamonds of *pamurí-gahsiru,* the mythical snake that brought men to earth, are also depicted. Sometimes these rock walls are true palimpsests with a superposition of drawings that, through the centuries, show changing styles. At times the figure of a jaguar dominates the multitude of representations, just as the fertilizing power of this divine beast dominates the jungle."[44]

All of this surely is amazing: 18,000 years and as many miles away from the Temple Caves of the Dordogne and Pyrenees!

485. On the Upper Inirida River, a rock shelter, painted with game animals and abstract symbols, where the Master of Animals dwells. Reichel-Dolmatoff explains: "In the rain forests of the Vaupés there exist, here and there, rock formations that stand out like dark islands on the horizon. These isolated hills or ridges often have steep walls and flat, mesa-like plateaus and are full of caverns and dark recesses. These uncanny places are the dwellings of *Vaí-mahsë (ëhtëngë ví'i,* "hill house"; *Vaí-mahsë ví'i,* "*Vaí-mahsë's* house"), where, surrounded by his animals, he dominates the forest."[57]

The Yurupari Cult

Yurupari is a word of unknown origin that appears in the literature of anthropology as the name of a ceremonial complex widely spread among the forest tribes of the upper Amazon. The dominant feature is an elaborate ritual exercise involving processions of initiated males to the accompaniment of bark trumpets. Females and males not yet initiated are forbidden the sight of these instruments. Distributions of fish, game, and wilderness fruits are associated with the ceremonies, which include as an essential feature the initiation of young men. (Compare the Mandan Okipa, I.2:226–231.) Theodor Koch-Grünberg, whose researches in these regions during the first decade of this century opened them to systematic scholarship, published in 1910 the following version of the Yurupari origin legend, obtained from the Yahúnga—a people of Tucanoan stock inhabiting (in his time) eight malocas at the junction of the Pirá-paraná and Apaporís rivers.

Many many years ago, there came out the great Water House, the dwelling of the Sun, a little boy who sang so beautifully that people flocked from near and far to see and to hear him. His name was Milómaki, the Son (*maki*) of Miló. But when the people who had heard him returned to their homes and ate fish, they all fell dead. Incensed, their relatives seized the boy, who had meanwhile become a youth, and, setting him on a great funeral pyre as an evil wretch who had slain their kin, set it afire.

The youth, however, continued to sing marvelously to the end. As the flames enveloped his body: "Now I die, my son," he sang; "now I am leaving this world!" As the body swelled with the heat, the song continued: "Now my body bursts. Now I am dead!" And indeed, the body exploded, Milómaki died, and the flames consumed him.

But his soul ascended to heaven, and that very day, from the ashes there grew a long green leaf that increased perceptibly as one watched, and, expanding, was by the next day a tall tree: the first paxiuba palm. There had been no such tree before that. Of its wood the people made large flutes that in a marvelous way reproduced the sound of Milómaki's singing. At the time of the ripening of wilderness fruits, men blow such flutes to this day, and dance thereby in honor of Milómaki, the producer of all edible fruits. Little boys and women are forbidden to see those instruments. Any woman who should do so would die. Any boy, would eat earth, become ill, and die, too.[45]

486. For most of the Amazon's riparian inhabitants, fishing (whether with spears, bows and arrows, traps, or, on significant festive occasions, such "fish poisons" as barbasco), although a continual pursuit that provides much of the protein in their daily diet, is considered an activity of a lower status and of less importance than hunting.

a

487. Played most often in association with men's rites and ceremonials, flutes made of twisted bark are pandemic in Amazonia: (**a**) a Yekuana plays the *wana*, twin flutes that, unlike sacred Yurupari flutes — a contemporary Tukano example of which (**b**) is remarkably similar to two Yahúnga models (**c–d**) drawn (c. 1903) by Theodor Koch-Grünberg — are not kept hidden from women and uninitiated males; (**e**) Kamyura versions of the instrument.

"In this myth," remarks Koch-Grünberg, "the tribal hero appears as the culture hero, the generator of vegetable growth, and is of a distinctly solar character. He is the Sun itself. He comes from the east, out of the great 'Water House,' wanders over the earth, and departs in flames to heaven. The burning of a hero to death because of his magical character is a feature common to many of the myths to be found in South America."[46] "Interesting," he adds, "is the reference here to the sea. The sea appears in the legends of many inland tribes, suggesting the probability of migrations, either of the peoples themselves, or of their legends."[47]

The Desana Snake Canoe, we recall, *ascended* the earthly rivers in its passage from the mythological River of Milk. Writing of the "Tropical Forest Tribes," Robert H. Lowie, in his introduction to Volume 3 of the *Handbook of South American Indians*,[48] makes a very strong point of the influence of river travel on the spread of both peoples and culture throughout this heavily forested part of the world. "The very wide distribution of certain traits in the area," he observes, "is correlated with navigation. Thanks to their mobility, the canoeing tribes were able to maintain themselves in the midst of boatless populations, to travel with ease over periodically inundated tracts, and to diffuse their arts and customs over enormous distances....Accordingly,

earthenware decoration in Santarém [on the lower Amazon] may precisely duplicate details from the Lesser Antilles."[49] And in the same way (I would add), the Yurupari bark trumpets that are being made today in the upper Amazon look very much like those depicted in de Bry's sixteenth-century engraving, *The Queen-Elect is Brought to the King* (See I.2:**387** and II.1:**45**), which was copied from a watercolor by Jacques de Moyne de Morgues, painted in Florida in 1564.

Two thoroughgoing studies of the Yurupari as practiced by the Barasana, a Tucanoan-speaking people on the Pirá-paraná river in the Vaupés area of Colombia—*The Palm and the Pleiades: Initiation and Cosmology in Northwest Amazonia*, by Stephen Hugh-Jones,[50] and *From the Milk River: Spatial and Temporal Processes in Northwest Amazonia*, by Christine Hugh-Jones,[51] his wife—opened the whole complex to view in a fresh light at the very moment of its imminent disappearance.

"In the Pirá-paraná area," writes C. Hugh-Jones, "the influence of the rubber trade was first felt in the latter half of the nineteenth century and the industry reached its height in the first decade of this century. After that it went into a gradual decline until the Second World War brought a sudden increase in demand. By 1970 there were rumours that the market was approaching total collapse and that

government support for the industry was to be withdrawn. White rubber gatherers (*caucheros*) entered the Pirá-paraná from the Vaupés and Apaporis and, in most cases, carried off the able men by force, often killing others and raping women. Many Indians tell how the reprisals against the brutal intruders were also extended to fellow Indians who had directed them to hidden longhouses. The location of longhouses was an indication of white activity, because Indians fled to the headwaters and concealed approaches to their longhouses when times were bad, and then moved back to the larger rivers as white people withdrew.

"Besides reducing the population and disrupting social life in these ways, the rubber trade introduced new diseases on a large scale. It also changed Indian culture and aspirations by creating new needs for white men's merchandise. But the *caucheros* did not purposefully attempt to change Indian culture from within by altering patterns of social and domestic life. Their very lack of interest in Indians as anything beyond a workforce to be ensnared in an eternal credit system meant that those who escaped their recruiting drives continued to live in a traditional way. By the period of our fieldwork, the methods of *caucheros* were less violent, but nevertheless very variable. Many Indians born in the upper Pirá-paraná were permanently living in rubber camps on the Vaupés and beyond, while others in the lower Pirá-paraná worked regularly on the Apaporis for a part of each year.

"The missionaries played a complementary role to the *caucheros*: proclaiming themselves to be against the economic exploitation of Indians, they set out to convert and 'civilise.' The first missionaries to enter the Colombian Vaupés area were Montfortians, who settled along the Papuri following an exploratory voyage in 1914. They destroyed longhouses and burnt ritual goods, and forced the inhabitants to build wattle-and-daub villages, each with its own church. The manner in which they waged their war against sin softened over the years, especially with the replacement of the Montfortians by Colombian Javierians in 1949, but the aims remained basically the same until around 1970 when there came a wave of radical questioning of missionary policy from within. As the methods of persuasion became more gentle, the bond between Indian and missionary strengthened in economic content. The labour required to build airstrips and to feed and maintain mission headquarters and boarding schools was bought with manufactured goods. As these became indispensable, Indians found themselves dependent on mission centers and so the inflationary spiral of demand for manufactured goods began. Such demands are met by working for the missions and this both accelerates the acquisition of mission values, and increases mission power by augmenting capital resources such as airstrips, buildings and so on. In this way, the act of earning manufactured goods strengthens the acculturative force and so creates the desire for more goods.

"Many Pirá-paraná Indians had visited mission centers outside the Pirá-paraná area long before missionaries visited them and all were familiar with the elements of

Christianity. The Vaupés marriage system, which requires each man to find a wife from beyond the area occupied by his own linguistic group, creates a network of alliances which facilitates the spread of missionary culture well beyond the limits of missionary activity. However, at the time of my fieldwork, the disparity between longhouse life in the Pirá-paraná and missionary village life in the surrounding areas seemed to have dampened the exchange of women across the divide, so that Pirá-paraná society taken as a whole was relatively endogamous and culturally distinct (in terms of existing culture rather than traditional culture) from the rest of the Vaupés."[52]

The Hugh-Joneses, after an initial survey trip down the length of the Pirá-paraná, made themselves at home in the maloca (situated on the Caño Colorado) of the Meni Masa sib of the Barasana. The Meni Masa is one of a group of five sibs, each with its maloca, separated from its neighbors by two or more hours of travel by trail or canoe. According to S. Hugh-Jones, the Meni Masa rank in the middle of this group of five, those sibs ranked above being referred to as "our elder brothers" and those below as "our younger brothers," each being associated with a specialist ritual role. The Meni Masa are "warriors." Of the two sibs above, the Koamona are "chiefs," the Rasegana, "dancers and chanters," and of the two below, the Daria are "shamans" (*kumua*, see pages 345–346) and the Wabea, "cigar lighters" or servants.[53]

"Barasana society is rigidly divided along lines of sex," Hugh-Jones points out. "Men and women use different doors to their house, spend most of their waking lives apart from each other and are periodically and forcefully reminded of their separateness by the Yurupary rites that form the subject of this book. Working amongst

them as a married couple was a distinct advantage. Minimally, it established that, in spite of being a foreign man, I was relatively safe and had not come there to take their women. It meant that we were recognized as being mature enough to be fully incorporated into adult life even though our lack of children was the subject of ribald comments. But most important of all, it meant that we became familiar with Barasana society from the point of view of both sexes. Though we never specifically divided topics of research between us, the nature of the society itself imposed a division on our work. Though my wife was barred from secret male ritual, she was able to talk freely with the men and to discuss topics normally kept secret from women. But for me, the world of women was relatively closed."[54]

The crucial finding of the Hugh-Joneses with respect to the Yurupari complex among the Barasana was that it culminates, not in one ceremonial, but in two: a minor, known as Fruit-House, and a major, known as *He*-House (*He*, pronounced as in *hen* with the *n* omitted). The term *He*, according to Hugh-Jones, "refers in particular to the sacred flutes and trumpets; more widely, it is perhaps best translated as 'ancestral' and refers to the past, to the spirit world and to the world of myth. At its widest range, it implies a whole conception of the cosmos and of the place of human society within it."[55] In other words, *He* means, "mythological."

"The Barasana have an unusually rich and varied corpus of myths which are treated with considerable respect," Hugh-Jones continues, "and which form the basis of shamanic knowledge and power. The myths describe the establishment of an ordered cosmos and the creation of human society within it; the human social order is seen as part of this wider order, as timeless and changeless and beyond the immediate control of human agency—it is, or should be, as it was created in the past."[56]

This, it is safe to say, is an Elementary Idea (see I.1:8, II.1:28, 73) informing *all* aboriginal mythologies. According to this view: to change in any way the form or manner of use of any myth, ritual, or artifact, breaks its connection with the mythological ground through which the energies of eternal life enter the empirical sphere of spatial and temporal processes. The astounding conservatism of aboriginal cultures can be attributed largely to this idea.

"The *He* state," Hugh-Jones goes on to explain, "implies a state of being prior to, and now parallel with, human existence.

488. Koch-Grünberg drawing (c. 1905) of Yurupari rites as celebrated by Tuyúka Indians on the Rio Tiguié. Advancing behind the warning calls of the sacred flutes, the men in file (some, with forehead straps, carrying woven baskets), make their way from the river to the ceremonial maloca.

Originally everything was *He* and the pre-human, man-animal characters of myth are the *He* People from whom human beings developed by a process of transformation. The *He* People and the *He* state, wherein lies the power of creation and order, are thus in the distant past. But it is also an ever-changeless present that encapsulates human society and which exists as another aspect of reality, another world. When *He* is viewed as the past, human society is in danger of becoming increasingly distant and separated from this wider reality and source of life—the effects of this [passage of] time must be overcome. As the present, this other world is seen as separated in space; human society is in danger of becoming out of phase with this other reality and spatial separation must be mediated. The *He* state is known through myth; it is experienced and manipulated through ritual and controlled through spatial and temporal metaphor."[57]

One more paragraph, and this elegant summary of what I would number as one of the fundamental Elementary Ideas of all aboriginal mythic thought and ritual procedure, can be concluded.

"At birth, people leave the *He* state and become human, ontogeny repeating phylogeny; at death, people once again enter the *He* state and become ancestors to be reborn at future births. In life, people enter into involuntary contact with the *He* state through dreaming and illness, through menstruation and childbirth and through the deaths of others. All such contact is uncontrolled and dangerous. [Hence, we may add, the rituals of protection.] It is also possible to enter into voluntary and controlled contact with the *He* state and to experience it directly. The power and position of the shaman lies precisely in his ability to experience and manipulate the *He* state at will; such people are seen as living on two planes of existence simultaneously. Other men can enter into contact with the *He* state through rituals at which the shamans act as mediators. Though all rituals involve such voluntary contact, it is during the rites at which *He* instruments are used that this contact is achieved to its fullest extent. The *He* instruments represent the living dead, the first ancestors of humanity. This regular and controlled contact with the outer world, which gives power to control life and which ensures the continuance of society in a healthy and ordered state, is reserved for adult men. Its complement lies in female fertility and powers of reproduction. Women ensure the reproduction of people; men ensure the reproduction of society."[58]

Where Sacred Things Are Seen

The most important and elaborate of all Barasana rituals is that known as *He wi*, "*He* House," or *He iaria wi*, "House where *He* are seen." It is also, of all the rites, the most dangerous, and very few shamans have the power to conduct it. At one level, it is the rite of initiation of young boys into the men's secret cult of the sacred flutes and trumpets. But since the sight of these is forbidden to women, the ritual also serves to underscore and maintain the tension between the sexes. Barasana marriage is exogamous. All the wives in every patrilocal maloca, consequently, are from other malocas, other sibs. But the instruments represent the ancestors, the descent line, of the local maloca and its sib, who, in the context of the ceremony are adopting into their substance a new generation of young men, so that the social organism grounded in *He* (the mythic past and mystic present) should continue alive into the future.[59]

As Hugh-Jones has observed: "Women ensure the reproduction of people; men ensure the reproduction of society." There are, accordingly, specific women's rites associated with menstruation, birth, and nourishment: moments of great mystery and, consequently, of danger. And the counterparts of these in the domain of the male sex are the dangerous *He* rites for the continuation of the culture. In fact, the ability of women to menstruate and the possession by initiated men of the *He* (the instruments) are seen as complementary and mutually exclusive. There was a time, it is even said, when the women stole the instruments and the men then menstruated. The women then had control. But the men regained the instruments and the women menstruated. Implied is the idea, as Hugh-Jones has noted, "that the sex that controls the *He* and which does not menstruate will be the one that is politically dominant."[60] But also implied is that the women have the *He* in themselves, and that it is this that causes them to menstruate. The *He*, as we learn from one of the myths, is in their hair.

"It is for this reason," Hugh-Jones points out, "that when the men took back the *He* from the women, their victory over them was double-edged. They regained only one kind of *He* (instruments) which implies political dominance, but they lost another (women's hair) which implies menstruation and the power to create children."[61]

"*He* House," he suggests, "can perhaps be interpreted as a symbolic act in which adult men give birth to the initiates. In order to give birth, men must first be opened up and made to menstruate."[62]

"It is entirely appropriate therefore," he concludes, "that after *He* House, the initiates should be confined in a compartment, as are menstruating women, and referred to by expressions which, in their feminine form, refer to women in this condition."[63]

The three-day ceremonial is preceded by a day of preparations, with increasing separation of the sexes: women in the rear of the house, making manioc beer, the boys to be initiated among them, and the men sitting in front of the house on the plaza. At dusk (which marks the beginning of the first day), the younger men come playing the *He* up from the river, where the instruments have been kept hidden. Immediately on hearing them, the women rush out the rear door to the surrounding scrub, and for the rest of the night the flutes and trumpets are played round and round, outside the maloca. The attendant shamans have meanwhile been chanting and flicking whips to drive away illness. One of them brings smoking beeswax on a potsherd out onto the plaza, where he fans the smoke to the four directions. Others blow their breaths over piles of tobacco snuff that is then blown in large quantities through tubes up the men's noses, causing them to vomit. All communication at this time is being held to a minimum, in whispers.

At the first light of dawn, the *He* are played into the house, where they circumambulate the men's area sunwise. The elders are now sitting in groups at either side of the men's door, the shamans on stools, the others on mats. The women have again rushed out the back door into the bush, to protect their power to menstruate and give birth.

Around 9 A.M., the leading shaman hands around a ceremonial cigar over which he has blown spells, together with a gourd of blown coca. Two more gourds are placed in the middle of the house, one containing red paint, the other snuff. The paint is known as the "blood and flesh of *He*." Any woman touching it would immediately menstruate. The men wipe it over their bodies, especially the temples and navel; for, as they say, "It makes us live." And the snuff, mixed with beeswax, they wipe with a stick over their legs and knees to protect against the stabbing pains of what are known as "water spears" which they would otherwise experience when ritually bathing—all other contact with anything of water being forbidden during the period of the rite.

Protected thus, the company now proceeds to the river in back of the maloca, to bathe. The shamans both lead the procession and follow, flicking their whips aggressively, and the instruments are played as far as to the edge of the clearing around the maloca. At the river they are placed in the water to give them a good sound, and in total silence (to protect against possible attacks by *He* jaguars) the elders bathe while the younger men wash only their face and hands. Back in the maloca, all drink amply of the beer (blown over by the shamans) which the women have prepared for them, and a long chanting session is held.

In the course of the afternoon of this first day, the long flutes known as Old Macaws are decorated with feather ruffs and their engraved designs are filled with manioc starch. Two elders then put on jaguar-tooth belts, elbow ornaments and feather crowns, and dance the decorated flutes up and down the middle of the house, after which the Old Macaws sound continuously, played by relays of elders.

Toward dusk the initiates are brought in. Their hair has been cut by the women, who have also painted them black from head to foot. Having been summoned by the shamans to appear, they are carried in on the shoulders of elders and set down to stand by the men's door in a row, linked by their little fingers. Here they are given kana berries (*Sabicea amazonensis*) to eat, to strengthen them for the rite's ordeal, and eating, each is looked over by an elder.

When the berries have been consumed, the boys are led to a mat before the shaman's enclosure and told to sit in a foetal posture, without moving. The ceremonial cigar and some blown coca are brought to them, after which each is served by the leading shaman a small sip of the hallucinogenic drink, yagé, drawn from a potion freshly prepared by himself at a station outside the maloca. Upon entering the building with it, he had paused at the door, to draw on the ground a figure known as the Yagé Mother [Figure 490], using pounded yagé bark as a paint and throwing the rest of the poundings up onto the maloca roof. Then he had entered

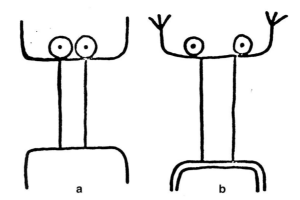

490. Yagé Mother: **(a)** figure drawn with pounded yagé bark on a Barasana longhouse floor during *He wi* ritual (recorded, 1970s, by S. Hugh-Jones); **(b)** petroglyph on a rock in the Vaupés river above Jauareté (recorded, 1900, by E. Stradelli).[58]

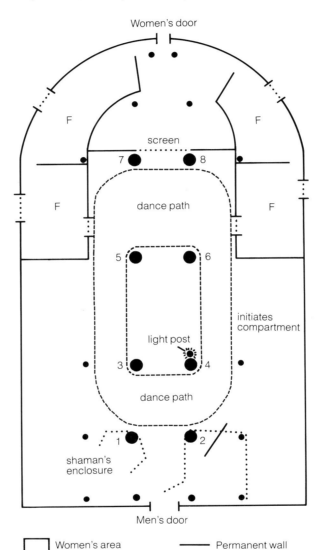

491. Maloca interior, as configured for the *He wi* rites: the temporary walls, special enclosures, and screen that separates the men from the women will remain for the duration of the event (see text).

and all the men had picked up *He* instruments for the moment of the revelation. Solemnly blowing the flutes and trumpets, walking very very slowly with the ends of the long instruments held very close to the ground, the men of the maloca pass before the initiates' eyes, showing to them each instrument, and the boys behold the *He* for the first time.

Following this event, there is a long session of chanting, and apart from the sounds of the chanting voices, the flutes and trumpets, almost total silence reigns in the house. Toward midnight, the conducting shaman carries his pot of yagé to a place between posts five and

six, calling to the company to come drink. One by one, the youngest first, clutching staves and acting out spearing, they advance in inverse order of seniority. Each is given yagé and blown coca, drinks, eats, and returns to his place, and when all have partaken, there follows another parade of the *He*.

When a chanting is heard, soon after midnight, of two voices within the shaman's enclosure, the guardian of the initiates ignites some beeswax taken from a gourd and proceeds twice around the dance path, sunwise, followed by the younger men blowing trumpets, and the initiates blowing short flutes. This procession is the climax of the festival. The women are out at the edge of the forest, listening for falling trees, and should any such sound be heard, it would be understood as an evil omen, presaging the wasting away and death of the participants.

The next events are of violence.

Two elders in full regalia (wearing bark-cloth aprons, belts of carved rose-colored shell, hanks of monkey-fur string on their backs, sacred elbow ornaments, and headdresses of egret and macaw feathers) step outside the building and sound out there the decorated Old Macaw flutes. Those are *He* spirits, fierce spirits, ancestors of the living and very dangerous. "I will kill you," they are saying. They are challenging the initiates to become as fierce as they. And the company, responding, grabs staves and whips, and lines up on either side of the room. The flutes enter, played with ends raised high in the air, and the company, rushing up and down the side aisles, acts out spearing.

Two gourds are next placed between posts one and two; one contains snuff, the other, beeswax mixed with coca. One by one, the members of the company, initiates first, the rest in inverse order of seniority, come up, wipe snuff on their knees, and eat pinches of coca. Then the episode of the challenging pipes and rushing about with staves and whips is played through a second time.

The two elders with the Old Macaw flutes now join the two chanting shamans, then return to playing the flutes, and during their playing blown coca from the beeswax gourd is passed to the older women, behind the screen between posts seven and eight. Receiving it, they eat the coca and apply blown red paint to their bodies. The Old Macaw flute men now are chanting with but one of the two shamans. The other has gone with a bundle of whips to stand before the women's screen.

All present run up the side aisles, acting out spearing, and stand in two groups by the shaman. One by one, starting with the youngest, they go forward and, standing with their legs apart and with their arms held above their heads clutching a staff horizontally in their hands, they are whipped on the leg, thigh, abdomen and chest. Holding their arms out in front of them, these are whipped too. After each person is whipped, he runs back to his place, acting out spearing as he goes. Finally the shaman comes back to the men's end of the house where he too is whipped by another elder.

After all this, more yagé is served and a chanting is commenced before the screen at the female end of the house that continues until dawn; at which time, the leading shaman comes with a pot of blown black paint, and the initiates and younger men begin to paint each other's legs and body. Those painting each other establish by this act a ritual brotherlike relationship and will speak of each other henceforth as *yu suori*, "my paint-partner." Formerly, according to report, the initiates were then made to stand in a row, their G-strings were cut, and the *He* instruments blown over their penises, after which they went out naked to greet the morning and to play the short flutes.

The morning of this second day is celebrated with another instrument parade, featuring Old Macaw, another long chanting session, and a general drinking of beer. About noon there is still another parade, during which the two leading shamans play a special type of trumpet (not otherwise seen in this ceremony) called Old Callecebus Monkey. Snuff to prevent illness now is served to everybody, men and women

as well, and finally, just before dark, the flutes and trumpets are again paraded twice around the room in a ceremony called "ending the dance." They are then taken outside and from the flutes the feather ruffs are removed. Mats are laid out near the women's screen and all but a few of the elders go to sleep there. It is thought dangerous for the initiates to sleep at the men's end of the house, where the Sun and the *He* people, having power there and desiring to keep the initiates with them forever, might send dreams of eating fish (a food forbidden at this time) and thus kill them.

The final day is of concluding rites. At dawn, the flutes are played inside the house, the trumpets around the outside. The shamans blow spells over snuff to be applied to the knees and water is drunk in small quantities, to prevent

danger both from the morning dew and from the bathing soon to follow. Then all go to the landing, where the instruments are immersed, the initiates and younger men bathe, and the shamans fill the Old Macaw flutes with water in such a way that it spurts out the sound holes. This is the flutes drinking and vomiting. The initiates drink water from the flutes, and what remains is poured over them to make them fierce. Certain leaves are crushed into water that is drunk to cause vomiting, to clean out the *He* poison and residual yagé, and the initiates then bathe, while two elders play the Old Macaw flutes.

The women have meanwhile prepared a meal and taken all the food and goods in the house out onto the plaza. When the men return, the feather ruffs are put back on the flutes, which are then played by various elders, the last being the two who had been the *He* spirits earlier in the festival. When they have finished and the shaman removes their feather headdresses, he blows spells on their heads and wipes his hands over them lightly, flicking off invisible, harmful substances. He does the same for everyone who wore headdresses during the services; for if this were not done, the men would be in danger of attack from jaguars and of headaches caused by the silverfish that eat feathers.

The meal is eaten on the plaza. The *He* instruments are wrapped in fresh leaves, taken down to the river, and hidden again in the mud under the water. The whole house is swept out thoroughly and fumigated; for it is saturated with *He* poison, which must be removed by shamanism, to protect the women from becoming ill. An enclosure of woven leaves is built just inside the men's door on the left and there the initiates sling their hammocks. The shamans blow spells on the hammock and, once the initiates have been installed there, the screen shutting off the women's quarter of the house is removed. The initiates' compartment is built in such a way that they can go in and out without seeing or being seen by the women at the other end of the house. The women fear the initiates, [Hugh-Jones explains] for if they have any contact with them, *He*, in the form of an anaconda, enters their bodies and they die.

For the initiates the end of this period [of seclusion and restrictions] is signalled by the total disappearance of the black paint applied to their bodies at the start of the rite. The end of the period is marked by the eating of capsicum pepper, blown over by the shamans. On seeing the *He*, the participants become *He* people (*He masa*) and *He* enters their bodies. This gradually leaves the body as the paint fades from the skin. For the elders, the period lasts one month; for the initiates and younger men it lasts two months. Pepper is thus blown twice, once for the elders, once for the initiates. During the period of restrictions, the men are described as *bedira*, a state when people fast and undergo restrictions. The same word also applies to menstruating women.[64]

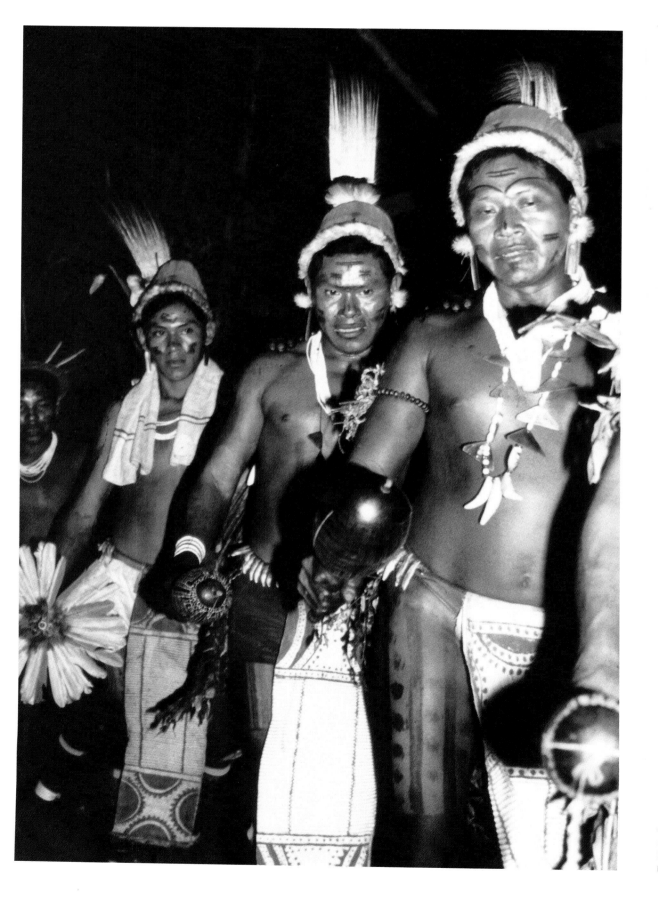

492. Barasana celebrants, dressed in ceremonial regalia and under the influence of yagé. When the Barasana put on feathers and paint, they enter into mythic time and become ancestral spirits.

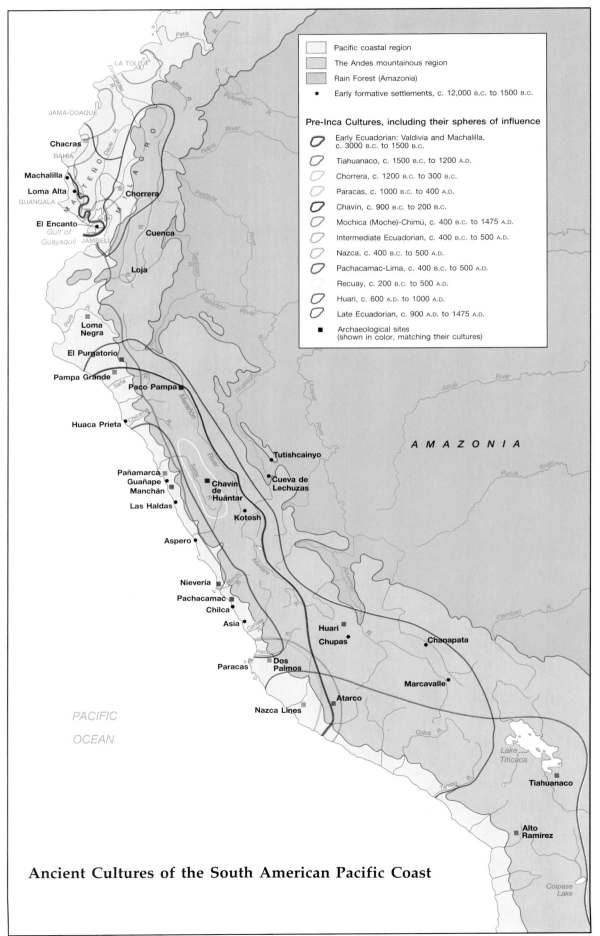

Ancient Cultures of the South American Pacific Coast

Valdivia (Ecuador) and the Old Pacific Culture

In December 1960, a door opened from the local North and South American scene to the much larger, of World History, when Emilio Estrada, a young Ecuadorian businessman who had adopted archaeology as a hobby, excavating at a rich pottery site near the little fishing village of Valdivia, on the Guayas coast of Ecuador, unearthed part of the castellated rim of a shattered ceramic vessel, which he recognized (no doubt with a shock) as similar in both form and decoration to a type of Middle Jomon ware (c. 3000 B.C.) from prehistoric Japan.

Estrada had already published in 1958 a monograph in Spanish classifying some 36,000 potsherds, numerous pottery figurines, and an assortment of artifacts, variously of stone, bone, and shell, uncovered at his site. Three carbon-14 dates had fixed the period of his finds between 2493 and 2093 B.C. Similarities had been noted, furthermore, to known potteries of matching date from two sites to the south, in coastal Peru, Guañape and Ancon, as well as two to the north, Monagrillo and Puerto Hormiga, on the Colombian Caribbean.[65]

Following his recognition of the Jomon connection, Estrada got in touch with Clifford Evans and Betty J. Meggers, at the Smithsonian Institution in Washington, D.C., who had done archaeological fieldwork in Ecuador, Brazil, Guyana, and Venezuela, as well as on Ponape in Micronesia. As she has told of their reaction to what for them was astounding news:

"Having been taught in graduate school that transpacific contacts were irrelevant to explaining the origins of New World traits, we reacted with skepticism. When we examined his sources, however, we found to our surprise that the similarities were closer and more numerous than anything we had been able to find within the Americas. Following the rules traditionally employed by archaeologists for establishing affiliations made it necessary to infer that Jomon and Valdivia were related. This

Map 39.

354

implied a transpacific contact about the beginning of the third millennium B.C."[66] For, as she declares: "If an ocean did not separate Japan and Ecuador, no archaeologist would hesitate to infer the common origin of 5000-year-old potteries from sites in these two countries."[67]

Estrada died in 1961 at the age of 45, three months before the publication of their co-authored announcement of this discovery in *Science*, February 2, 1962.[68] In 1963, Meggers and Evans, on a special visit to Japan, were there able to inspect and to compare the collections of excavated materials from Early and Middle Jomon sites, both on Honshu and on Kyushu, and, after analyzing the evidence, came to the conclusion "that pottery was introduced from western Japan to Ecuador, and that other early occurences in the Americas were derived from the Valdivia complex."[69] In 1965 their final report was published,[70] and from every quarter of the academic community expressions came, and have come flying ever since, of incredulity, indignation, and even insult.

The first question, of course, is of the possibility of a transoceanic voyage at that early date from Kyushu to Ecuador. Meggers and Estrada had modestly suggested "a boatload of Early Middle Jomon fishermen," caught by a storm too far from shore and carried by currents along the great circle route, eastward and then southward to the Guayas coast.[71] But they need not have been so modest. The voyage could have been intentional and of many more craft than one.

The opening, formative years of the Jomon culture of earliest post-Paleolithic Japan date from c. 11,000 B.C. Ocean levels at that time were some fifty feet lower than today, but rising as the last of the glaciers melted. The people of the islands were not of the race of the historic Japanese, but of unrelated stocks as different from each other as the Caucasoid Ainu from Siberia and the Southeast Asian Austronesians from the island world then coming into being with the gradual flooding of Old Melanesia (see I.1:30, and I.1:**Map 8**).

From the very start of this earliest postglacial age, a number of distinct Jomon traditions were already in formation in various parts of the islands, suggesting, as

Chester S. Chard has observed, "the existence of separate ethnic or tribal groupings."[72] What now appears to be the earliest ware is from the Fukui Cave in Kyushu, radiocarbon dated at 12,700 ± 500 years ago,[73] which is equivalent to c. 11,200–10,200 B.C., the earliest date for pottery (as far as I have learned) in any part of the world. The origins of the art are unknown. The people of the time were of a hunting-fishing-gathering stage. Evidence of deepwater fishing at the Natsushima site, near the mouth of Tokyo Bay, "indicates," says Chard, "that at least some coastal groups in Japan must have had adequate watercraft over 9000 years ago, and a late Initial Jomon site on one of the Izu Islands," he adds, "is even more convincing evidence of maritime capabilities, probably at least as early as 7500 years before the present. By around 6500 B.P. [that is, about 4500 B.C.] there is clear evidence of occasional trade between Kyushu and the Pusan area of Korea."[74]

Chard's tentative chronology for the more than 10,000 years of Jomon ceramic manufacture and (let us add) Jomon seafaring is as follows:[75]

Incipient Jomon ..... c. 11000–7500 B.C.
Initial Jomon .... c. 7500–5300 B.C.
Early Jomon .... c. 5300–3600 B.C.
Middle Jomon .... c. 3600–2500 B.C.
Late Jomon .... c. 2500–1000 B.C.
Final Jomon .... c. 1000– 400 B.C.

Very cautiously and noncommitally, Chard makes reference to the announcement of Jomon pottery in Ecuador, neither affirming nor denying his belief in its possibility, though recognizing that in the vast region of the Pacific world, of which Jomon Japan was a part, "seafaring," as he writes, "must have reached a fairly high development thousands of years ago in order to account for the evidence of human occupation throughout the western Pacific from the Kyukyus, Taiwan, and the Philippines on out to Micronesia."[76]

a

b

493. (**a**) Japanese earthenware vessel, 11⅝" tall with a 35½" girth, Middle Jomon period, c. 3000 B.C.; (**b**) Ecuadorian pottery jar, c. 2¾" high, Valdivia phase 6, c. 1850–1700 B.C.

To the unstudied eye, these two pots might appear extremely dissimilar, but to Emilio Estrada (and, subsequently, to various ceramic specialists) key fragments of such Jomon and Valdivian vessels as these exhibited sufficient similarities of form, decorative motif, and technique of manufacture to suggest strongly that they were of common origin.

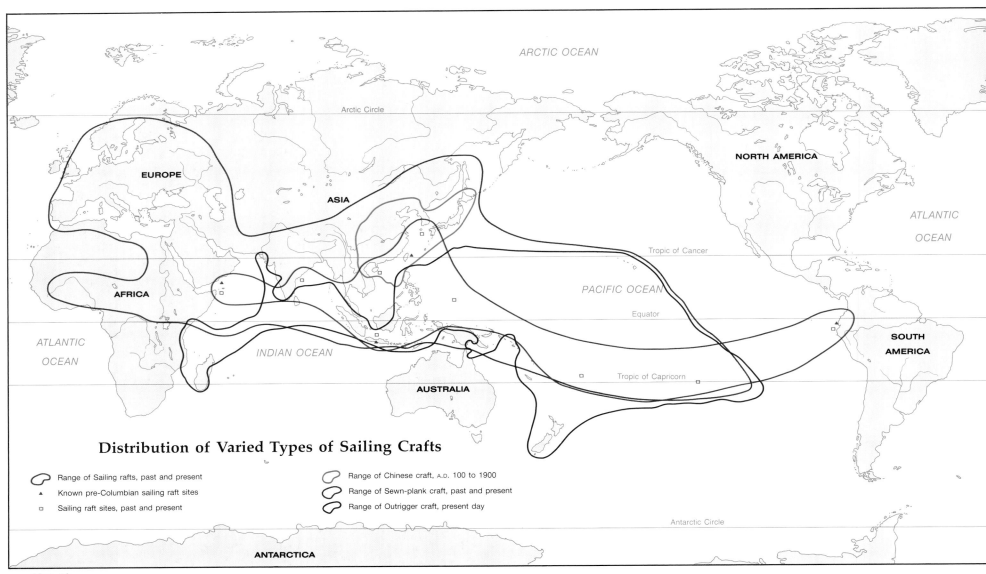

Distribution of Varied Types of Sailing Crafts

⌒ Range of Sailing rafts, past and present   ⌒ Range of Chinese craft, A.D. 100 to 1900

▲ Known pre-Columbian sailing raft sites   ⌒ Range of Sewn-plank craft, past and present

□ Sailing raft sites, past and present   ⌒ Range of Outrigger craft, present day

Map 40.

In Map 40 the occurrences and distributions of seaworthy rafts, sailing rafts, and outrigger canoes throughout the world can be seen to match in large part the areas outlined in Baumann's map (I.2:**Map 33**) showing the world-distribution of the mythologies of bisexual gods. Intriguing questions are also raised by a comparison of various sailing rafts from diverse locations—especially from the Coromandel Indian Coast (Figure 494), Java (Figure 495), Annam (Figure 496), Formosa (Figure 499), and Brazil (Figure 497)—with a similar craft from pre-Columbian Ecuador (Figure 498), recorded from exactly the site of Estrada's discovery of Early Middle Jomon pottery

sherds. The Brazilian example is, in Doran's view, post-Columbian. However, its local name, *jangada,* is Tamil, derived from Sanskrit, and the support for its mast is of a kind found otherwise only in India and Annam.[77] Its position (it is worth noting) is at the mouth of the river Amazon, several of the numerous headwaters of which originate in the Andean highlands, just across the mountains from coastal Ecuador and proximate to the sources of rivers that flow toward the Pacific. These rivers, cutting through the prodigious Andes mountain range, provide possible connective routes between the Ecuadorian coast and the Upper Amazonian rain forest, where the

494. From the Coromandel coast (India), a sailing raft with two leeway boards and a steering paddle.

495. This panel on the stupa of Borobudur (Java) depicts, in bas-relief, a sailing raft caught in a fierce storm. Assisting in the rescue of a mate being threatened by a sea monster, sailors fore and aft manipulate the craft's daggerboards.

496. From the Vietnamese state of Annam, this bamboo raft makes use of multiple daggerboards.

great latticework of river- and canoe-ways are thoroughfares for the Arawakan, Cariban, and Tupi-Guarani tribes.

Many observers have noted what appear to be more than coincidental likenesses between the cultures and racial features of the riverine tribes of the Amazonian Basin and those of the waterways of Southeast Asia: specifically, Malaysia, Borneo, the Celebes and Moluccas. Stephen C. Jett points out that physical anthropological data on the tribes of interior Borneo and on the Caribs and Arawaks of equatorial South America demonstrate between these two groups greater similarity than between either group and its neighbors. By way of explanation, some physical anthropologists have suggested convergence (following established biological "rules") under similar conditions of heat and humidity. But Jett concludes: "This greater similarity suggests actual migrations."[78]

"It is possible," he states further, "that the entire system of vegetative-reproduction-shifting cultivation in the New World owes its origin to Malaysian or other Southeast Asian immigrants. If so, local plants—such as sweet potato, yantia, and manioc—were largely substituted for similar Asian ones, such as yams and taro. However, there is evidence (of variable quality) that certain Southeast Asian food plants, such as the plantain, were brought to pre-Columbian tropical America…

"The old cultural pattern of Indonesia," he continues, "and that of equatorial America are strikingly similar. Points in common range from longhouses to head-hunting, and include a host of specific traits. Of these the blowgun complex has been studied in detail and was found to share a very large number of common points in the two areas concerned.[79] It may also be relevant that the Tucano of southern Colombia, though an inland tribe, have a tradition of having come from across the Pacific.[80]

"The aforementioned similarities," he then notes, "have been attributed by some to similar physical environments. Many of the shared traits, however, have no specific adaptive value in such environments. Further, the distribution pattern of the relevant traits—decreasing in frequency as one moves away from northwesternmost South America—is suggestive of transpacific introduction over a long period and sequential diffusion into the Amazon Basin, the Guianas, and Central America. As to those traits which clearly *are* adaptive, Malaysians' earlier adaptation to equatorial environments in Asia is exactly what would have enabled them to occupy such environments successfully in the New World while at the same time excluding them from other environments."[81] For the dating of these movements, Jett suggests "a probable time range from 3600 to 300 B.C. and a possible principal Malaysian source area on the shores of the Celebes Sea."[82]

Concerning the feasibility of trans-oceanic voyages by raft or dugout canoe, there is today no longer question. Thor Heyerdahl's drift voyage from Peru to the Tuamotus on the unguided raft, *Kon-Tiki,* and the passage from Hawaii to Tahiti and back of the large, double-hull, Polynesian type sailing canoe, *Hokuleia,* have put a term to that argument. However, as Jett points out, our academic colleagues need not have waited for those two demonstrations for the cure of their thalassophobia. The sea, for boatmen, is not a barrier but a highway; indeed, a challenge and invitation. J. Merrien, he reminds us, published a catalogue, following the *Kon-Tiki* adven-

ture, of no less than 120 modern intentional solo and two-man ocean voyages,[83] which included: a solo ninety-three-day crossing from Japan to San Francisco in a nineteen-foot sloop; a sixty-eight-day raft drift from California to Hawaii; a solo voyage in a converted Indian dugout canoe (bottom length, thirty feet) from Vancouver to the Cook Islands (5500 miles in fifty-six days), followed by an ultimate landing in England; a solo journey in a nineteen-and-a-half-foot schooner from San Francisco to Australian waters without a single port of call (6500 miles in 162 days). Also included in Merrien's formidable catalogue were three solo round-the-world tours: one, a solo by Joshua Slocum in the *Spray* (thirty-six feet nine inches) of 46,000 miles in three years; another, by Vito Dumas in a thirty-two-foot ketch, which included a 7200-mile run from the Cape of Good Hope to New Zealand and a continuation to Valparaiso, Chile (5400 miles in seventy-two days), followed by a trip around the Horn; the third, sixty-two-year-old Francis Chichester's one-stop circumnavigation of the globe (28,500 miles with only one stop) in a fifty-four-foot ketch. Notable, also, were the voyages of Eric de Bisschop: first, in a double canoe with one companion, from Hawaii to Cannes in 264 days; next, some 5000 miles by bamboo sailing raft from Tahiti into the southeastern Pacific; and finally, 5500 miles by raft from Peru to Rakahanga. Among the 110 other examples cited and described was the pontoon raft journey of seventy-year-old William Willis in 1965, from Peru, 7450 miles to Samoa, and an additional 3000 miles, then, to Australia, though suffering (following various accidents and a wind that had ripped his mainsail apart) from an abdominal hernia, fractured sacrum, and paralysis from the waist down.[84]

Could a Jomon Japanese dugout canoe or sailing raft have landed in Ecuador, safely and intentionally, c. 3000 B.C.?

497. The jangada, the post-Columbian sailing raft of Brazil, has a single daggerboard and a steering paddle, as well as multiple steps for the mast, a feature also found only in India and Annam, where the most complex of all sailing rafts are located.

498. A drawing made in 1619 showing an early Ecuadorian sailing raft with multiple daggerboards.

499. This sailing raft of bamboo, from Formosa, features multiple leeway boards that, when thrust down into the water, prevent the raft from being blown sideways, thus enabling it to make headway in any direction for unlimited periods of time.

That America was already known to the seafaring people of East Asia is almost certain. For, as Robert von Heine-Geldern pointed out over thirty years ago, after reviewing an article published in 1875 in the Proceedings of the California Academy of Sciences,[85] *in the course of a single year,* no fewer than twenty Japanese junks, having lost in storms their masts or rudders, were carried by currents toward the North American coast, which they reached at various points from the Aleutian Islands to Mexico. And this sort of thing, Heine-Geldern infers, must have happened (if one thinks back to that period of Early Jomon maritime activities recognized by Chester Chard as occurring no less than 9000 years ago) to many many times twenty shipwrecked Japanese craft — not to mention similar craft from other East Asian shores. Accordingly, Heine-Geldern has reasoned, if the occupants of a single one of those many hundreds of shipwrecked craft had contrived to return home, that would have sufficed to reveal the existence of a continent on the other side of the ocean.[86]

Moreover, evidence that this continent must indeed have been known to Asia at an early date has been lately dependably reported from two sites near the southern Chinese coast (in Kiangsu and Chekiang provinces), where the peanut, a South American domesticate, now appears to have been cultivated c. 3300–2800 B.C.[87] — which is exactly the period of Estrada's and Meggers' Valdivia. Furthermore, the fashioning of bark cloth (Polynesian, *tapa*) in southern China no later than c. 2400 B.C. is made known by the appearance in Taiwan at that date of stone bark-beaters almost identical in form to those of Central and Western Mexico, Costa Rica, and El Salvador.[88] And still further: the presence throughout South America of chickens of Asian—not European—breeds at the time of the Spanish and Portuguese first arrivals indicates, as George F. Carter has observed, that at least some of the transoceanic voyages were made, not only intentionally, but with "such speed that they allowed the carriage of animals who had to be fed and watered and would surely not have survived a long drift voyage."[89]

On November 30, 1980, six Japanese scientists brought their forty-three-foot catamaran to land at Arica, Chile, terminating a six-and-a-half-month voyage. Their craft, the *Yasei-Gō,* "Wild Adventure," had set sail from Shimoda on May 8, following the Japanese Current (*Kuroshio,* the "Black Current"), which, they reasoned, might have carried the Jomon fishermen to America. And indeed, it brought them to San Francisco on July 5, and then carried them south to Ecuador, Peru, and Chile.

"We have proved," said the happy, though weary, Captain Kazunobu Fumimoto, "that such a voyage can be made in a boat like those used by Japanese fishermen 5000 years before Christ."[90]

Map 41.

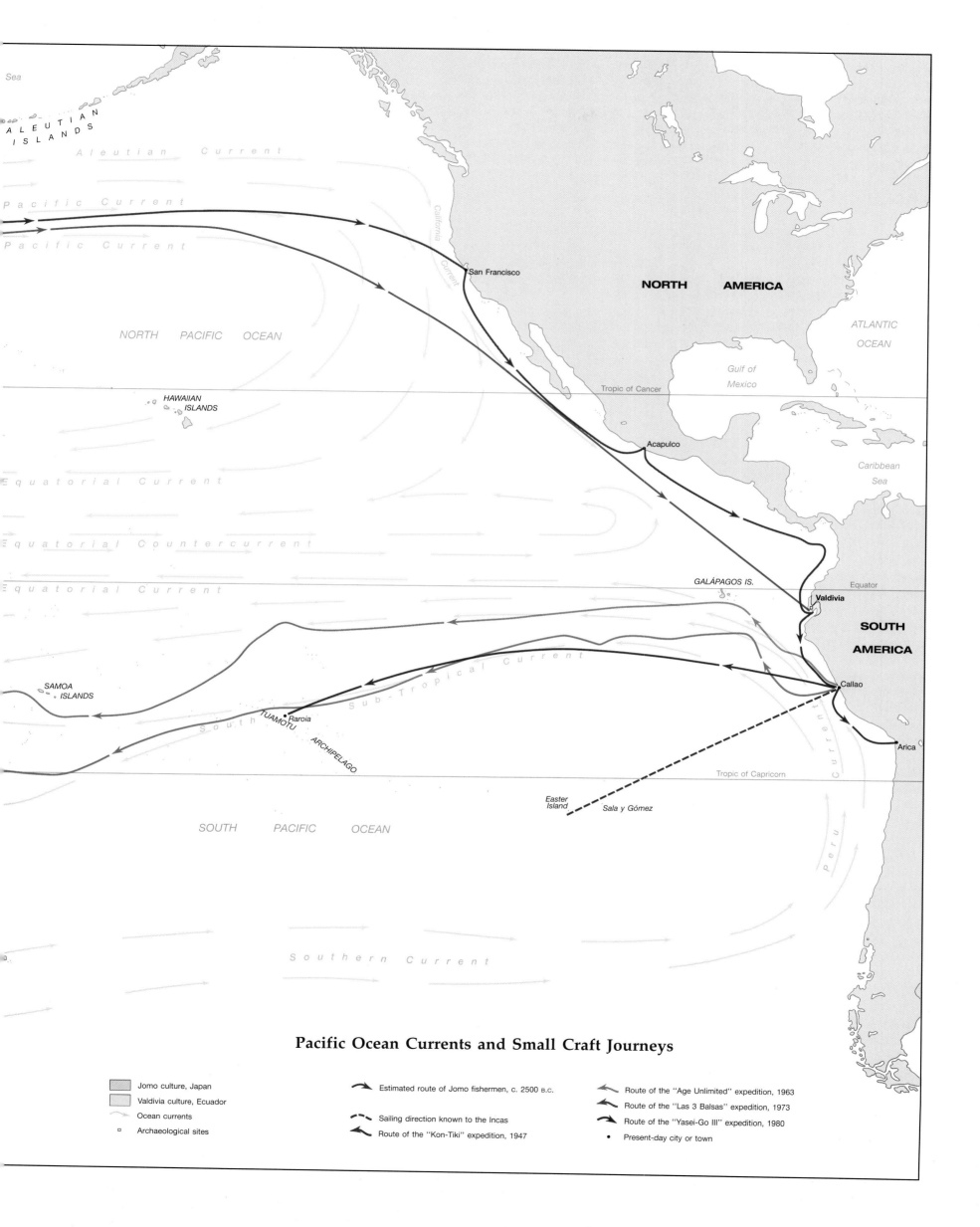

Pacific Ocean Currents and Small Craft Journeys

Jomo culture, Japan	
Valdivia culture, Ecuador	
Ocean currents	
▫ Archaeological sites	

Estimated route of Jomo fishermen, c. 2500 B.C.

Sailing direction known to the Incas

Route of the "Kon-Tiki" expedition, 1947

Route of the "Age Unlimited" expedition, 1963

Route of the "Las 3 Balsas" expedition, 1973

Route of the "Yasei-Go III" expedition, 1980

• Present-day city or town

359

Ecuador As the American Formative Matrix

Comparisons between Jomon pottery from Japan (fragments, left column) and Valdivian shards from Ecuador (right) evidence numerous similarities in design and manufacturing techniques (see below). Consideration of these similarities, some experts argue, as well as the apparent absence of any clearly antecedent indigenous ceramic tradition, suggests that the art of pottery-making might have been introduced into the Americas by some prehistoric, trans-Pacific voyagers. The question has not been resolved.

The work of Meggers, Evans, and Estrada[91] suggests that, together with the primary idea and technique of pottery manufacture, there had crossed the sea, c. 3000 B.C., a distinctive cluster of secondary ideas and techniques for the non-functional embellishment of the ceramic vessels produced. Meggers has compiled a list of twenty-eight Valdivia traits that are shared, on the one hand, by the Jomon wares of Japan and, on the other, by potteries of the very same early period from Panama and the Colombian Caribbean coast.[92] Further evidence of Ecuador's seminal position in Early Formative America is provided by Valdivia figurines (Figures 505 and 506)—the earlier in stone, the later in clay—that are (by many centuries) *the earliest known female statuettes in the Americas.*

In 1969 the Smithsonian Institution published James A. Ford's *A Comparison of Formative Cultures in the Americas,*[93] which contained twenty-two charts that displayed essentially similar patterns of distribution throughout the Americas for bent-knee figurines, ceremonial centers and planned villages, grinding stones, bark-beaters, particular forms of bowls and pots, red-slip and zoned-relief decorations, and so forth. The distribution patterns pictured in these charts (which served as a principal source for portions of "From Nomadism to Seed Gardening" in this volume; see II.2:122–127) tend only to confirm the very strong impression already given by the distribution of the figurines, namely that coastal Ecuador was a matrix—possibly even *the* matrix—of Early Formative culture impulses in the Americas. The bark-beaters represent, almost certainly, a transoceanic influence; the grinding stones, for the preparation of vegetable food, suggest an agricultural background; while the ceremonial centers (notwithstanding earlier similar findings on the coast of Peru)[94] testify to an astonishingly early unfoldment toward the Classic temple forms of the South and Middle American civilizations.

A veritable gold rush of scientific teams to the Ecuadorian region shortly followed the appearance of the Meggers, Evans, and Estrada publication, and it was then not very long before claims were staked to evidences of potteries purportedly of an earlier date than certain of Estrada's sherds, although controversy continues over the accuracy of various so-called calibrated and uncalibrated datings.[95] Nothing, however, has yet been found of earlier figurines. Nor have possible sources for any of the antecedent techniques and wares been adduced, though many have been postulated. Some have piously hoped, of course, that an indisputably American origin for these earliest potteries might be uncovered, an antecedent in demonstrable independence of transoceanic inspiration.

500. Broad-line incisions with square-ended tool.

501. Row of punctuations at lower margin of an incised zone.

502. Combination of crosshatch at rim, horizontal incised lines on neck, and zigzag lines on body.

503. Zoned punctuation and incised lines.

Should that prove to be the case, however, a new and far more mysterious conundrum will have emerged, a mystery more perplexing than that of prehistoric transoceanic travel. As Clinton Edwards has remarked in comment on the papers

504. An array of early-Valdivian stone figurines.

collected in *Man across the Sea*: "We do have the problem of explaining how and why, after tens of thousands of years of very slow technological change and lack of any attributes of civilization anywhere in the world, both of the world's great land masses should rather suddenly and in many similar ways experience almost contemporaneously the phenomenon of change from the precivilized to the civilized state." He continues: "Students of Old World prehistory and history seem fairly well in accord that the major generator of change is the dispersal and interchange of ideas within a single, uncompartmented *oikumene*. On the other hand, many scholars in the United States assume that the forces and processes engendering change stem predominantly from the individual group itself, not from outsiders. The result of this latter theoretical persuasion was the compartmentalization of cultures as distinct entities in the Americas."[96]

To date, some of the more extensive of the reported researches in coastal Ecuador have been those of the expeditions organized by the University of Illinois at Urbana, directed by Donald W. Lathrap of the Field Museum of Chicago, and supported by both the United States National Science Foundation and the Banco Central of Ecuador. Among the sites excavated, two have been of outstanding consequence: Loma Alta, situated on a hill fifteen kilometers up the Valdivia River; and Real Alta, a coastal site southeast of Punta Concepción (see II.2: Map 16). From the materials accumulated, classified, and interpreted, Lathrap and his colleagues—recognizing three distinctive stages of development—have attempted to formulate a chronological reconstruction of one of the initiating culture-complexes of the American Formative era.[97]

505. These early-Valdivian ceramic figurines are distinguished by their elaborate hair treatments.

The first period they distinguish was of a *preceramic culture, dating from possibly 4000—certainly 3000—to c. 2450* B.C.,[98] when the Valdivians dwelt in small, beehivelike oval houses and practiced an intensive agriculture, which included cultivation of the bottle gourd. A finding of what appears to be spindle whorls at the bottom of one of the excavated trenches suggests that the Valdivians may already have been growing and spinning cotton, although they could equally well have been working with another wild fiber such as kapok. Their figurines were of the crudest kind, and of stone (see Figure 504).

What is generally known to American archaeology as the Formative stage of civilization (or Civilization) generally corresponds to what in Europe is known as the Neolithic (see II.2:122). Lathrap has described it as "the stage in cultural evolution...defined by the appearance of large permanent communities that derived the greater part of their food from farming."[99] Ford's charts—especially those showing

506. Detail of an enigmatic, dual-headed, early-Valdivian stone figurine, one of the earliest representations of the distinctive, universal, bifocal, mythological perspective that would later inform such aboriginal, American graphic metaphors as the Tlatilcan "pretty ladies" (see **342**), the Huichol sky goddess Our Mother Young Eagle Girl (see **404**), and certain early-Antillean zemis (see **430**).

507. The presence of the bottle gourd already in the garden plots of earliest Ecuador (Valdivia 1, c. 4000/3000–2450 B.C.) is suggested by the discovery there of bowls, with incised faces and rims carved in imitation of a carved gourd, similar to the examples pictured above: the top bowl has a diameter of c. 7¼", while the bottom is c. 3⁵⁄₁₆" high.

For the bottle gourd, or calabash, is native not to America, where it is known only as a cultigen, but to tropical Africa.[59] Its dissemination has been attributed by some to waves and currents, but as Carl Sauer pointed out some thirty years ago: "It is a cultigen as we know it in America and depends on the care of man for its preservation. It is in no sense a strand or marsh plant. The theory of its accidental dissemination involves, in addition to the undamaged transit of an ocean, a waiting agriculturalist who carried it from the seashore to a suitable spot of cultivation. It is at any rate an anciently grown plant in the New World, as many gourds in archaeological sites attest."[60] Two more recent authorities, Thomas W. Whitaker and Herbert G. Baker, have suggested in reply to this point that a gourd washed up by waves might have been picked up simply by a beach-comber and carried to the finder's village to be opened out of curiosity, with the contents finally thrown onto a trash pile, where the seeds took root.[61] So that, in Whitaker's considered view, "The gourd could have been introduced into the Americas by drift from Africa or Polynesia, but introduction by human transportation remains a distinct possibility."[62]

Lathrap's date of 4000/3000 B.C. eliminates Polynesia, however, which at that time was uninhabited. "On the northern border of Mesoamerica," Whitaker reports, "*L. siceraria* [the bottle gourd] is reported from strata radiocarbon dated at 7000–5000 B.C. This is the earliest date for this species in the Americas."[63] But here again, as in Ecuador, we are on the Pacific side of the continent; so that, one way or the other, either by ocean current or by sailing raft on the same current, the odds are for a trans-Pacific voyage of the bottle gourd from that part of the world around the Celebes Sea from which Stephen Jett has presumed the long-house, blowgun, bark-cloth beater, panpipe, and dugout canoe to have come to South America, together with the idea itself of vegetative-reproduction-shifting cultivation. Consideration, with Map 41 in view, of the distance that a bottle gourd would have had to have floated undamaged from the Celebes Sea to the American coast, to be picked up there by a beachcomber, opened out of curiosity, and thrown onto a trash pile, where its seeds (still alive and well) took root, will, one should think, suffice to settle the case for deliberate transportation by an agriculturalist who knew what he had.

the distribution of grinding stones, figurines, and ceremonial constructions—strongly suggest that in Formative Ecuador the passage from an economy of nomadic hunting and gathering to a sedentary life and to agriculture (a cultural transition that has elsewhere been viewed as being a prerequisite to the development of an archaic high civilization: literate and monumental, aristocratic and city-based) had already occurred in Ecuador by c. 3000 B.C., a date arguably earlier than any recorded elsewhere in the Americas. Lathrap's excavations both suggested and enlarged upon this demonstration: "One should consider," he declares, "even earliest Valdivia fully Formative."[100]

The origin of this agriculture is itself, of course, a question. Lathrap holds that both the agriculture and the life-style of the earliest Valdivians represented "an extension of Tropical Forest culture, which itself expanded out of the Amazon Basin, first to the Guayas Basin, and then on west to the coast. It was a Tropical Forest economy further enriched by the presence of developed races of corn."[101] Others counter, however, that "all evidence indicates settlement was earlier on the coast. Preceramic complexes—for example, the Vega—extend to 7000 B.C."[102]

If we accept Lathrap's reading of the evidence, it only presses back the origin of this agricultural development to the Amazonian Basin and the (undated) appearance there of what Stephen Jett suggested was a type of vegetative-reproduction-shifting cultivation possibly exported from insular Southeast Asia and applied in tropical South America to plants of the local forest: manioc, peanuts, and potatoes, in place of taro and yams.

The second stage of culture defined in Lathrap's reconstruction of the prehistory of coastal Ecuador was of a *pottery-fashioning population, during a period extending from c. 2450–1850 B.C.* (Valdivia 2 through 5, according to his reckoning), when large, elliptical houses appear (Figure 508), which by 2300 B.C. (Valdivia 3), at the coastal site of Real Alto, stood arranged along a central

509. Jar fragment with an incised and mottled design representing corn ears, c. 6⁵⁄₁₆" tall, from San Pablo, Valdivia phase 6, c. 1850–1700 B.C.

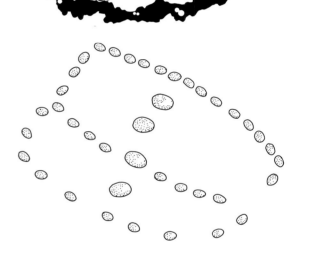

508. Hypothetical drawing (top) of a large early-Valdivian house, the frame of which was built of hardwood posts, up to c. 8" in diameter, deeply embedded in a trench serving as the foundation for an outer wall that encircled an oval area, 33'9" × 26'2½"; reconstruction based on one complete floor plan (middle), as well as traces of several others, from the site of Real Alto (bottom), a village, according to Donald W. Lathrap, of numerous similar dwellings "oriented around a central open plaza containing the remains of what appears to have been a somewhat larger structure."[64]

plaza by way of a well-planned village (length, north-south, about 330 yards; breadth about 220). Two matching mounds, projecting from the house rows, divided the plaza into north and south. Potsherds decorated with what could plausibly be corn-kernel impressions (Figure 509) suggest that maize may have been in cultivation at the time. Other sherds have been interpreted as being in imitation of bottle gourds.[103] The figurines—no longer of stone, but of clay—appear to be of a totally different tradition from the earlier, beehivehut period; they are exactly those which Estrada found associated with nearly 40,000 pottery sherds suggesting some connection with the Early Middle Jomon ware of contemporary Japan.

Another reading of the archaeological record in Ecuador at this time points to increasing evidence of an enduring, landward, Tropical Forest connection that suggests a remarkably full and convincing reconstruction by analogy of the social manners of the period.

At the Real Alto site, for example, the complete floor plan of one of the dwellings was uncovered. It had been a large building, with walls enclosing an oval area some forty feet long and thirty feet wide. Massive hardwood posts, eight inches in diameter, forming the frame of the structure, were deeply embedded in a trench that served as the foundation for the outer wall. "The size of the house," states Lathrap, "is not compatible with the interpretation that it sheltered a single nuclear family. Rather, the structure is comparable to the *malocas* of the Upper Amazon which house large groups, several families related through the male line. A population of thirty people for the house does not seem excessive."[104]

Lathrap estimates a community of fifty to one hundred of such longhouses, all oriented according to an overall plan that has its closest parallels (in his view) "in modern Indian communities occurring in a broad belt from the highlands of northeastern Brazil to the south and west on up to the eastern foothills of the Andes in Bolivia....It is legitimate," he concludes, "to look to the village plans of Ge and Bororo communities and the social order they exemplify for clues to the interpretation of Valdivia society."[105]

And not only the social order, the religious practices, too, can be postulated to have been of the Upper Amazonian Tropical Forest type; for instance, in the ritualized use of hallucinogenic drugs, and in the prominence of the role and figure of the shaman. As discussed by Lathrap:

"Tropical Forest cultures of South America are remarkable in that they use far more hallucinogenic drugs and integrate the use of such drugs into their religion in a more complex way than any other peoples on earth. More species of plants containing chemicals which can alter the physiological or psychological state of the human organism have been identified and used by Indian groups of the Amazon than by any other people. Both species of domesticated tobacco were clearly brought under cultivation in the Amazon drainage. Coca, the source of the modern drug cocaine, was domesticated on the eastern slope of the Andes. The tropical vine, *Banisteriopsis*, frequently referred to as *ayahuasca*, and the seeds of the mimosa-like tree, *Anadenanthera*, are two of the most powerful vision-producing agents known, resulting in particularly intense and complex colored hallucinations. These are only a few of the most widespread and powerful mind-expanding drugs in the arsenal of the Tropical Forest religious practitioners. The visions and experiences achieved through

the use of these drugs are of great religious importance, both in ceremonials binding the living group to the collective body of dead relatives, and in curing rituals. The most common religious practitioner in the Amazon Basin is the shaman, who gets his power through repeated sacramental use of *ayahuasca* and/or the snuff ground from seeds of the *Anadenanthera*. It is believed that while under the influence of these elements, the shaman is possessed by or turns into a ferocious animal, most typically a cayman [a kind of South American alligator] or a jaguar. While possessed by or transformed into his supernatural helper, or alter-ego, he is believed to be capable of traveling at incredible speed through both time and space and in this state can retrieve the soul of his patient or determine what other conditions must be met to insure the recovery of his patient.

"Over most of tropical South America east of the Andes the symbol of this kind of shaman is a wooden stool that is carved in the form of the ferocious creature who is the alter-ego of the individual shaman. Most typically the stool is in the form of a jaguar, although the cayman is also frequent and there are even examples implying a double load of power, with one end carved as a cayman and the other as a jaguar.

510. Two shaman's stools: top, a Valdivian ceramic miniature, c. 2⅜" long, featureless now, probably once represented a jaguar; below, from Cerrojupa, Manabi province, Ecuador, a full-sized stone seat with a jaguar in relief on the base.

511. A striking ceramic, c. 18¼" high, that is an outstanding representation of the anthropomorphic jaguar god, who, as has been demonstrated over and over again, is a dominant figure in the mythologies of most South American peoples; from coastal Ecuador, the La Tolita-Tuymaco culture, c. A.D. 1000.

"The uniformity of this complex of beliefs and practices throughout South America indicates that it is a very old system of thought and can be projected back to the earliest variants of the Tropical Forest culture. It is thus of tremendous interest that along with the solid human figurines of Valdivia, which may have served in curing rituals, we find exact miniature replicas of the zoomorphic wooden shaman's stools which are the prerogative of the Tropical Forest curer. One of the Valdivia examples is even clearly a jaguar, and is identical except in scale to a recently carved wooden stool from the upper Xingu Basin in Brazil...The presence of this kind of shaman's stool implies the use of either *ayahuasca* or the snuff from the *Anadenanthera* tree."[106]

"The Buena Vista series," he reported, "associated with a pottery-making culture, represents a very homogeneous brachycranic [broad-headed] type that probably corresponds to a family group…The Buena Vista physical type is totally different from the earlier preceramic Peruvian coastal population of Cabezas Largas, leading to the inference that the introduction of pottery also brought a new physical type. This new group may be to a large degree the source of the brachycrany observed in populations associated with the later pottery-making periods of the Peruvian coast."[109]

Another body of evidence to be taken into account is of the shell fishhooks found among Valdivia remains already from the earliest period (see Figure 513). As noticed by Meggers, Evans, and Estrada, "All are of pearl oyster (*Pinctada mazatlanica*) and similar in general size, proportions, and construction."[110] And as Lathrap has observed of the same: "It has been noted

512. An anthropomorphic grotesque jaguar head with deeply hooded eyes, a wry smile, prominent incisors, and a distinctive, cowl-like headdress; made of brownware pottery, c. 5¼" high × 7" wide, this suggestive specimen was recovered from an area located in the state of Manabi (Ecuador) near the confluence of the Peripa and Daule rivers; it is of the Jama-Coaque Culture.

All of this we recognize from what we have already learned of the Amazonian tribes. It is necessary to note, however, that the cultures of those tribes are not generally classified by anthropologists as being representative of the Formative stage of civilization. Furthermore, other scholars have difficulty accepting the certainty with which Lathrap pursues his Tropical Forest connection; they argue that equally plausible antecedent cultures can be found elsewhere.

During the period of occupation of the excavated longhouse at the coastal site of Real Alto, there gradually built up on the dirt floor some eight inches of trash and, as Lathrap reports: "This cultural deposit contains the remains of hundreds of pots and dozens of figurines made, used, and discarded by the inhabitants."[107]

Ceramic figurines are not characteristic features of Tropical Forest religious usage, but belong, on the contrary, to the complex represented in the ceramic wares of Jomon affiliation discovered by Estrada. If their association here is also with the Tropical Forest folkways, as Lathrap suggested, then early Ecuador may have been an arena for just such a coming together of two distinct traditions as can usually be found wherever significant formative cultural transformations have come to pass. As Heine-Geldern points out in his article on the origin of ancient civilizations: "How-

ever original and unique each of the ancient civilizations may appear to be, not one of them came into being independently. Fecundation by another civilization was always necessary.… Even the oldest of the higher civilizations, that of Babylonia, ancestor of all others, did not come into being through 'mutation'…but emerged as the result of mutual contacts of a whole series of cultures which had preceded it."[108]

From the now numerous sites of coastal and inland Ecuador, the reported evidence suggests very strongly a conjunction of two distinct traditions, one of the land, the other of the sea. The Guayas area is especially well suited for meetings of this kind, with its riverways affording passage to the trans-Andean interior and the trans-Pacific *Kuroshio*, "Black Current" (see Map 41), coming to land precisely at the well-named promontory of Punta Concepción. Its geographical location, then, is surely a major reason why coastal Ecuador might well have been a, if not the, Formative matrix of the New World civilizations; and why, during its initial centuries (from c. 3000 B.C. or earlier, to c. 1000 B.C.), with new influences arriving not once simply, but repeatedly, from Asia, it appears to have stood far in advance of any of its neighbors.

This judgment is reinforced by the skeletal remains unearthed by Meggers, Evans, and Estrada at their coastal Valdivia sites. Juan R. Munizaga, of the Universidad de Chile, Santiago, to whom these remains were entrusted for analysis, arrived at the conclusion that the Valdivia skulls taken from the site of Buena Vista were of a totally different physical type from skulls one thousand years older, unearthed at the *preceramic* Cabezas Largas site on the south coast of Peru.

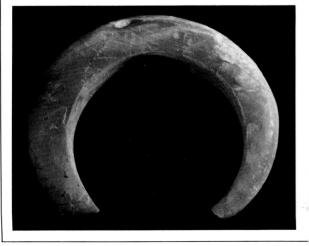

frequently that the hook of mother-of-pearl shell which functions both to engage the fish's mouth and to serve as lure, is remarkably similar over the whole Pacific. In the New World," he continues, "such hooks of an early date are known from the preceramic occupation of the north coast of Chile [about where, by the way, the Japanese drift expedition of 1980 came to land]. The fishing equipment of the late prehistoric and historic Chumash Indians of Southern California is also remarkably similar. Comparable hooks were also in use on most of the Polynesian and Micronesian islands."[111] Such a distribution of evidence through immense reaches of both time and space speaks certainly of a long continued oceanic (Old Pacific) order of life in which a good part of the American Pacific Coast participated. And that this oceanic culture made its contribution to the Formative transformations of the Punta Concepción domain is surely evident as well. A little

ceramic bowl in the form of a dugout canoe (Figure 514), which Lathrap assigns to Valdivia 4, c. 2150–2000 B.C.,[112] and which might have represented either a vessel for coastal fishing or one for travel on the riverways that penetrate the Andes and lead to the Amazon, may be taken as a reminder, at this point, of the adaptability of artifacts to new purposes.

514. Restored ceramic bowl fragment with red slip, suggestive of a dugout canoe, c. 2" high, Valdivia phase 4, c. 2250–2000 B.C.

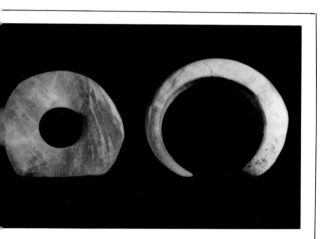

513. The sequence above depicts shell fishhooks in several stages of fabrication; beginning as a circular shell fragment, the hook is formed using stone reamers to make a central perforation that is gradually enlarged and shaped — a method of manufacture that is remarkably similar throughout the entire Pacific. That the early Ecuadorians were involved with marine fishing is evidenced by the recovery from Valdivia Phase excavations of seventeen such fishhooks or fishhook fragments (two exemplary, intact specimens are pictured below). These deeply recurved fishhooks — fabricated from the disklike, glistening shells of the pearl oyster (left, *Pinctada mazatlanica*), which is found in coastal waters from the Gulf of California to Peru — served a dual function, being both tantalizing lures that attracted fish and effective tools for ensnaring them.

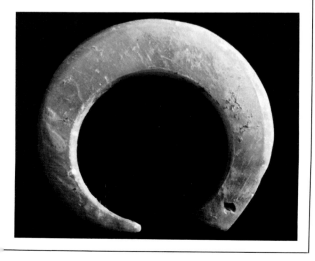

Generally sociologists recognize that, complementary to the influences (no matter how strong) of what is known as *diffusion*, are the responses of *acculturation*, the processes of change that occur in any native culture following an alien infusion. These changes are of two orders: (1) "directed change," where the influence is of one people establishing, with its institutions, dominance over another through military conquest or political control, as, for example, in the instance of the Christian conquest of America and, centuries earlier, of Europe; and (2) "voluntary incorporation," where, through cultural interchange, borrowings occur without the exercise of military or political domination, as, for example, in the receptions by China and Japan of the Buddhism of India. In developments of this second kind the diffused complex or idea serves largely as a catalyst, releasing reactions which finally are of the society affected. And indeed, even in cases of a massively "directed change," the native character is what is definitive, finally, of the consequence. The Christianity of the Indians of Peru or Brazil today, for example, is hardly that of Ignatius Loyola in sixteenth-century Spain or of Oliver Cromwell in seventeenth-century England; not to mention Saint Paul. Indeed, even in Matthew, Mark, Luke, and John, there are differences enough to give one thought.

The term *diffusion*, that is to say, is misconstrued when taken to imply the annulment, rather than activation, of native creativity. As one distracted theoretician has complained: "If all the world can be linked in a single one-way claim of diffusion, comparison is unnecessary. Why compare the rise of civilization in Mesopotamia, China, Mexico, and Peru if China

received all its significant ideas from Mesopotamia, Mexico from China, and Peru from Mexico (or Peru from Ecuador from Japan)?"[113] To which the elementary answer is, of course, that the virtue of a scientist lies, in contrast to that of a theologian, in recognizing a fact, not in defending an idea. Moreover, no one has ever claimed that *all* of the significant ideas of China and Japan, Mexico and Peru, must have come from the Near East; or even that all those ideas which clearly *are* from that earliest source of what is known as "archaic high civilization" (literate and monumental, aristocratic and city-based) remained in sense and form unchanged in Egypt, India, China, Japan, Mexico, and Peru. There is such a thing, moreover, as "stimulus diffusion," where a dispersed idea becomes variously embodied, as in the instance recognized by Stephen Jett, of the idea of vegetative-reproduction-shifting cultivation carried from tropical Southeast Asia to tropical America, to be applied there to plants of the local scene.

For a date some time within the period of Valdivia 6 (c. 1850–1700 B.C.), the "impressions of two textiles of different weave," states Lathrap, "have been noted on a lump of partially fired clay from Real Alto.... It is conceivable," he adds, "that a plant other than the New World cultivated cotton was the source of the fiber that went into the yarn of the textile, but the very fine and even character of this yarn makes such an alternative unlikely...given the firmness of the yarn and the high warp count per centimeter, it is most likely that a heddle loom was used."[114]

Now, as reported by S. G. Stephens, "Of more than twenty species of *Gossipium* that have been recognized, only four include cultivated forms....Two of the species, *G. arboreum* L. and *G. herbaceum* L., have thirteen pairs of chromosomes and are confined to the Old World continents and neighboring islands. So far there is no convincing evidence that these species, or any nearly related wild species, have existed in the New World except in recent experimental culture....The other two species, *G. hirsutum* L. and *G. barbadense* L., have twenty-six pairs of chromosomes. They are commonly known as the New World cottons, because their centers of variability and archaeological prehistory lie in Mesoamerica and northern South America, respectively. Cultivated forms of both [American] species, however, are widely distributed in the subtropics of both Eastern and Western hemispheres and in Polynesia....There are two puzzling cases of cotton distribution that might be related to early transoceanic contacts, though alternative interpretations cannot be excluded. They are of particular interest because one case (cotton in the Cape Verde Islands) requires some form of transatlantic distribution; the other (cotton in the Marquesas Islands) may involve a transpacific contact."[115]

How these contacts might have been effected, Stephens does not pretend to know, though he does have a couple of quaint suggestions. One is of "transport by birds";[116] so that those who tremble to think of pre-Columbian passages by human navigation may now entertain the more likely idea of some bird of powerful wing consuming a cargo of durable seeds and then taking off in all haste, with neck outstretched, to attain some unseen distant land before nature would have worked the cycle of its usual course and discharged the burden into the ocean. The other suggestion was of European seamen of the sixteenth century or later throwing overboard their old worn-out mattresses, which, being stuffed with seed-bearing New World cotton, might then have floated to hospitable shores.[117]

The valuable observation here is of a New World cultigen distributed to coastal Africa and to Polynesia. The datings seem not to be known, but there is the obvious implication of pre-Columbian two-way voyaging, at least across the Pacific, where the evidence is in accord with that of Heyerdahl's drift-voyage from the Peruvian coast to the Tuamotus on the raft *Kon-Tiki*.

Cultivated cotton is one thing, however; a cotton fabric finely woven is another. Fragments of a cotton textile, dyed red and sticking to the side of a silver vase, were recovered from excavations at Mohenjo-daro in Sind: of the period, that is to say, of India's pre-Vedic, Indus Valley Civilization, c. 2300–1750 B.C. The yarn was of *Gossypium arboreum*. Textiles in Egypt, finely woven of flax, and in Mesopotamia, of wool, are of dates a millennium earlier. But the earliest known cotton has been, up to now, from Mohenjo-daro. Remarkably, half the world away, the Valdivia date, c. 1850–1700 B.C., is a close match.

Striking changes in the forms and ornamentation of Valdivian ceramic wares, from c. 2000 B.C., occurred at about the same time as, but seemingly were not influenced by, a substantial influx of potteries from a newly arrived ceramic tradition which was named by Meggers, Evans, and Estrada—after a type site north of Valdivia village—the Machalilla Phase. "The area occupied by these sites extends along the coast," they reported, "from South Manabi Province into northern Guayas Province."[118] And among the human skeletal remains associated with these sites there appeared a feature formerly unknown to the American Pacific Coast, namely, *artificial deformation of the human skull* (see II.2:**312**). Again quoting Munizaga, who analyzed these remains:

"Cranial deformation appears for the first time on the Pacific coast of South America in Ecuador at about 4000 years ago, as part of the Machalilla Phase. The type of deformation is fronto-vertico-occipital or tabular erecta, of the variety known as 'cuneiform' or 'Chavín.'

515. Machalilla solid ceramic figurines from the Barcelona site, c. 1500–1000 B.C.; both feature red-on-tan painting, coffee-bean eyes, and salient noses: left figure, c. 5″ tall; right fragment, c. 4¼″ high.

516. Two Chacras-style (Terminal Valdivia) ceramics: left, red-slip figurine of seated woman, c. 5½″ tall, from Valdivia Heights; right, fragment, 2½″ high, from Miguelillo, Manabi.

"Tabular erecta deformation appears along most of coastal Peru in the late Preceramic, at a date subsequent to its occurrence in Ecuador, permitting the inference that it was diffused from north to south.

"The North-South diffusion current is most clearly demonstrated by the Formative Period complexes (Machalilla, Cupisnique, Early Ancon-Supe, Paracas Cavernas), in which identity in the variety of deformation implies diffusion of the same deforming apparatus, a rather complicated system that seems to be correlated with this time period and zone."[119]

"The different shapes that a normal skull can acquire by deformation have been classified into types and varieties according to the manner in which pressures were applied. This permits us to infer from the characteristics of a skull the kind of apparatus by which it was molded. The tabular erecta deformation shown by the Machalilla Phase skulls is the result of strong compression of the back of the head against a hard surface, to which it is fastened by appropriate binding. The 'cuneiform' variety of this type indicated that the head was held so that the face invariably looked forward; the pronounced occipital flattening shows that the bindings were tightly applied; the concavity of the occipital permits the inference that a pillow-like object was placed between the skull and the board."[120]

By 1700 B.C. (Valdivia 7, according to Lathrap's reckoning) the village at Real Alto had become, as he described it, "an administrative and religious center controlling several farmsteads scattered along the Rio Verde and other lesser rivers such as El Rio Real, thus managing some six hundred acres of riverine agricultural bottom lands. This system of a control center with satellite settlements," he adds, "implies a stratified society."[121]

517. This hollow figurine of a naked man, c. 11½″ tall, is noteworthy for its face and body painting (including incised designs that have been filled with white pigment), its distinctive hair (or headdress) treatment, and its prominent circular ear-spools, an ornamentation most often associated with Indians living in the Amazon Basin and eastern Brazil; Chorrera, c. 1000–200 B.C., from Cerro Verde, state of Manabi, Ecuador.

It appears thus probable, from the look of things, that a governing priestly caste (or perhaps race) was now in charge, such as in the classic periods of both the South and Middle American hieratic civilizations of the first millennium A.D. maintained in great ceremonial centers a formal ceremonial order of social festivals and observances, while a rural agricultural population, residing in villages round about, provided both the economic support and the required manual labor for the maintenance of a manner of life established equally in the energies of nature and the forms of a society oriented to cosmological coordinations. Two completely different types of figurine now appear: one quite crude and markedly stylized (Figure 515), with coffee-bean eyes and a salient nose; the other, of hollow forms (Figure 516)— as were the later, so-called Chorrera figurines of c. 1000–300 B.C. (named for an inland site in the Guayas Basin)— represents what Lathrap declares to be "the artistic climax of the Ecuadorian Formative."[122]

Across the Pacific the civilization of China had by now attained maturity. The dates of the Shang dynasty are from c. 1523–1027 B.C. Lathrap dates the Machalilla phase in Ecuador from c. 1500–1000 B.C. and the culminating Chorrera phase from c. 1000–300 B.C., which is the period in China of the Chou dynasty (c. 1057–250 B.C.). Among the hollow ceramic Chorrera figures Lathrap remarks a beautifully rendered dog forming the body of a whistling bottle (Figure 519). "This particular dog representation," he declares, "…is the ancestor of the whole range of delightful dog effigies from the state of Colima in western Mexico. Similar figures of dogs are particularly common in the late prehistoric Chimu empire on the North Coast of Peru where they are executed in a burnished black ware. All of these dog representations seem to form a single artistic tradition of which this Chorrera vessel is the oldest known example. It also appears to depict the particular breed of dog so faithfully portrayed by Colima and Chimu potters. This is the breed usually referred to as the Mexican hairless.

"The Mexican hairless was bred as a source of meat, its low massive body having the same relationship to the contours of a normal dog as our own Angus steer has to the basic configuration of wild cattle. The presence of this highly specialized breed of dog in Chorrera before 500 B.C. suggests a long prior history of attention to the food potential of this oldest of domesticated animals and argues that the breed first appeared in Ecuador and from there spread to Northern Peru and West Mexico. A dog is known from China where it was bred for eating before 2000 B.C. Some people have suggested that the presence of this particular breed in the New World is the result of contact eastward across the Pacific

518. Late Preclassic ceramic representations of Colima dogs that were interred with the dead for food and for companionship.

around 1000 B.C. Such transpacific diffusion might account not only for the dog but also for the peculiar ceramic pillows to be discussed later, and for certain kinds of human figurines and house effigies that are peculiarly East Asian in appearance."[123]

It might account also, one might add, for a number of other novelties that appeared in the New World at just this time. For the date, c. 1000 B.C., is of the greatest moment as marking the almost simultaneous appearances in Middle and South America of *two monumental cultures,* one, the Olmec, in Mexico, on the torrid Gulf coast of Tabasco and Veracruz; the other, the Chavín, in the northern highlands and neighboring Pacific coast of Peru. The manifestation in Mexico was suddenly of a sculptural art, already of the highest standard, rendering colossi in basalt and miniatures in jade, associated (at La Venta) with a ceremonial compound containing a fluted pyramid. That in Peru was of a massive temple complex built of dressed rectangular stone blocks, honeycombed with galleries at different levels, ventilated by shafts and decorated with mythological figures carved in low relief on its stone pillars and lintels. Prominent in both art contexts is the figure of a jaguar-mask or -man, suggesting shamanic associations, but also, as Garry J. Tee has shown,[124] there is evidence

519. Chorrera whistling bottle in the form of a dog, c. 10¾" high, Manabi, Ecuador. "Similar figures of dogs," notes Donald W. Lathrap, "are particularly common in the late prehistoric Chimu empire on the North Coast of Peru where they are executed in a burnished black ware. All of these dog representations seem to form a single artistic tradition of which this Chorrera vessel is the oldest known example....This is the breed usually referred to as the Mexican hairless."[65]

in the aesthetic handling of these forms of an influence from China.

Schematically, the dating of these two new cultures may be registered as from c. 1000 B.C. to c. 200 B.C., with the Olmec as perhaps the earlier. They are regarded as representing the initial phases of the monumental high civilizations of Mexico and Peru. In Ecuador the contemporary development, c. 1000–400 B.C., was of the Chorrera phase already mentioned, where, in addition to the superb unfoldment in ceramic wares, a number of signs appear of a cluster of ideas that can only have arrived from elsewhere: not only dogs bred for eating, ceramic pillows, and house effigies, but also, roller stamps of a kind long known in southeast Asia, large ear spools, and the flute.

The cultural lead at this time passes from Ecuador to Mexico and Peru, in both of which later centers the timeless, village-based, Neolithic order of life is irrevocably surpassed—through a time-factored acceleration of developments which, like an organic process working through its inevitable course, is to unfold, mature, and come to its period of full ripening, when, like a thunderbolt, the fire of the Spanish Inquisition arrives and by a handful of incredibly courageous, gold-maddened thugs, two civilizations are laid waste.

The Civilization and Despoliation of Peru

Reconstruction of the mythologies of the Pre-Incan peoples of present-day Peru is rendered difficult, first, by the fact that there are no written documents, either from their time, or from the period of the Incas; second, by the fact that the Incas, though their reign was short (hardly 150 years, c. A.D. 1380–1532), imposed their own mythology on the whole area, either eliminating or assimilating local cults and traditions; and finally by the fact that what late reports we do possess are from the pens of Spanish chroniclers, who were neither well informed nor particularly interested — with, however, two exceptions:

Garcilasso Inca de la Vega was the son of a young Spanish nobleman who had served under Alvarado as a captain of infantry and in 1538, in Peru, six years after the conquest, married a baptized granddaughter of Tupac Yupanqui, the eleventh Inca (fl. c. 1439). Garcilasso was born in 1540, in Cuzco, of which city his father was then governor. His mother died when he was twelve; his father, when he was twenty. Sailing to Spain, he served in the army, from which he retired when thirty or thirty-five, to settle in Cordova and devote himself there to writing, until his death, 1616, the year of the deaths, also, of Shakespeare and Cervantes. Garcilasso's principal opus, *The Royal Commentaries of the Incas*, reviews in Part 1 the history of Peru before the Conquest, and, in Part 2, the history of the Conquest and of the wars, thereafter, among the Conquistadores themselves for monopoly of the spoils.[125]

The second valuable chronicler, Pedro de Cieza de León, who was born in Seville about 1519, came to the New World at the age of thirteen and remained until 1550, during which season of seventeen years, while serving in various armies, he began in 1541 to keep diligently a journal, with intention of publication in four parts.[126]

"The attempt savors of temerity in so unlearned a man," he wrote, "but others of more learning are too much occupied in the wars to write. Oftentimes when the other soldiers were reposing, I was tiring myself by writing. Neither fatigue nor the ruggedness of the country, nor the mountains and rivers, nor intolerable hunger and suffering have ever been sufficient to obstruct my two duties, namely, writing and following my flag and my captain without fault....Much that I have written I saw with my own eyes, and I traveled over many countries in order to learn more concerning them. Of those things which I did not see, I took great pains to inform myself, from persons of good repute, both Christians and Indians."[127]

Of the people of those times before the founding of the Empire, however, not even this good man could learn. "From what I gathered from the accounts of the Indians around Cuzco," he recorded, "it would seem that in olden times there was great disorder in this kingdom we call Peru, and that the natives were stupid and brutish beyond belief. They say they were like animals, and that many ate human flesh, and others took their daughters and mothers to wife, and committed even greater sins, and had great traffic with the devil, whom they served and held in great esteem. Aside from this they had strongholds and fortresses in the mountains and hills, and on the least pretext, they sallied forth from them to make war on one another, and killed and took prisoner as many as they could. In spite of the fact that they were given over to these sins and worked these evils, they also say that some of them were religiously inclined, and for that reason in many parts of this kingdom they built great temples, where they prayed, performing their rites and superstitions before big idols, and the devil appeared to them and was worshipped. And while the people of this kingdom were living in this way, great tyrants arose in the provinces of Colla and in the valleys of the Yungas and elsewhere, who carried on war against one another, and committed many killings and thefts, and they all suffered great calamities. Many fortresses and castles were destroyed, but the struggle between them went on, at which the devil, the enemy of mankind, rejoiced to see so many souls lost."[128]

Cieza's own Roman Catholic mythology shows through here. For him, the devil was an actual personage who wandered through the world for the ruin of souls, as God too was a living, albeit invisible, personage. Invisible both, they are the ultimate antagonists in the great theater of world history, in competition for the capture of souls with which to populate their kingdoms: the one, of dark and total torment; the other, radiant of God's presence. Many peoples have ideas about God, but only Roman Catholics have true knowledge, namely, of God as three divine Persons: Father, Son, and Holy Spirit.

The first, the Father, created not only heaven and earth, but also hell, to receive that once luminous prince of the host of his angels, Lucifer, who in pride had set his own will above that of his Creator and so incurred the terrible wrath of God, who flung at him that awful sentence of rejection [undoubtedly in Latin]: "Depart from me, thou cursed, into everlasting fire!" And together with him went those of the heavenly host who had joined him in rebellion.

But God the Father created, also, Adam and Eve, male and female, in his own image, to live in timeless happiness in a timeless Earthly Paradise, out of which four rivers ran in the four directions. And Lucifer, now Satan, to avenge himself on his Creator's indignation, took the form of a serpent—wisest and therefore least trustworthy of God's creatures—wherewith to seduce the "weaker vessel," Eve (who had been fashioned from one of her husband's ribs), into tasting the fruit of a certain tree of the knowledge of good and evil, which by God's command, was the one tree in the garden the fruit of which had been expressly forbidden to the couple. Whereupon, having eaten, their eyes were opened to the knowledge, not only of good and evil, but also of male and female, and with leaves they clothed their nakedness. So that when the Father, whose pleasure it was to walk in the garden in the cool of the day, discovered them thus attired, he realized what they had done. And [as we read in the Book] lest they should eat of the fruit of a second tree, which also grew in that garden, the Tree of Eternal Life [compare the Bo-Tree of the Buddha; folklore motif: World Tree *axis mundi*, Tree of Life] and so become immortal and omniscient as himself, he withdrew from their sight and expelled them from the garden, setting to guard its gate two angels with a flaming sword between, to block the way to the Tree of Life.

Thus Satan, the devil, had mankind in his keep, and the Father, offended in wrath withdrawn, had abandoned the whole of creation to the malice and deceptions of that Antagonist and his ubiquitous host. It was he and his imps who inhabited all the idols of heathenness; he and they who appeared to shamanic seers in visions; and again, he and they, who, having thus deluded the progeny of fallen Adam and Eve, were harvesting souls unnumbered to the torments of their hell-pit of dark fire.

In heaven, however, a program of redemption had been conceived—at once to recover mankind from the devil's keep, and to atone mankind with the inaccessible Father—and the Son, Second Person of the Trinity, became the agent of this feat of rescue. Begotten of the Holy Spirit, Third Person of the Trinity, in the blessed womb of an immaculate daughter of the chosen race of Israel [a holy, priestly race, which had

520. Pope Alexander VI, Rodrigo Borgia, father of a dozen or more illegitimate offspring—some in Spain, others in Italy—of whom Juan, Cesare, Jofre, and Lucrezia Borgia are the best known. *Inter Cetera*, his 1493 Bull (see pp. 308–309), divided New World lands between Portugal and Spain (the last remaining great Catholic powers of Europe).

been set apart by God to become the vessel of the Incarnation; but which, alas!, on accomplishment of the Event, had shut its eyes and ears to the Word become Flesh, and so, having become accursed to God, was now, in this sixteenth century of the Years of Our Lord, to be scoured out of Catholic Spain, together with the devil's heretic brood of Mohamet], the Son had become Man, and, as at once True God and True Man, had been crucified, taken down from the Cross, and buried: by which Sacrifice the Father had been atoned in his wrath and mankind redeemed from the devil's keep. Not all of mankind was redeemed, however [and here, of course, was the crucial historical point], only those baptized into the One True Church, which the Son had founded in his lifetime and committed to the infallible charge of his disciples under Peter: wherein, by virtue of the sacraments, participation in the reconciliation of mankind with the Father was attained, and salvation thereby from the devil. *Extra ecclesia nulla salus.* Only under the sign of the Cross are the devices of the devil and his host undone.

Therefore, for the healing of mankind, frustration of the devil, and accomplishment of God's purpose in the world, the work of history was to enlarge the bourn of Peter's Church, which task, since the devil's recent calamitous triumphs in accomplishing the heresies of Luther and Henry VIII, had fallen upon the only two remaining great Catholic powers in God's Europe, namely Portugal and Spain. The Bull of Pope Alexander VI, Rodrigo Borgia (see Figure 520) had conferred God's charge upon these most Catholic nations, that (as therein written) "the health of souls should be procured and the barbarous nations subdued and brought to the faith."[129]

It is little likely that a sincere participant in such a world-restructuring enterprise should be able to understand anything of mythologies not his own. Moreover, in the matter of mythologies earlier than the Inca, Cieza's informants (as may be judged from the passage above quoted, page 368) were quite as ignorant as himself. An idea can be gained of the sense the Incas entertained of the superiority of themselves and their civilization to the tribal cultures, not only in former times, but also still around them, from an account recorded by Cieza of the subjugation of an aboriginal Colombian tribe by the Lord-Inca Huayna Capac (fl. c. A.D. 1475).

Having subdued in Ecuador "certain nations [to use Cieza's words] who had never wished to accept his friendship," he proceeded northward and "went exploring as far as the Angasmayo River, which was the boundary of his empire. And he learned from the natives that farther on there were many peoples, and that they all went naked without the least shame, and that all, all of them, ate human flesh, and he built several strongholds in the region of the Pastos. [See Map 39.] He sent word to their headmen that they were to pay him tribute, and they replied that they had

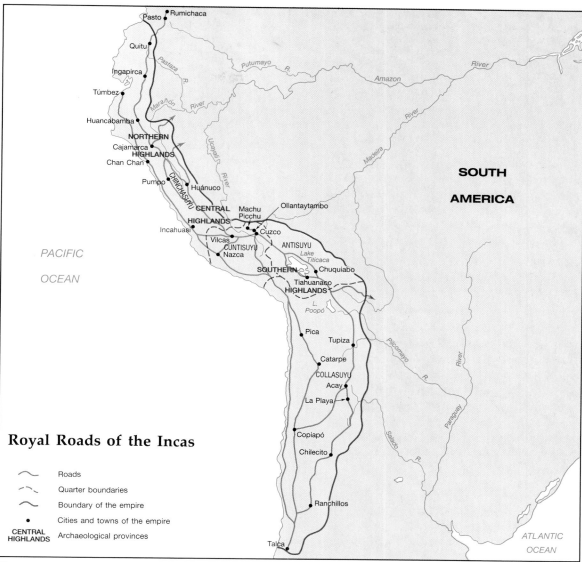

Royal Roads of the Incas

- ∿ Roads
- ∿ Quarter boundaries
- ∿ Boundary of the empire
- • Cities and towns of the empire
- CENTRAL HIGHLANDS — Archaeological provinces

Map 42.

nothing to give him. Whereupon, to bring them to reason, he ordered that every house in the land, every so many moons, must give him in tribute a large quill of lice. At first they laughed at his order; but afterwards, however lousy they were, they found they could not fill so many quills. So they tended the flocks the Inca had ordered left with them, and paid with those that were born of the foods and tubers grown in their lands."[130]

*   *   *

It was not until about 1940 that the archaeological investigation of Pre-Inca Peru began to be seriously pursued by university-supported expeditions, and although much remains to be learned, the chronology that has already emerged of earlier kingdoms and empires belies the reports that were given to Cieza of barbarism and chaos. The period under investigation is roughly dated from c. 1000 B.C. to A.D. 1380, when the Lord-Inca Viracocha consolidated the empire, and the geographical view extends from the Angasmayo River in Colombia, where the Inca Huayna-Capac discovered the above-noticed louse-bearing tribe, to Talca (below Santiago, Chile) in the south. The Royal Road to the Incas covered the greater part of this distance in two branches: one, the Highland Road, from Quito (Ecuador), through Cuzco (seat of the Inca Empire), to Talca, a distance of

3250 miles;[131] the other, the Coastal Road, from the Port of Tumbes (in northern Peru) again to Talca, 2250 miles.

At the time of the Spanish Conquest, the three outstanding peoples of the South American west coast were the Chebcha in Colombia, the Inca in Peru, and in Chile the Araucanians, nomadic, fiercely fighting hunting-and-gathering tribes who remained unsubdued by the Incas, or even by the Spaniards, until defeated in the Araucanian War (1880–82), after which they were settled on reservations.

At the first coming of the Spaniards, Araucanian-speaking peoples occupied the area west of the Andean highlands from the Rio Choapa, south, to the southern tip of the island of Chiloé (see Map 39). About the beginning of the eighteenth century, they began to spill over into Argentina, along the Andean foothills and into the western Pampa. As recognized today they are in five divisions: (1) the Picunche (*picun* "north," *che* "people"), (2) the Mapuche (*mapu* "land"), and (3) the Huilliche (*huilli* "south"), (4) the Pehuenche (*pehuen* "pine") in the Andean highlands; and finally, east of the Andes, (5) the Argentine Araucanians, who have been called by a number of names: Araucanos de Pampas, Patagon, Pampa, Mapuche, Puelche (*puel* "east"), Ranguelche (*rangh* "reed"), Hombres del Manzanar (*manzano* "apple tree"), Moluche, Pinunche, Huilliche, and Piche ("small") Huilliche.[132]

Archaeologically the Incan Highlands are now reckoned to consist of three geographical divisions: (1) the Northern Highlands, from the southern border of Ecuador to Huanuco, the most important site of this region being at Chavín de Huántar; (2) the Central Highlands, from Huánuco to Cuzco, seat of the Inca Empire; and (3) the Southern Highlands, from Cuzco into Bolivia along an extensive high plateau (the *altiplano*), which includes the vast Lake Titicaca, out of which, according to Inca legend, the first light came, when the sun rose from its waters. In the southern part of that lake are a number of isles, of which the largest was regarded by the Inca (according to Garcilasso) as their place of origin. For it was there, according to this legend, that Manco Capac, the first Inca, received from the Sun-God his cultural commission. On that island therefore, in memory of that moment, a great temple was constructed, the ruins of which are said to be in the Late Inca style (A.D. 1400–1500) and still in a fair state of preservation.[133] Cieza wrote:

The name of this great lake of the Colla [the Southern Highland] is Titicaca, from the temple that was built in the center of the lake. About this the natives had an idea that was pure superstition, and this is that they say their forebears asserted for a fact, like the other nonsense they tell, that for many days they were without light, and when they were all in darkness and gloom, there arose from this island of Titicaca the sun in all its splendor, for which reason they hold the island to be a hallowed spot, and the Incas built there a temple…which was one of the most venerated, in honor of their sun, bringing to it vestals and priests and great treasure. Although the Spaniards on different occasions have removed much of this, it is believed that most of it has not been discovered. And if these Indians were without light, as they say, it might have been caused by an eclipse of the sun.[134]

The vestals here mentioned, who were known as Chosen Women, or *mamaconas*, Virgins of the Sun, had been selected from the age of about ten for the promise of their beauty and intelligence. As described by G. H. S. Bushnell in his classic introduction to the cultures of pre-Pizarro Peru:

521. Portrait of Manco Capac, the first Inca, who received his commission from Inti, the Sun God.

522. Peruvians panicking during a solar eclipse, in Picart's *The Religious Ceremonies and Customs of the Several Nations of the Known World* (1731–37).

"An Inca official visited the villages at regular intervals to inspect any girls who had reached the age of about ten. He divided them into two classes; those of special beauty or promise were sent away to be educated in special institutions by the State, or reserved for sacrifice on special occasions or in emergencies, such as the accession or serious illness of an Emperor, and the remainder were left behind, to be married in due course to the boys of the village by the curaca [local supervisor], who picked their mates for them. Those who were taken away were placed in convents called Accla Huasi, the Houses of the Chosen Women in the provincial capitals or in Cuzco, and here they learnt such things as spinning, weaving, and cooking. Those destined for sacrifice were regarded as fortunate, since they were assured of a life of ease and comfort in the world to come. The others were divided into those who would be given as wives to nobles or successful warriors by grace of the Emperor, and the Mamaconas, some of whom would be secondary wives or servants to the Emperor, and some dedicated in perpetual chastity to the service of temples and shrines. Those who served the Emperor included specially skilled weavers, who made fine clothing for him. It is difficult to exaggerate the importance of cloth in the Inca polity, and examples like the textiles found in Paracas mummies [527–528] suggest strongly that this was nothing new, in fact the general excellence of Peruvian weaving would make it surprising if it were otherwise. In Inca times the weavers had to make cloth for the ruler and the goods from materials provided by the State, and in return the State gave them the materials from which to weave their own clothes. The finest fabrics were reserved for the ruler, and gifts of them from him were highly appreciated. Cloth was used in all sorts of gift exchanges, in the crises of life and for sacrifice. It was second only to food in the army's rations, and enormous quantities were found by the Spaniards in the storehouses, in addition to those which were burnt to keep them out of their hands."[135]

At Tomebamba, in the Northern Highlands, there was a temple of the Sun, the splendor of which so impressed Cieza, as he passed through, along the Highland Road, that he paused to write of it at length.

The lodgings of Tomebamba are situated at the joining of two small rivers in a plain having a circumference of over twelve leagues. It is a chilly land, abounding in game such as deer, rabbits, and partridges, turtle doves, and other birds. The temple of the sun was of stones put together with the subtlest skill, some of them large, black, and rough, and others that seemed of jasper. Some of the Indians claimed that most of the stones used in the construction of these lodgings and the temple of the sun had been brought all the way from the city of Cuzco by order of the Lord-Inca Huayna Capac and his father, the great Topa Inca, pulled with great cables. If this is true, it is a remarkable thing, considering the size and number of the stones, and the distance. The fronts of many of the buildings are beautiful and highly decorative, some of them set with precious stones and emeralds, and, inside, the walls of the temple of the sun and the palaces of the Lord-Incas were covered with sheets of the finest gold and incrusted with many statues, all of this metal. The roof of these buildings was of thatch, so well laid that barring a fire, it would last for ages. Inside the dwelling there were sheafs of golden straw, and on the walls carved figures of the same rich metal, and birds, and many other things. In addition to this, it was said that there was a great sum of treasure in jugs and pots and other receptacles, and many rich blankets covered with silver and beadwork. Whatever I say I cannot give an idea of the wealth the Incas possessed in these royal palaces, in which they took great pride, where many silversmiths were kept busy making the things I have described and many others. The woolen clothing in the storehouses was so numerous and so fine that if it had been kept and not lost, it would be worth a fortune. The virgins dedicated to the service of the temple were numbered more than two hundred, and were very beautiful, chosen from among the Cañari [the people of this province] and the region of the district governed by the high steward of the Incas, who lived in these dwellings. They and the priests were well supplied by those in charge of the maintenance of the temple, at whose gate there were gate keepers (some of whom were said to be eunuchs), whose duty it was to watch over the *manaconas,* as the virgins living in the temple were called. Besides the temple and the palaces of the Lord-Incas there were a great number of dwellings where the soldiers were garrisoned, and still greater storehouses filled with the provisions I have described, howevermuch was used. For the stewards kept careful account after their fashion of all that entered and all that was given out, and the will of the Lord-Inca was observed in all things. The natives of this province, known as the Cañari, are well built and of goodly countenance. They wear their hair very long and coil it around their head, so by it and the round crown of wood, as fine as sieve wire, they can be recognized as Cañari wherever they go, and this is their identification.[136]

From Tomebamba there was a turn, a spur, from the Royal Highway west to the port of Guayaquil, on the coast of Ecuador, in the Guayas province of Estrada's Valdivia finds from c. 3000 B.C. And again, a little south of Tomebamba, there was another turn, southwestward, to Tumbes, at the head of the Coastal Road.

This valley of Tumbes was once thickly settled and cultivated, covered with fine, cool irrigation canals, channeled from the river, with which they watered their crops abundantly and harvested much corn and the other things needed for human consumption, and many delicious fruits. The ancient rulers, before they were subdued by the Incas, were more feared and obeyed by their subjects than any of those described, as they all state and recall, and they were served with great ceremony. Their clothing consisted of a shirt and blanket, and they wore a headdress which was a round affair made of wool, and sometimes of gold or silver

523. Picart's fanciful interpretations of Inca sun worship: above, inside the sun temple, an offering is made of a sacred vessel; below, the Peruvians celebrate their annual Grand Festival of the Sun.

or of small beads, which were known as *chaquira*. These Indians were much given to their religion, and performed great sacrifices…they are more self-indulgent and comfort-loving than the mountain-dwelling Indians. They are very industrious in the cultivation of their fields, and carry heavy loads. The fields are excellently cultivated, with much forethought, and they are very orderly in their watering of them. They raise many varieties of fruit and well-flavored roots. Corn is harvested twice a year, it and beans, and broad beans yield abundantly when planted. Their clothing is made of cotton, of which they gather as much as they need in the valley. In addition, these Indians of Tumbes are great fishermen…for by this and the other products they sell to the highland dwellers they have always been rich.

From this valley of Tumbes it is a two days' journey to the valley of Solana, which in ancient times was thickly settled, and had lodgings and storehouses. The highway of the Incas runs… between groves and cool, pleasant glades. through their valleys between groves and cool, pleasant glades.

From Solana one comes to Poechos, though some called it the Maicabilca, because beyond this valley there was a chieftain or lord by that name. This valley was very thickly populated, and beyond doubt many were the people who dwelt there, to judge by the numerous large buildings. These, though now in ruins, bear out what was told of them, and the esteem in which the Incas held them, for in this valley they had their royal palaces and other lodgings and storehouses. Time and wars have so wasted all that the only thing to be seen in proof of what is told are the many and very large burial places, and how the many fields that lie in the valley were cultivated by them that were alive.[137]

Like the highland sites, those of this coastal strip traversed by the Royal Coastal Road are distinguished archaeologically as of three zones, north to south. At the mouth of each of the valleys of the numerous short rivers that come down from the highlands to the sea, there had been before the Incan conquest a relatively independent local agricultural community. The three zones archaeologically distinguished are: (1) *The North Coast,* from Piura to Casma, which included the Moche, where, from c. 250 B.C. to c. A.D. 750, there had flourished one of the finest ceramic-sculpture traditions in the whole history of pottery, and where, from perhaps the twelfth to the late fourteenth century (when the city was entered and sacked by the Inca Capac Yupanqui) the opulent capital, Chauchan, of the empire of Chimu or Chimor, held dominion over a coastal range that extended from Tumbes south to the river Rimac; (2) *The Central Coast,* from Huarmay to Lurín, which included, just south of the river Rimac (near Lima), a very great pilgrimage center and temple dedicated to a deity, Pachacamac, whose age is unknown, but whose cult was of such antiquity and importance that the Incas accepted and assimilated its deity as an aspect of their own Virecocha.

This valley [of Pachacamac] is pleasant and fertile [Cieza wrote], and there stood there one of the most sumptuous temples to be found in these regions. They say of it that, despite the fact that the Inca lords built many temples, aside from those of Cuzco, and glorified and embellished them with riches, there was none to compare with this of Pachacamac, which was built upon a small, man-made hill of adobes and earth, and on its summit stood the temple which began at the foot and had many gates, which, like the walls, were adorned with figures of wild animals. Inside, where the idol stood, were the priests who feigned great sanctimoniousness. And when they performed their sacrifices before the people, they kept their faces toward the door of the temple and their backs to the figure of the idol, with their eyes on the ground and all trembling and overcome, according to certain Indians still alive today, so that it could almost be compared to what one reads of the priests of Apollo when the Gentiles [i.e. the Greeks] sought their vain oracles. And they say more: that before the figure of this devil they sacrificed many animals, and human blood of persons they killed; and that on the occasion of their most solemn feasts they made utterances which were believed and held to be true. In the terraces and foundations of this temple great sums of gold and silver were buried. The priests were greatly venerated, and the lords and caciques obeyed them in many things that they ordered. And it is told that beside the temple there were many and spacious lodgings for those who came there in pilgrimage, and no one was deemed worthy nor allowed to be buried in its vicinity except the lords or priests or pilgrims who came bearing gifts to the temple.

When the great yearly feasts were celebrated, many people assembled, carrying on their diversions to the sound of the musical instru-

ments they possessed. And as the Incas, powerful lords that they were, made themselves the masters of the kingdom and came to this valley of Pachacamac, and, as was their custom in all the lands they conquered, they ordered temples and shrines built to the sun. And when they saw the splendor of this temple, and how old it was, and the sway it held over all the people of the surrounding lands, and the devotion they paid it, holding that it would be difficult to do away with this, they agreed with the native lords and the ministers of their god or devil that this temple of Pachacamac should remain with the authority and cult it possessed, provided they built another temple to the sun which should take precedence. And when the temple of the sun had been built, as the Incas ordered, they filled it with riches and put many virgins in it. The devil Pachacamac, highly pleased with this arrangement, they say revealed his satisfaction in his replies, for the one and the other served his ends, and the souls of the misguided remained fast in his power....

The name of this devil meant "maker of the world," for *camac* means "maker," and *pacha,* "world." And when the Governor Don Francisco Pizarro (because God so willed it) took Atahualpa prisoner in the province of Cajamarca, as he had heard about this temple and the riches it contained, he sent Captain Hernando Pizarro, his brother, with a force of Spaniards to this valley to remove all the gold from that cursed temple, and return to Cajamarca. And although Captain Hernando Pizarro made his way to Pachacamac with all possible speed, it is common knowledge among the Indians that the headmen and priests of the temple carried away more than four hundred loads of gold which was never seen again, nor do the Indians alive today know where it is.

Notwithstanding, Hernando Pizarro (who, as I have said, was the first Spanish captain to enter the temple) found considerable gold and silver. Later on, Captain Rodrigo Orgoñez and Francisco de Godoy and others found a great quantity of gold and silver in the burial sites, and it is believed and held certain that there is much more. But as no one knows where it is buried, unless it is stumbled on by chance it will be lost. From the moment Hernando Pizarro and the other Spaniards entered this temple the devil was defeated and his power destroyed, and the idols in it cast down, and the buildings and the temple to the sun were lost, and most of the Indians have disappeared, so that there are very few left.

This valley is as lush and full of vegetation as those which border upon it, and in the fields much cattle and other livestock and mares are raised, which breed a number of good horses.[138]

Over 400 drawings such as these were included by the Cholo (part Inca, part Spanish) chronicler Felipe Guaman Poma de Ayalia (born 1534) in his *Nueva Cronica y buen gobierno,* a 1200-page letter addressed to the King of Spain, which was forgotten until 1908, when it was discovered in the Royal Library at Copenhagen. Pomo de Ayalia's illustrations are a primary source of information about Inca festivals, daily life, and ethnic groups. Top to bottom: (**524**) In the western part of the empire, an Indian brings offerings to a local *huaca* (anything imbued with spiritual force) honored along with Inca deities. (**525**) "Tupa Inca Speaks with All the *Huacas,*" in order to learn of the past and divine the future. (**526**) "The Great Sorcerer" of the Inca ceremoniously burns a devil clearly drawn from the European imagination (see **428**).

The last of the coastal valleys, namely (3) *The South Coast,* from the river Mala to the river Lomas, includes, besides the important archaeological site of Paracas, with its rich burials dating from c. 500 B.C. to about the second and third centuries A.D., the no less important center of the classic Nazca Culture, which flourished from c. A.D. 250–750 and differs from the contemporary Mochica of the north, as Bushnell has remarked, "in not providing any evidence for expansion or aggressive tendencies."[139] "The pottery," he states further, "does not provide the same sort of evidence about the structure of society as that of the Mochica, but, such as it is, it indicates an interest rather in the supernatural than in the rank and occupations of men."[140]

"When the traveller by air looks down on the desolate pampas round Nazca," observes Bushnell, "he sees a multitude of long straight lines, geometrical figures and other markings on the ground, a phenomenon which has also been observed, but on a small scale, in the Virú valley and in North Chile. They were formed by removing the dark brown pebbles which cover the yellow sandy surface in this neighborhood, and piling them up round the exposed areas. The lines may radiate from a point in almost any direction, form parallel groups, or be distributed irregularly, and they vary from half a kilometre to more than eight kilometres in length. They are associated with elongated, solid areas of more or less rectangular, trapezoidal or triangular form, one of the largest being 1700 metres long with a mean width of 50 metres. Spirals and zigzag lines are frequent, and there are irregular forms besides occasional birds and fish. Lines frequently intersect and figures may be superimposed on one another, but examples of the various types are associated in a way which suggests that no great time-difference is involved. An indication of their age is given by radiocarbon date of c. A.D. 500 for a post at the intersection of two lines, and some animal forms have appendages which recall in a vague way those of some Nazca monsters. Their object has not been satisfactorily explained....Whatever the explanation, the setting out and execution of these perfectly straight lines and other figures must have required a great deal of skill and not a little disciplined labor."[141]

The Paracas culture is arguably best known for wrapping its mummies in burial cloths that are considered preeminent examples of the art of textile making. Above left (**527**), a painted cotton shroud, Paracas-Cavernas culture, c. 1000–400 B.C.; above right (**528**), an embroidered sample, Paracas Necropolis culture, c. A.D. 1–400.

529. No satisfactory explanation of purpose has yet been given for the profusion of mysterious lines that covers the arid, otherwise empty pampas near Nazca. Clearly visible only from the air, some are straight, while others form trapezoids, spirals, and giant figures of such animals as spiders, monkeys, fish, and the hummingbird pictured below.

*   *   *

The general history of the cultures of this Inca zone of six archaeological provinces (three highland and three coastal) unfolds from c. 3000 B.C. to the year of the Spanish Conquest through a sequence of four periods (variously named by various authorities) that date about as follows: *Formative* (c. 3000–300 B.C.), *Pre-Classic* (c. 300–1 B.C.), *Classic* (c. A.D. 1–900), and *Post-Classic* (c. A.D. 900–1532).

Following an indefinite, almost timeless era, first, of nomadic Paleolithic hunting, gathering, and fishing tribes, such as survived into the early twentieth century in the "marginal areas" of southeastern Brazil, Argentina, and Tierra del Fuego; then, during an as yet undefined period of what do appear to have been influences from Southeast and East Asia (the pearl-oyster shell fishhook, dugout canoe, longhouse, blowgun, panpipe, tapa cloth, bottle gourd, and so forth, in association with vegetative-reproduction-shifting cultivation) and the emergence of that tropical-rain-forest type of village life that still prevails throughout the Amazon Basin, there occurred in coastal Ecuador, c. 3000 B.C. (or perhaps earlier), a transformation of the local extension of the Amazonian style of village life (with deep-sea fishing as an added feature) which is now taken to mark the beginning of what is known in American archaeological circles as the Formative Period of New World high cultures. Donald Lathrap describes the criterion by which this culture-stage or -period is recognized and defined. "It is necessary," he declares, "to distinguish clearly between man's first manipulation of the plants naturally available to him as a source of food and his later achievement of a system of agricultural production that yielded a dependable supply of food."[142] "Man," he continues, "was transplanting and protecting particular species of plants long before he really achieved productive agriculture."[143]

With the achievement of such a dependable system of food production there followed an increase in both the size and the complexity of the village settlements and, with that, a specialization of the inhabitants' social functions. Among nomadic and tropical-village tribes, where every competent adult is in possession, or at least has some knowledge, of the whole cultural heritage, there is no more than a natural distinction of social roles according to sex, age, and individual talents—with the only radical separation being of the shaman, linked to a subliminal psychological, instead of immediately practical social-economic, ground of values and concern. With the improved economy and consequent enrichment and expansion of the agriculturally supported community, however, there followed such a differentiation of socially required specializations that the community was one, no longer of generally equivalent adults, but of distinct classes of specialists; and from that there followed a sociological mutation, from the condition, so to say, of an association of amateurs, to that of an enterprise of professionals: a quantum leap, immediately evident archaeologically in the appearance of a distinctive, monumental art informed by an advanced order of both cosmological and psychological insights, and characterized by a distinctive style which thereafter endures, develops, and degenerates

530. Before being fired, this stirrup-spouted funerary vessel portraying a Mochica flautist was burnished, covered with cream slip, and painted with an iron-oxide pigment. Of particular note is the striking verisimilitude with which the texture of the skin had been rendered.

During the Early Intermediate Period (c. 200 B.C.–A.D. 900, approximately synchronous with Bennett and Bird's "Mastercraftsman Period"), on the North Coast, the Mochica civilization, with a sharply divided class system given to warfare and expansion, flourished A.D. 200–700, developed a tradition of realistically modeled and painted pottery that spread into all the other coastal valleys, and was typified archaeologically by the remains of immense public buildings, "which," as Bennett and Bird remark, "display only limited architectural skill, but certainly suggest well organized mass labor."[66] On the South Coast, the contemporaneous Nazca culture was devoted, apparently, less to warcraft and expansion than to religious interests and the arts, the chief remains of the culture being not large buildings, but beautiful pottery and those enigmatic Nazca lines (see **529**).

531. Double-spouted Nazca stirrup vessel in the shape of a decorated trophy head, c. 8⅝" high.

through the relevant lifetime of the culture.

So defined, the Formative Period comprises those centuries during the course of which such an elite, time-factored culture acquired its form, from the moment of its inception to the first monumental manifestations of its achieved style.

In the New World this Formative Period (particulars of which we have already reviewed) extended, as now construed, from c. 3000 to 300 B.C., and was comprised of three phases: an *Early Formative* (Valdivia), c. 3000–1500 B.C.; *Middle Formative* (Machalilla), c. 1500–1000 B.C.; and a *Late* or *Culminating Formative* (Chorrera-Chavín) phase, c. 1000–300 B.C.

During the Early and Middle Formative periods, influences from Southeast and East Asia seem to have mixed with indigenous traditions and to have contributed substantially to the stimulation of the native imagination. From the period, on the other hand, of the Late or Culminating Formative phase, with the almost simultaneous appearance (at Chavín de Huántar in the Northern Highlands of Peru and at various sites in the swamplands of the Mexican states of Veracruz and Tabasco) of the earliest monumental ceremonial centers of two distinct yet related civilizations, the epochal transition was made from the timeless idyll of village horticulture, hunting, and fishing to the time-factored unfolding, maturing, and aging of distinct historical cultures. It was as though a spiritual threshold had been crossed and a self-consistent development initiated, with such a will and destination of its own that no influence whatsoever could now significantly alter its course.

In Peru, the first great phase of this culminating development was of a cultural unfoldment and maturation in two stages: (1) a *Pre-Classic* stage (c. 300–1 B.C.), termed by Wendell Bennett and Junius Bird in their exposition of Andean history, the "Experimenter Period," and described as characterized by "experimentation in new techniques and new controls...in the crafts, in building, and in the agricultural methods";[144] and then, (2) a *Classic* stage (c. A.D. 1–900), the "Mastercraftsman Period," described as characterized by "the mastery of agricultural techniques, by ambitious monumental architecture, by skilled craftsmanship in ceramics, weaving, and metallurgy, and by a florescence of art styles."[145] The period is represented by hundreds of sites and a number of major cultures, each covering an extensive area; notably, the Mochica culture in the North Coast Valley and the Nazca culture of the South Coast, alongside the closely related necropolis culture at Paracas; in the Southern Highlands, the Pucara and Early Tiahuanaco cultures, and in the Northern Highlands, the Recuay. It was a period of achieved civilization, accomplishment in the arts, abundance in the necessities of life, and stable, orderly states.

Toward the close of the ninth century and beginning of the tenth there occurred what Bennett and Bird have described as a shift from "technological advancement to manipulation of man-hour units and political organization," and with this change in emphasis, "expansion in the form of conquests in new regions became profitable." Moreover, "this general tendency for expansion and aggression was not limited to one region, but, except for the Nazca culture, seems to have been general throughout the Central Andes."[146]

With this we pass from the early to the late stages of the cultures of the area, from their centuries of maturation to age and disintegration—from cultivation to violence—through a sequence of three increasingly brutal phases:

(1) An *Early Post-Classic* phase (c. A.D. 900–1200), the "Expansionist Period," when from a center in the Southern Highlands around Tiahuanaco and Lake Titicaca some sort of "culture wave" somehow issued forth and along the whole coast left its mark in monuments of a distinctive "Tiahuanaco" stamp; whether this wave was military and political or purely aesthetic and religious is unknown, but its look and timing suggests a sort of Napoleonic or Alexandrian shaping of a sudden but ephemeral empire.

(2) A *Middle Post-Classic* phase (c. A.D. 1200–1450), the "City Builder Period," when "the disintegration of whatever type of unity the Expansionists had imposed was succeeded by new struggles for power....There is now evidence for large, well organized populations living in planned building units in a pattern which can be designated as urban, even though large cities are not found everywhere.

...Since all cultures now possess adequate technology and all are concentrating on political controls, the balance of power depends largely on the extent of territory. Consequently, it is not surprising that the North Coast cultures became stronger than those of the Central and South Coasts, since the northern valleys are larger and have a more permanent water supply."[147] In this "period of contending states," the empire of Chimu with its capital Chan-chan, expanded from the valleys formerly of the Mochica to dominate an area extending some six hundred miles, from Tumbes south to the Chillón. To the south of that, a small but powerful state occupied the Rimac and Lurin valleys. Farther south the people in the Mula, Cañete and Chincha valleys also were united. Still farther south—in the Ica, Nazca, and Acari valleys—a fourth center was established. And it was over this whole arena, not of chaos (as Cieza told of it: see page 368), but of contending city- and state-building powers, that the armies of the Incas, proceeding from the Central Highlands, rapidly imposed through a few ferocious campaigns, the order of a Roman state.

Thus was initiated (3) the *Final Post-Classic* phase of the civilization (c. A.D. 1450–1532), the "Imperialist Period," the political genius and practical efficiency of which are demonstrated in those two Royal Roads, the length of the Empire, 3150 miles, from Quito in the north to Talca in the south, over which relays of runners could bear messages and orders at a constant speed of some ten miles an hour. As Cieza wrote of this marvel:

In the memory of people I doubt there is record of another highway comparable to this,

running through deep valleys and over high mountains, through piles of snow, quagmires, living rock, along turbulent rivers; in some places it ran smooth and paved, carefully laid out; in others over sierras, cut through the rock, with walls skirting the rivers, and steps and rests through the snow; everywhere it was clean-swept and kept free of rubbish, with lodgings, storehouses, temples to the sun, and posts along the way. Oh, can anything comparable be said of Alexander, or of any of the mighty kings who ruled the world, that they built such a road, or provided the supplies to be found on this one! The road built by the Romans that runs through Spain and the others we read of were as nothing in comparison to this. And it was built in the shortest space of time imaginable, for the Incas took longer to order it than their people in carrying it out.[148]

The kingdom of Peru was so vast that, if the Lord-Inca happened to be at one end of his territory, he had to be informed of what was going on at the other by a messenger, who, if he had to make the trip alone, however much he traveled each day, by the time he had covered the thousand leagues it would be too late to do what needed to be done or to make the necessary decisions. For this reason, and the better to rule the provinces, the Incas devised a system of posts which was the best that could be thought of or imagined, and this was the invention of Pachacuti, the son of Viracocha Inca, father of Topa Inca, according to the songs of the Indians, which the *orejones* confirm [the aristocrats, called by the Spaniards "long eared," because of lobes stretched to receive the large earspools of their rank]. Not only did Pachacuti invent these posts, but he did other great things, as we shall relate. Thus, from the time of his reign along all the highways every half league, more or less, there were little houses well built of wood and straw, and in the mountains they were built along the hillsides and cliffs, so the roads were full of these little houses every so often, as has been said above. And in

532. A section of the eroded, cast adobe or adobe brick walls (right), some up to 50 feet high, as well as a detail of one of the many varied designs in molded clay plaster (below) with which they were adorned, that were used in the construction of Chan Chan, the capital city of the Chimú empire. Founded c. A.D. 800 at the northern end of the Moche valley, Chan Chan was comprised of a civic center covering some 3.5 square miles and an 11 additional square miles of outlying buildings.[67] The Chimú seemingly mass-produced pottery, textiles, and metalworks at Chan Chan. They began to seize control of other coastal valleys c. A.D. 1200, and the empire continued to expand its territorial holdings and to consolidate its power until conquered by the Incas in A.D. 1465.

each of them two Indians were to be stationed, with supplies, and these Indians were to be drawn from the neighboring settlements, and were not to be there permanently, but replaced from time to time by others. This was so carefully observed that all that was necessary was to order it, and it never failed during all the time the Incas reigned.

Each province took care to supply the posts which came within its confines, whether in the wastelands and snow-covered highlands or near the highway. And when word had to be sent to the Lord-Inca in Cuzco or anywhere else of something that had happened or was required for his service, a runner set out from Quito or Tomebamba, or Chile, or Caranqui, or any other part of the kingdom, whether plains or mountains, and at full speed ran that half-league without stopping, for the Indians selected for these posts must have been the swiftest and most agile of all. And when he came near the other post he began to call to the one in it, saying to him, "Set out at once, and go to such and such a place, and tell that this and that has happened, or that this governor begs to inform the Inca...." And as soon as the one who was there heard this, he set out at full speed, and the one who had come went into the little house to rest and eat and drink of what was always kept there, and the other did the same when he reached the next post.

Thus in a short time the news had been carried three hundred leagues and five hundred, and eight hundred, of what had happened or was needed and should be ordered. And those who carried these messages observed such secrecy on their mission that neither plea nor threat could make them reveal the news they were bearing, even though the message had already been passed on to the next messenger. It is a known fact that over such roads, through rough sierras and perilous mountains, snow-covered peaks, and rocky wastes overgrown with every kind of briar and thorn, neither swift horses nor mules could carry the news with more speed than these messengers on foot. For they are very swift, and one of them could cover more ground in a day than a messenger on horse or mule in three; I do not mean to say a single Indian, but by the system they used, which was for each to travel half a league. And never, because of a storm or anything else that might happen, was any post deserted, but the Indians I have mentioned were always there, and never left until others had come to take their place.

In this manner the rulers were notified of all that happened in their kingdom and realm, and took the measures the situation called for. Nowhere in the world does one read that such an invention existed, although I do know that when Xerxes the Great was defeated, the news was carried in this way, by runners, in a short time. There is no doubt that this organization of the posts was very important in Peru, and it can be seen from this how good was the government of its rulers. Even today in many parts of the uplands, alongside the highways, certain of these post houses can be seen, and they bear out the truth of what is said. I have seen certain *topos*, which are like boundary markers, except that these here are large and better made, and by them they counted the leagues, and the distance between each was a league and a half by the measure of Castile.[149]

*   *   *

533. Artifacts crafted of gold, in the pursuit of which the conquistadors would come to ravage the continent and decimate its native inhabitants, first appear during the Early Horizon phase (c. 900–250 B.C.), when the distinctive style of the Chavín culture crystallized at the type-site of Chavín de Huántar in the Mosne valley and then began to spread rapidly throughout the northern highlands and along the northern and central parts of the coast, and, apparently, even into southern coastal regions, where it affected the ceramics there being made.[68]

Herewith, several outstanding early examples of craftsmanship in gold: (**a**) Chavín crown with a grimacing, jaguar-fanged, claw-footed deity (and many snakes) wearing a breast plate suggestive of the Chinese *t'ao-t'ieh* (see p. 383 and **549**); (**b**) Chavín disk, c. 4¾" in diameter, in the center of which is a similar feline face with snakes; (**c**) Chavín spoon, c. 4⁵⁄₁₆" long, the handle of which was made by soldering together two sheets of metal to form a hollow man (also a rattle), either blowing into or drinking from a silver conch shell; (**d**) Mochica plaque showing two masked warriors—each with an animal headdress and a belt terminating in an animal head, one with a conch shell hanging from his elbow—dancing around a pole surmounted by a grinning head.

a

b

c

d

As clues to the mythology or mythologies of the Pre-Inca eras of this great domain, we have, first, the evidence brought forth by Lathrap (see above, page 363) of shamanic practices supported by hallucinogenic drugs and visions, featuring were-jaguar and -cayman associations of the shaman, such as are carried on today among the Amazonian forest tribes. The prominence of ceramic female figurines, however, among the Early and Middle Formative artifacts of this culture zone cannot but represent an accent of some kind upon what in the Orient is known as the "female energy or power" (Sanskrit, *śakti*), however interpreted in local mythology or cult practice. In the myths and rites of every one of the Old World Neolithic cultures personifications of this energy are not only prominent but dominant. They are not reflections of shamanic thought and experience, but arrive from another quarter. Indeed, among the Paleolithic remains already reviewed of the Dordogne (see I.1:66–79), a separation of the female and male energy fields and cultic associations is already evident, with the figurines (Paleolithic Venuses) assigned to dwelling sites and the representations of shamans (as semi-animal presences) confined to the temple-caves of the male initiation rites. Thereafter, in the later, Neolithic periods, when intensive agriculture had become the main support of society and the analogy was not only recognized, but stressed, of the power of Nature to bring forth and nourish life with the power of the female body to do exactly the same, representations of the shaman disappear from the iconography and there is a multiplication of female figurines beyond measure. In the accumulated rubbish in the dirt floor of the Valdivia *maloca* that Lathrap excavated he found "hundreds of pots and dozens of figurines made, used, and discarded by the inhabitants."[150] An interesting detail to know would be the relative density of fragment distribution in the rear and front of the *maloca*, since we know (pages 351–353) that during the house ceremonials of the Amazonian Barasana the women sit apart, screened away in the rear of the *maloca*, while the men and the youths being initiated partake of their hallucinogens and sound their various bark trumpets. Further, one of the outstanding characteristics of the cultures of both North and South America (as also, by the way, of both China and Japan) is a persistence even into the late high-culture stages of a robust shamanic strain, even along with the inevitable *śakti* observances of their agriculturally grounded seasonal ceremonials. I am inclined to see a prefiguration of this disposition in the observed conjunction, already in earliest Formative Ecuador, of the shamanic jaguar cult with its kit of hallucinogens and the multitude of little ceramic personifications of the *śakti*.

Around 1200–1000 B.C., however, at the opening of the Late or Culminating phase of the New World Formative development, something decisive occurred which has not been explained. Not only was there (as has already been remarked) the almost simultaneous, sudden appearance of two monumental ceremonial centers showing an immediate mastery of the arts of architecture and sculpture in stone, but there was also evident in the monuments of all of these Late Formative ceremonial centers an order of symbolic thinking, translated into symbolic art forms, that is altogether beyond the range of what, in contrast, can only be called "primitive art."

The astonishing Raimondi stela (now in the National Museum at Pueblo Libre near Lima), which is far and away the most *mysterious* iconographic image yet discovered anywhere, either in the New World or the Old, marks decisively the quantum leap that had been accomplished in the inward life and experience of the priestly élite of this Native American civilization in the period of its initial manifestation.

*　　*　　*

534. The mystery of the Raimondi Stela lies not only in the sophistication of its symbolic form, for which we have not a word of explanation (since during the whole history of this Andean civilization there was never developed a system of writing), but also in its early date (c. 1000 B.C.), which centuries earlier than any known work of comparable sophistication either in Europe or in Asia—though not, be it noted, in Egypt. The god that it shows (known to archaeology as the Staff God) is almost certainly the same as that represented, centuries later, on the great Monolithic Gateway at Tiahuanaco, where the deity appears to be weeping. A vase painting from Peru (Figure 539) exhibits the same interesting feature, and related, certainly, is the weeping Argentinian god shown in the copper plaque of the Frontispiece to Volume I. We have also seen weeping visages from the Antilles (see page 314).

All of these are popular representations, apparently, of the same dominant divinity, in various aspects, adapted to the folklore and conditions of the various local cultures, whereas in the remarkable stela at Chavín de Huántar, the initial ceremonial center of the widely spread civilization, the inward reality and transcendent import of the personification are disclosed.

As described by G. H. S. Bushnell, the revelation is of "a standing figure with feline face, holding an elaborate staff in each claw-like hand, while from the head projects a monstrous appendage facing upwards and consisting of a series of fantastic snouts with feline fangs and snakes projecting on either side."[69]

Observe the picture upside down (Figure 535) and the "fantastic snouts with feline fangs" will appear. There are three—each proceeding, as it were, from the tongue of the one above—all of which emanate from a tongue or snout that descends from the rectangle which, when right side up, is the head of what appears then as the god. Regarded upside down again, this rectangle shows two faces, one above the other, that below, of a bird, from which the trinity of faces proceeds, the other, of a jaguar. And we notice now that in each of the two elaborate staves there is a jaguar-face just above the bend of the god's elbows.

Now there is certainly a hidden doctrine here, as in the universe there is hidden divinity. Right side up, all that the icon shows is an image of the popular Staff God wearing an extraordinary headdress; whereas, upside down (and no one could possibly have turned this great stone stela upside down), an esoteric revelation appears of the one god's three aspects or faces proceeding from the composition's only readily visible image of a bird, its beak precisely at the top of the axial vertical (at the bottom of which are the twined serpents of a caduceus), while above the bird-face is again our old friend the jaguar, whose fangs, at either side of his jaw, are not centered like the bird's beak, and who, when we again turn the icon right side up, stands before us holding, right and left, the two staves of the one world-governing god's contrary powers: Justice and Mercy, in the vocabulary of the Christian cult. What they were at Chavín, c. 1000 B.C., we do not know. But that the Jaguar aspect here confronting us holds with his two staves sway over this temporal world where all things are experienced as pairs of opposites—male and female, light and dark, future and past, good and evil, and so on—is clear; and further, that at that centering point in mid-forehead, where the inner eye of vision opens to the way of spiritual flight, transcending all dualities in axial ascent, there occurs an overturning of insights and values, and where only enigmatic shapes had been seen, now the forms are beheld of three divine faces.

Serpents, meanwhile, are everywhere: two hanging from either side of the god's belt, eight along either side of the quadrangle of his head, eight more along each side of the tower of his headdress, and then two at the summit, interlaced as a caduceus, bringing thus the two ranges of opposites together as aspects of one entity. At the top of each of the staves, furthermore, there are again two serpents, and a caduceus is an element at the base of each staff. Finally, along the snout of the first of the three faces are two runs of three serpents each, bringing the total number of serpents (if I have caught them all) to fifty two, which just happens to be the number of years in what was to be known as

535. Inverted drawing of Raimondi Stela.

a Knot or Bundle of Years in the much later Mayan calendar; and if this is not merely a coincidence, then the deity of this mystical early-Andean stela is a counterpart symbolically of the Platonic *Aion* and Zoroastrian *Zervan Akarana* ("Endless Time"), as a personification of the ever-returning, self-renewing round of the passing years.

The relevance of the serpent symbol to the pictorial exposition of this mythological "archetype" or "elementary idea" (see II.1:28) can be substantiated through a consideration of the serpent in other mythological associations.

The motif of a raptorial bird killing a snake is depicted in one of the powerful stone statues that have been found in the neighborhood of San Agustín (Colombia), in the highland Huila district, at the headwaters of the Magdalena river. These monuments are of the date, approximately, of the mystic Staff God of Chavín de Huántar, the Olmec ceremonial centers in southern Mexico, and the Chorrera ceramics of contemporary Ecuador. Figure 536 is of a Chorrera jar, where again we see a raptorial bird killing a snake. The motif appears today on the Mexican national flag, in memory of the Aztec legend of their settlement, after long wandering, at the site of Tenochtitlan (now Mexico City). They had halted there, by the waters of Lake Tezcuco, when they beheld an eagle perched on a tall cactus that was growing from a wave-washed rock; and while they watched, the bird rose to the rising sun bearing a serpent in its talons. This being taken as an augury, it was there that they founded their city of the Sun, Tenochtitlan.

Across the Pacific, in Southeast Asia and Indonesia, this same theme of the sun-bird (*garuda*) with a serpent (*nāga*) in its talons is paramount in the arts, both of the classical Hindu-Buddhist centuries (A.D. 800–1200) and of today. And do we not find in the *Iliad* the legendary account of an eagle soaring above the fleet of the Greek heroes approaching Troy, bearing in its talons a bleeding snake which was interpreted by Kalchas, the soothsaying priest of the expedition, as an augury of the victory of the patriarchal Greeks over luxurious Aphrodite's Troy?

One of the earliest known symbolic juxtapositions of the serpent and the winged solar bird is from ancient Mesopotamia, c. 2000 B.C., in an engraving on the libation vase of a certain King Gudea of Lagash. Two serpents interlaced across an axial staff, in the way of a caduceus, are flanked by a pair of lion-birds or cherubim, who are either opening the portals of a shrine to reveal its symbol of the mystery of life, or closing the same to contain the symbol's force. In the biblical version, according to Genesis 3, the gates are closed, the serpent with its life-wisdom is cursed, and two cherubim are stationed at the gate to guard the way to the tree of the knowledge of eternal life. In the Hindu and Buddhist traditions, on the other hand, the serpent power is to be fostered and increased.

The ability of the serpent to shed its skin and thus to renew itself, as the moon is renewed by sloughing its shadow, has recommended it, throughout the world, as an obvious image of the mystery of the will in nature, which is ever self-renewing in its generation of living beings. But also, in its threatening character, as a traveling aesophagus, the serpent is equally an image of the consuming power of the same will, foreboding death to all that lives. In its flowing form, the serpent suggests water. The forked flashing of its tongue, however, is flamelike. But in water, too, there is fire, a generative fire which carries life to deserts parched by the unmitigated fire of the sun.

For the solar fire is like a raptorial bird, a killer. The sun desiccates, evaporates, and draws to itself the waters of life, and can be thus appropriately pictured metaphorically as a raptorial bird bearing off and consuming the serpent of the earth-fertilizing waters.

The image is given in nature (see I.1:**68**). Anyone, anywhere in the world where there are serpents and raptorial birds, might be struck by this dramatic manifestation in the spectacle of nature, of its two extremes in conflict: the earthbound serpent and the bird of celestial flight. Anyone, anywhere in the world, might be struck, furthermore, by the analogy of the sun absorbing the waters of the earth and this bird dispatching a serpent. And still further, since there is more to a myth—or even to a poem—than the observation of similitudes in the spectacle of nature, we must add that anyone, anywhere in the world, might experience in himself an empathetic participation in the fascinating conflict, and go on to render in a work of art an image of the opposition of earthly and celestial energies as something to be experienced equally within oneself and in the constitution of the universe. And then finally, of course, anywhere in the world, once this image has been rendered by a creative poet or artist, others might experience its force and assimilate it to the local mythological vocabulary as a pictorial metaphor appropriate for representation in religious monuments.

Hypothetically, from the point of view of an abstract system of psychological suppositions, such imagined occasions might be thought to account for the unrelated appearances, here and there in the world, of identical mythological motifs. But in fact, then, why do we not find in the Paleolithic temple caves any painting of a raptorial bird killing a serpent? Might there be required some sort of psychological readiness for the insight? And would this readiness, then, be somehow a function of local social conditions?

The association of the image of the bird with shamanic flight is already evident in the art of the caves, specifically in that painting, for example, in the crypt of Lascaux, of a shaman in trance wearing a bird mask and with the figure of a bird on the shaman's staff by his side (see I.1:**105**). In the paintings of the Bushman trance-dancers, too, the imagery of flight is present in

their figures of flying bucks (see I.1:**176–177**). The earliest serpents, on the other hand, appear to be those three engraved cobras on the buckle of mammoth ivory discovered at Ma'lta (Siberia) in the grave of an elaborately ornamented boy (see I.1:**127**). Significantly, there were a number of ivory female figurines in that grave as well, besides ivory images of wild geese in full flight.

536. From Manabi, a Chorrera effigy jar, c. 10¾" tall, showing a laughing falcon (*Herpetotheres cachinnians*) holding in its beak and claws a snake, probably a fer-de-lance (*Bothrops*).

I know of no earlier raptorial bird and serpent image than that, already mentioned, of the *Iliad*, except one, engraved on a cylinder seal from Mesopotamia, showing an eagle clutching *two* serpents. The date of this seal is of King Gudea of Lagash, c. 2000 B.C., on whose libation vase we have already noted the earliest caduceus. The eagle is the sun-bird of Lagash, Im-gig, who is shown frequently with a lion's head, since the lion, like the eagle, was in antiquity metaphoric of the sun, which, in turn, is metaphoric of spiritual light. The teaching of the Buddha is known as his Lion Roar; for as the great sound of a lion's voice scatters the grazing herds, or as the light of a rising sun dispels the herd of stars of a moonlit night, so the word of the Buddha annihilates the lustful delusions of the unilluminated will. Waxing and waning, the light of the moon is of the sun, but tempered to the cycles of time: for the fire of the sun, full blast, annihilates. The moon is lord of the tides of life, but the sun, lord of an enduring light, is disengaged from the waxing and waning of time's ruins. Sloughing its skin, the serpent is an earthly counterpart of the moon shedding its shadow, and so, as illustrated in the Buddhist image of the World Enlightener and Teacher protected by the five- or seven-headed cobra, Muchalinda, there is a balance to be achieved in life between the blast of absolute illumination and the covering, tempering, life-sustaining and -loving wisdom of the serpent. The internal fire of the serpent that is evident in the flashing of its tongue is to be increased through reflection of the solar blaze, but not to such a degree as to incinerate the serpent. And so it was that Nietzsche, who understood such mysteries, in his *Thus Spake Zarathustra* gave as boon companions to his nineteenth-century prophet of a new wisdom for mankind an eagle and a serpent, "the proudest and the shrewdest among the beasts."

Thus the apparent polarity of spirit and will, celestial light and the values of earthly nature, is what in the earliest historic periods the bird and serpent duo symbolized. And the inward, psychological application and realization of the import of this mythologized symbolization is what is intended in the Indian practice of yoga—the earliest evidences of which appear on seals from the Indus Valley, of the period, exactly, of the libation vase of King Gudea of Lagash. The relationship of the symbolism of this piece to that of the Muchalinda Buddha (three thousand years later) is obvious. A little less obvious, but nevertheless discoverable through an exercise of the comparative imagination, is a relationship of the symbolism of the Indus seal, as well, to that of the great American stela (c. 1000 B.C.) at Chavín de Huántar, where the awakened (Buddha) eye at the center of the god's forehead is represented as the visage of a bird and, instead of two serpents rising, one at either hand, we have fifty-two. Turn the monument upside down and, just above the triad of benign faces is the visage of the bird with its beak indicating the axial meridian, while at the base of this axial line is the caduceus. The symbolism is of the universal World Tree, as represented, for example, in the Icelandic Eddic Yggdrasil, with the eagle, perched on its peak, the dragon, Midhogg, gnawing at its root, and the busy squirrel, Ratatosk, running up and down the trunk between, bearing to each the words and messages of abuse from the other.

What can be said of all these likenesses? Too close to be disregarded, they have to be explained, if not by evidences of diffusion, then by a psychology of archetypes. The pictorial vocabulary of the Indian system of yoga by which they are most cogently interpreted is late, of the Tantric period, fourth century A.D., or later; so that diffusion is ruled out, unless (which is not impossible) there was a controlled verbal communication of some kind that was carried without fault across a vast ocean, not only of space, but of time. Alternately, one may conjecture that the extravagant use of hallucinogens in American shamanic practice must have produced transformations of consciousness, very like, if not identical with, those of the experiences of Indian yogis. The parallels, in any case, are much too numerous, too close and exquisite, to be attributable to chance or to undirected convergence.

Briefly resumed: The controlling image of what is known as Kundalini Yoga is of an awakening and unfolding of the "Serpent Power" (śakti, the will in nature), through breath control and other intentional exercises, rousing it from its animal lethargy in the lower, pelvic centers of the cerebro-spinal nervous system, to ascend through nodes of psychological transformation toward a realization, finally, of a full spiritual awakening, symbolized as the dissolution of the fully uncoiled serpent into the light by which it was waked.

The word yoga is from the Sanskrit root yuj, "to yoke, to join, to link"; specifically, to yoke one's waking consciousness to the ultimate source of consciousness, or, mythologically expressed, to unite the will of the individual with that of the Lord of the universe, whether known as Shiva, Aion, Zervan Akarana, or the Staff God of Chavín de Huántar.

The feminine noun kuṇḍaliní means, "that which is coiled"; for in this yoga the cosmic energy (śakti), which is of each of us the life, is symbolized as a coiled serpent lodged at the base of the spinal column, asleep until awakened, when it will uncoil and ascend along an inward spinal nerve to the ceiling of the brain, passing on the way five centers, nodes, or chakras ("circles"), at each of which the mode of consciousness of the yogi is transformed.

The total number of centers is thus seven. Three are of the pelvic region, three are of the head, and one, between, as the node of transformation, is of the great area between the diaphragm and shoulder yoke of the heart and the lungs:

1. Near the base of the spinal column, between the rectum and the genitals, where the kuṇḍaliní sleeps;

2. At the level of the genitals, where the will becomes of an erotic cast; and

3. At the level of the navel, where the wakened serpent's aim is to eat (consume), to master, and to control.

4. At the next center of the heart, a radical transformation occurs with an awakening to the prospects of a life given, not to torpor, physical lust, or conquest, but to further spiritual unfoldment and realizations. At this center of the heart, that is to say, there occurs what has been in many cultures recognized and mythologically symbolized as a "virgin birth," that is, the inception of an eminently human lifetime, addressed to ends unknown to the lower animal (pelvic motivated) orders of consciousness. Whereupon a tension is generated between two now contrary natures, one addressed to the popular world, the other to the inner life.

In the Raimondi stela of Chavín de Huántar these are represented by the two faces in the quadrangle of the deity's heads: that below, of the jaguar god, addressing the world with his two symbolic staves, and that above, at the point in the forehead of the opening of the Buddha eye, of a bird, turned upward to the towering revelation of an inward dimension of three successive transformations.

In the imagery of India the heart center of this transformation is symbolized as a lotus of twelve vermilion petals, each inscribed with a letter of the Sanskrit alphabet, and with the sign of the syllable yam at the center, enclosing a lingam-yoni symbol in gold, symbolic of the "virgin birth," as representing the male and female organs (lingam and yoni) in conjunction. At this level, at this station of indrawn consciousness, the sound OM is heard of the world-creating radiance of the immanent-transcendent ground (brahman). Once heard, this sound is recognized in all things. The six-pointed star enclosing the golden central symbol is of the color of smoke from the solar fire of this resounding sound. Its two triangles, upward and downward pointing, are significant of the tension and the relevant decision now to be marked between effort and inertia, ascent along the way of increasing consciousness and rapture against the impeding down-draft of the unregenerate senses. The two deities, upper right, are the gods patron of this center (Shiva and his śakti), personifications of the powers symbolized in the golden triangle at the center. And the animal is the black antelope on which (unseen) the wind god of the breath (prāna, spiritus) rides with his hands extended in the gestures known as "fear not" and "granting boons."[70]

Finally, the channel shown rising from the golden triangle is to be the passageway of the unfolding Serpent Power to the transforming raptures of further ascent. Leading to, and passing through, the three remaining centers of transformation, all of which are of the head, it matches in the Raimondi stela the towering "appendage facing upwards" in which are to be seen three faces. No practiced Freudian will have difficulty in recognizing in the inverted bird-face at the root of the towering gloriole a counterpart of the lingam and yoni in the Indian symbol. The bird is the golden sun-bird. Its position on the forehead of the rectangular head of the Andean Staff God is exactly at that point above the eyes where, in Hindu and Buddhist images, the eye of awakening uncloses. The second, the lower and principal face in this large, rectangular head is of the powerful were-jaguar, who, with his two symbolic shaman staves, is governing this temporal world of dualities. The downward-pointing triangle and the upward-pointing of the Indian heart chakra correspond in sense to the sense of these two faces. "Two souls," wrote Goethe, "dwell within my breast." And here they are.

Thus the interesting head of the Andean Staff God matches in its symbolic details the glorious lotus of the resounding syllable OM of the Indian symbolic system. The panel on the god's chest shows three pairs of volutes (Chakras 1, 2, and 3). The gloriole above his head is about to reveal three faces (Chakras 5, 6, and 7). The eight serpents on either side of the head are sideways reaching and small. Those above, upward reaching, are magnified (as in rapture), as are, also, the volutes. And if we now, once again, turn the icon upside down, to consider, stage by stage, the transformations represented in the faces, their messages from the silences of our own most inward space come loud and clear, in three transformations:

5. "This region," states an Indian text, "is the gateway of the great Liberation."[71] Its station is at the level of the larynx (the Voice, the Word, the Lion Roar). There is a purgation to be accomplished here: to put down, to quell, and to be quit of all the temporal lusts and fears of the lower centers, and so to become cleared for untrammeled spiritual flight. Accordingly, the snout is overcast of the first of the Raimondi stela's three faces, and it is crossed by threatening, tusk-like spikes and marked by the heads of six serpents.

6. Whereas here, at that point above and between the eyes where full awakening is achieved and the rapture experienced of what is known in the Christian vocabulary as the Beatific Vision of God, what are shown on the forehead of the second Raimondi face are the heads of a pair of eagles. Chakra 6, that is to say, corresponds to the experience that the angels know of the vision of God in heaven; as Chakra 5 was of purgatory. And since what is here beheld is a personification of the infinite, the Sanskrit term for the good is saguṇa brahman, "the infinite qualified," while the rapture known is of savikalpa samādhi, "qualified union with the infinite."

7. "The most difficult leave-taking," said the mystic Meister Eckhart, "is the leaving of God for G O D";[72] overcoming the name and form of the historical "Ethnic Idea," that is to say, for an experience of transcendence. At Chakra 7, at the crown of the head, the mind-annihilating rapture is experienced of nirvikalpa samādhi, "unqualified identity" with nirguṇa brahman, "unqualified transcendence"; and accordingly, in the Raimondi stone, whereas the first revealed face showed six serpent forms and the second two eagle's heads, the last carries only an abstract design. For we have here gone beyond all names and forms—the names and form even of what had been earlier feared and revered as "God."

Turn the image right side up again!

537. Drawing of the Raimondi stela right side up.

All that we now see is a popular anthropomorphic god, represented as the avatāra, "descent into temporality," of a supreme power whose horned visage appears mysteriously near the summit of the radiant crown.

And one more detail: the menacing mouth of the were-jaguar turns into the cat-like grin of an amusing face with smiling eyes, when the panel is reversed and the beatifying revelation exposed of the mystic tower.

Mythology in the domain of any of the high civilizations will be of three orders, which, though they may appear to be of the same constitution, are not; nor can they ever be. They are, namely, mythology, (1) as experienced by the mystics; (2) as applied by governing authorities; and (3) as idolized by the folk. The aim of the first is rapture; of the second, power; and of the last, health, progeny, and wealth: or, in terms of the chakra system just reviewed, these aims are those proper, respectively, to Chakras 4, 3, and 2 (see pages 378–379). Mystics and the folk have in common the ability to turn to their use any mythology whatsoever. Politicians, on the other hand, not only are committed to one system, but also have the necessity to impose their system on others; for it is by engaging the folk mind in the idolization of the deities they propose that they engage the worshippers to themselves. Mystics can become an inconvenience, since their ability and need to read past the "ethnic idea" to the "elementary idea" disempowers the image politically intended to be idolized. And yet, paradoxically, as I believe we have found in the evidence of this *Atlas*, it has been out of mystic states that mythologies are derived.

Among the most primitive hunting and gathering tribes, of course, there is no place for the political factor. With the enlargement of settled communities, however, during Neolithic (Formative) eras, class distinctions originate, and ruling élites then emerge and take charge.

From the evidence, c. 1000 B.C., at Chavín de Huántar it appears that in Highland Peru this Formative élitism was not only of a social order, but also intellectual, vocational, of craftsmanship in the arts, and of inward spiritual insights. There has been discussion as to whether the distinctive style of Chavín art and thought, with its characteristic symbols, was in any way linked to a context of political domination. The influence became spread over broad areas, both in the Northern Highlands and along the North, Central, and South Coasts, but whether by political force or by some other manner of influence is unknown. As Bushnell has remarked of the archaeology of this culture:

"It is united by the presence of similar pottery types, and by evidence of a religion of animal worship, in which the cult of a feline god held the foremost place. There are a number of ceremonial centers which show a considerable variety in detail, and each seems to have been the nucleus of a group of scattered settlements, but there is no indication that the centers were united by any sort of political organization. Weapons are not common; flanged and spiked stone mace-heads and polished stone mace-heads occur in the graves of the Chicama region, the spear-thrower was in use, and a single long palm-wood bow was found at Ancón, but some of these must have been used for hunting. Fortifications

538. Mochica effigy vessel depicting an anthropomorphic creature that some suggest was a "bat god," holding a human head in its left hand and a knife in its right.

539. Ceremonial urn of the Tiahuanaco-Epigonal period, decorated with a figure — probably the Inca deity Viracocha — who wears a snake headdress, carries two staffs, and is seen to be weeping.

are unknown, as fighting can hardly have amounted to more than small-scale local raiding, and the carvings at Sechín indicate that head-hunting may have played some part in this. With a small population in a few scattered settlements, there cannot have been any of the competition for land which so often provokes wars.

"An important question which remains," Bushnell adds, "is, where did the bearers of the religious cult, ceremonial pottery and other new features come from?"[151]

Now "animal worship" is not at all the proper term for anything of which we have learned in the course of our review of the "primitive" cultures of mankind, let alone for such a figure as the Staff God of the Chavín de Huántar stela. As told by the Pawnee Letokots Lasa: "Tirawa, the One Above, did not speak directly to man. He sent certain animals to tell man that he showed himself through the beasts, and that from them, and from the stars and the sun and the moon should man learn. Tirawa spoke to man through his works, and the Pawnee understands the heavens, the beasts, and the plants. For all things tell of Tirawa" (see I.1: 8, 10, 25, 48–49).

Too many of our best scholars, themselves indoctrinated from infancy in a religion of one kind or another based upon the Bible, are so locked into the idea of their own god as a supernatural fact—something final, not symbolic of transcendence, but a personage with a character and will of *his* own—that they are unable to grasp the idea of a worship that is not of the symbol but of its reference, which is of a mystery of much greater age and of more immediate inward reality than the name-and-form of any historical ethnic idea of a deity, whatsoever. The feline god of the Andean Chavín Culture, accordingly, is not in any way evidence of "animal worship," but is of a sophistication that makes the sentimentalism of our popular Bible-story theology seem undeveloped. Where did the bearers of this truly mystical, profoundly poetic mythology then come from?

A rubbing from Chavín de Huántar (Figure 541) shows the symbolical were-jaguar holding two marine shells in his hands, a *Malea* in the right and a *Spondylus* in the left. Shells, as Lathrap has recognized, are important elements in Chavín religious art and are almost always presented as a pair: the conical univalve, *Malea*, being an obvious male symbol, and the bivalve, *Spondylus*, female.[152] Right, male; left, female: a worldwide archetypal association! The god in whose image the male and female aspects of the will in nature are comprised is also of an enormous domain (see I.2: Map 33). Another rubbing of a relief at Chavín de Huántar (Figure 542) shows an eagle, the claws of whose feet are exactly those of the feet of the jaguar god. Donald Lathrap has suggested that the birds represented in the symbolic arts of northwest-

540. Mochica ceramic effigy vessel, c. 4⅝" tall, depicting an anthropomorphic being about to consume a supine figure with a feline helmet (see 551–555).

ern South America at this date are the monkey-eating harpy eagle (*Harpia larpyga*), which is native to the Amazonian Basin and "by far the most impressive and powerful raptorial bird in South America....Many of the Tropical Forest tribes," he states further, "held the harpy eagle in great veneration, raising the young for their feathers and for purposes of ceremonial exchange and trade."[153] The serpent represented, he posits, is the prodigious Amazonian anaconda, whose mythological role as the Water Mistress, sister of the Moon, we have learned from the Makiritare of the Orinoco (see page 331); the Barasana of the Upper Orinoco Vaupés region tell tales of the same great snake in the character of the Manioc-stick Anaconda: of his birth as child of the Primal Sun (precursor of the visible sun and moon of today), of his marriage to Jaguar Woman, and of his death when he broke into flame and burned himself to ashes. From his bones were made the original trumpets of the men's rites, and from the ashes of his other remains grew manioc, edible fungi, and various other plants.[154] "It would appear appropriate," states Lathrap in comment

on the imagery of Chavín, "...that the attributes of the most powerful known carnivore, the jaguar, were combined with the attributes of the most powerful raptorial bird, the harpy eagle, and the most powerful constrictor, the anaconda."[155]

These were all creatures of the neighboring Amazonian forest. The two seashells, *Malea* and *Spondylus*, on the other hand, were not only from a remote coast, but also difficult to obtain. Neither occurs along the coast south of Ecuador, and, as Lathrap points out, "large specimens of *Spondylus*, in particular, can be obtained only by diving to reefs at depths of fifty feet or more.

"Chavín art demonstrates," he continues, "that as early as 800 B.C. *Malea* and *Spondylus* were accepted as essential parts of the sacramental system. Indeed, there are representations of the *Spondylus* from a slightly earlier context at the site of Kotosh in the Huánuco Basin. The people of Chavín and Kotosh had to obtain these shells by long-distance trade from coastal Ecuador.... The Formative people of Ecuador used the bright red rims of the *Spondylus* shell for their own jewelry. They also traded this material to their southern neighbors as a most profoundly sacred and necessary commodity." And further: "In economic rituals of the modern highland Peruvian communities these marine shells still play an important part in ensuring proper rainfall and crop fertility."[156]

Uniting in his one person, thus, not only the powers of the male and female, as well as those of the celestial eagle and aqueous anaconda, but also the influences of two distinct mythological traditions, one of the neighboring rain forests to the east, the other of the sea to the west, the jaguar god of Chavín de Huántar appears and stands before us as a mystery god indeed, compounding in his one commanding presence practically all the enigmas and pairs-of-opposites of our subject. He is in no way the grotesque idol, merely, of some primitive local cult. Neither is he, finally, local—despite the appearances in the make-up of his person of the three most powerful animals of the nearby Rain Forest myths.

541. Rubbing from Chavín de Huántar of the principal Chavín deity, who holds a strombus shell in his right hand and a spondylus in his left.

542. Rubbing of one of a row of harpy eagles on a stone slab that once may have rested over the entrance to the main temple at Chavín de Huántar.

a

544. A tusked deity and his tiny companion, atop a ceremonial digging stick in a Mochica warrior-priest's grave at Huaca de la Cruz, the Virú valley.

545. Stela 2 from La Venta, Tabasco, Mexico.

543. Of note, but inexplicable, is the similarity of the headgear on such widely dispersed figures as these three: (**a**) stone figure, c. 18″ high, from Tiahuanaco, once on the shore of Lake Titicaca in Bolivia; (**b**) Tres Zapotes Monument A (see **350**); (**c**) stone sculpture from San Agustín, Colombia.

b

c

546. Valdivian bowl fragment with a diameter of c. 7¼″, an undulating rim, and incised mask-like facial treatments (see **507**).

547. Chilcat blanket of the Tlingit featuring an iconographic representation (arguably of a bear) that is suggestive of a *t'ao-t'ieh* mask.

The three figures shown in Figure 543 are wearing similar headgear. The first is from Bolivia, the second from Tres Zapotes, Mexico, and the third from San Agustín, Colombia. The posture of the Colombian figure is matched in a miniature, six inches high, from the Virú Valley (Figure 544). It is matched again at La Venta in a large stela, eleven feet five inches high (Figure 545), which is evidently the image of a god surrounded by a cloud company of attendants. Above the head of this figure is an immense headdress. Above the heads of the Colombia and Virú Valley figures are the apparitions of their feline "alter-egos." The shape of the headpiece of the Colombian apparition is exactly that of the jaguar-boy and jaguar-god heads and faces in Olmec art (Figure 356), where the boys are represented as sacrifices to the god. The earliest example of the mask in America, apparently, is from Ecuador, c. 2150–2000 B.C., on a piece of Valdivia pottery (Figure 546). It appears again, about a thousand years later, engraved and painted on two small bottle gourds (Figure 548) unearthed by Junius Bird in the late 1940s at Huaca Prieta, a site on the Peruvian North Coast, in the Chicama Valley. The radiocarbon date here was 1016 ± 300 B.C., and associated were some bits of bark cloth, cotton string, twined cotton fabric, looped and knotted pouches, fishing nets, and even true weavings: a context definitely of the sea.[157] And finally, of course, on the North American Northwest Coast, in the arts of the Haida, Kwakiutl and Tlingit wood carvers, the same unmistakable face appears on totem poles, carved boxes, and Chilcat blankets (Figure 547).

Across the Pacific, on bronze ceremonial vessels of the Shang Dynasty (c. 1523–1027 B.C.) and Early (Western) Chou (c. 1027–772 B.C.), something very like this South and Middle American jaguar mask was an essential ornamental feature. Known as *t'ao-t'ieh*, the "Glutton," its earliest form is shown on the bronze *ting* (tripod with two ears: sacrificial cauldron regarded as a type of imperial power)[158] reproduced in Figure 549. It is here composed of two confronting dragons of the one-legged kind known as *k'uei*. "There is a difference of opinion," William Willetts states in discussion of this image, "as to how it originated; whether the confrontation of two animals or animal heads seen in profile first suggested the idea of a frontal mask, that is, or whether an original mask acquired, by a fanciful proliferation of its form, a *double entendre* in the shape of two confronting animals seen in side view....Chinese accounts as to the meaning of *t'ao-t'ieh*," he goes on to report, "are conflicting. A passage in *Tso chuan* [a fourth-century B.C. history] speaks of noxious spirits at large in the hills and wastes,

549. Schematic drawing (above) explicating the iconography of one of the three *t'ao-t'ieh* masks (each formed from a pair of confronting *k'uei* dragons), all on a ground of squared spirals, on the Shang Dynasty bronze *ting*, c. 9¼" high, pictured in full at the right.

548. Carved gourd vessel with cover, from the Huaca Prieta site on the north coast of Peru.

and tells how these were depicted on the Nine Cauldrons of the legendary Yü the Great, to give people a fair idea of what they look like. By the third century A.D. the commentator Ku P'o is identifying the *t'ao-t'ieh* with one of these. But a passage in *Lü shih ch'un ch'in*, attributed to the third-century B.C. writer Lü Pe-wei, runs: 'On Chou vessels there was put a *t'ao-t'ieh* with a head, but no body. He is eating a man and thinks he is going to swallow him; but already the *t'ao-t'ieh's* body is destroyed."[159]

There is in Indian art and myth a comparable symbolic glutton called *Kīrttimukha*, "Face of Glory," also represented as a mask (Figure 550), of which the legend tells:

As a manifestation of Shiva's invincible majesty, Glutton was born of a lightning flash of wrath from the deity's third eye, whence he appeared as a ravenous monster avid to consume whatever was before him. And when nothing was seen available, Shiva ordered him to consume himself, which he promptly did. Commencing at his feet, he came chopping up the line until nothing was left but a face without a lower jaw, whereupon Shiva, delighted by this epitome of the nature of life, which lives on life, namely on itself, declared: "I name you 'Face of Glory,' *Kīrttimukha*, and shall place you above the entrances to my shrine. No one who cannot bow in obeisance to you is worthy to come to me."[160]

550. *Kīrttimukha*, as pictured in a detail of a larger work entitled *Durga Slayer of the Titan Buffalo*, Bhuvanesvara Vaital Deul, c. 1000 A.D.

There is thus represented in this image a fierce philosophy of unqualified affirmation of the nature of life; a *yea!* that breaks past the barrier of fear to a recognition of sublimity. The mask appears over shrines, not only of Shiva, but also of his goddess, and in later Buddhist art, over images even of the Buddha with right hand lifted in the "fear not" posture.

551. Chinese bronze Yu vessel, Shang Dynasty, 1523–1027 B.C. On the back of this piece is an exceptionally fine *t'ao-t'ieh* design. Interpreters have differed as to whether the animal is meant to be eating or protecting the human being, who appears, indeed, to be rather more pleased than discomposed by what is happening. However, the tiger in China, like the jaguar in the Americas, is a beast symbolic of earth, and as such representative of the female, receptive, *yin* principle in nature; the *yang*, the male, being represented by the dragon — as by the Feathered Serpent. And we perceive that in this wonderful piece, symbolic of the sacrifice it was designed to serve, there are serpents of many kinds curling everywhere over the two bodies, together with auspicious spiral, thunder, and labyrinth motifs.

553. Ceramic Classical Recuay jar, found in a stone-lined grave in the Callejón de Huaylas Valley in the north highlands of Peru. Dating from the Early Intermediate Period (c. 200 B.C.–A.D. 600, contemporaneous with the Mochica), this vessel, painted with black negative designs over white and red, is typical of most extant Recuay pottery, both in its style of modeling and in its distinctive decoration.

Enlarged to a world-mythological perspective, the imagery of these alter-ego pieces can be compared to that in Mesopotamian and Indian art where gods are shown riding or standing on their animal vehicles. The animal in such an image is the alter-ego — the operative aspect in time — of the immortal, whose higher aspect is of eternity, disengaged from this field of birth, suffering, and death. Accordingly, where a god is slain by a beast, as was Adonis by a boar, the animal is in fact the alter-ego of the personification slain; representing the active, timebound and thus death-bound aspect of an immortal that has condescended to assume a form and play a mythic or historic role. The animal is thus an agent of the active aspect of the power that appears to be slain.

And so, too, in relation to a human being: the mythic alter-ego, where it appears, is symbolic of the person's active will and effective power in the field of space and time, the endowed person himself (like the Buddha seated beneath *Kīrtti-mukha*) being at once at one with and transcendent of the temporal manifestations.

This is an idea that was implicit in all of the archaic high mythologies where ceremonials of human sacrifice played an important role. It is what was implied in the Early Christian understanding of the Crucifixion, as stated in what has been called "the great Christological passage" of Paul's epistle to the Philippians 2:6–9, where the sacrificed God-Man is celebrated as one.

> *Who, being in the form of God, thought it not robbery to be equal with God:*
>
> *But made himself of no reputation, and took upon him the form of a servant, and was made in the likeness of men:*
>
> *And being found in fashion as a man, he humbled himself, and became obedient unto death, even the death of the cross.*
>
> *Wherefore God also hath highly exalted him, and given him a name which is above every name.*

Augustine states somewhere that Jesus "went to the Cross as a bridegroom to his bride," and so, too, we must suppose, those many who in Antiquity were sacrificed voluntarily must have greeted the grim threshold of their return from time to eternity. There is a famous Shang sacrificial bronze vessel, shown in Figure 551, in which this idea appears to be rendered. It will be noted that on the back of the symbolic beast there is an unmistakable *t'ao-t'ieh*. Figure 552 is a Mochica stirrup-spout jar from the Peruvian North Coast; Figure 553, a representation of the same theme from the Classical Recuay Culture of the Highlands; Figure 554 is a bone club from a Salishan tribe of Washington State; and Figure 555 a Chimú bronze.

552. Polished clay stirrup-jar, showing a man in the consumptive embrace of an anthropomorphic, cayman-like creature, having special mythological significance to its Mochica creators (see **541**).

554. Detail of the head of a bone club, Salish tribe, Washington State.

Whatever the explanation may be, it seems to me to be evident beyond question that, in the monuments of the great were-jaguar god of the Formative Cultures of South and Middle America, features appear that are of a kind with those of the equivalent high gods in Asia. How this came to be, we can only surmise; for the evidence that we have (and we have a lot) has been consistently interpreted in contrary senses by those qualified to judge. However, there can be, in fact, only three possibilities: (1) massive, politically directed influence; (2) completely independent, parallel development; and (3) creative native incorporation of unenforced influences from Asia.

For number (1), it seems to me, there is no evidence whatsoever; against (2), it seems to me, there is too much evidence of analogies to make any judgment of complete independence possible only as an article of blind faith (which for some, I understand, is a requirement of their school). And so, that leaves number (3)—which has been evident, of course, for over a century to most European scholars of this subject. The only remaining questions, then, must be of the period or periods, and of the kinds and extent of the Asian influences—to which the answers separate into two clusters. The first has to do with the period preceding c. 3000 B.C., and the second, with the Formative Period thereafter.

With respect to the first, there is the whole longhouse (maloca) complex to consider, along with the dugout canoe, pearl-oyster shell fishhook, blowgun, panpipe, headhunt, vegetative-reproduction-shifting cultivation, men's secret societies, and the rest. The key myth is of a deity killed and buried, from whose remains the food plants arose; and in the South American rain forests, the myths and rites of this horticultural tradition coalesced with a powerful, shamanic, hunting-and-gathering heritage, to which a lavish exploitation of the abundant hallucinogenic plants of the region had given a special accent.

And with respect, then, to the questions touching the Formative innovations fol-

556. Plan of grave from Sitio Conté; Skeleton 12, the Cacique, has fallen from his seated position.

555. Chimú bronze figurine from North Peru.

lowing c. 3000 B.C. first to be noticed are the Valdivia-Jomon affiliations of the earliest ceramic female figurines in the New World; next the appearance in Ecuador, c. 1500 B.C., of the custom of artificial skull deformation. With the appearance of stone monuments in the Late Formative phase, from c. 1000 B.C., the signs of Asia greatly multiply, with ceramic pillows, ceramic roller stamps and flat stamps, dogs for eating, and, at Chavín de Huántar, an elegant esoteric art, comprising *double-entendre* motifs. At Paracas, on the South Coast, in the barren sandy wastes around the hill called Cerro Colorado, Julio C. Tello, in 1925, excavated a wall-enclosed necropolis, where the tombs were subterranean houses from which he extracted 429 mummy bundles, in an amazingly good state of preservation,

many of the skulls of which had been trephined.[161] The represented culture, contemporary with the Chavín, seems to have been culturally related to the Nazca. And finally, over three thousand miles to the north, on the western coast of Panama, by the Rio Grande de Coclé, in the tombs of a now famous burial ground known as Sitio Conte, from which over two hundred pottery vessels have been recovered, the graves of the Caciques contained, besides the dignitary himself (buried in a sitting posture, as though still in authority), the skeletons of over twenty retainers who had been sent along with him to eternal life (Figure 556).[162]

557. From Sitió Conte, Coclé, Panama, a beaten gold plaque, 6¼" x 6⅝", showing an anthropomorphic deity, depicted as an almost-prototypical "hocker" (German, "squatter"), with cayman-like claws, a spine rendered visible in "x-ray" style, and a headdress comprised of a pair of confronting mouths, with attached eyes and extended fish-like bodies, that some suggest are representations of hammerhead sharks. Miguel Covarrubias notes that the hocker motif "is a circum-Pacific element and is [found in] early China, Malaysia, Melanesia, and Polynesia [see I.2:**324–326**]. It appears with dots or disks between knees and elbows; in series, often losing the head and becoming a decorative pattern; or as hockers with claws, horns, death's head, and visible spinal columns, suggesting that it represents a spirit of the dead.... In some cases (Northwest Coast, Mexico, Peru, Borneo) hockers are flanked by two animals, which [another scholar] identifies with the guardians of the sun god in Mexico and Peru."[73]

Robert von Heine-Geldern (1885–1968), who for some five decades waged an almost solitary battle against the American Anthropological establishment, to demonstrate what, as an Orientalist, he had recognized of Asia in the Americas, identified the South Chinese coastal states of Wu and Yüeh as the probable seats of the influences evident in Chavín. In 333 B.C., however, when Yüeh, which had subdued Wu, was itself subdued, the Chinese transpacific voyaging ceased, and the adventure passed to their southern neighbors in northeastern Indo-China, the Dong-son, ancestors of the present day Vietnamese. "Traces of Dong-son influence are far more numerous in South America," Heine-Geldern claimed, "than those of Chinese influence. One finds them throughout the Andean region from Panama to northern Chile and northwestern Argentina....The trans-Pacific voyages of the Dong-son people may have come to an end as the result of the final conquest of Tonkin and North Annam by China toward the middle of the first century A.D."[163] Later Chinese evidences in Mexico and Guatemala suggest, however, to quote Heine-Geldern again, that the relations of China with Mesoamerica either continued after the fall of Yüeh or, as seems more likely, were resumed under the Han. They may have terminated as a result of the political troubles which, in the third century A.D., culminated in the fall of the Han dynasty."[164]

In working out the links between Asia and Mesoamerica, Heine-Geldern collaborated in research with Gordon F. Eckholm of the American Museum of Natural History, and, as he tells: "we experienced one surprise after another. The architecture and the art, the religious symbols, the cosmological ideas, the institutions of the states and the royal courts, the insignia of kings and dignitaries, even the games—all this to an unsuspected and overwhelming extent—reminded us of the civilizations of Southeast Asia and India."[165]

Although the high-civilization Mayan-Toltec-Aztec development cannot be dealt with properly in this context until we review the origins of writing and of solar and lunar calendric calculations in the Old World, the unfoldment of Peruvian civilizations—developed without writing and without any calendar, so far as we know—has been considered as a special curiosity, not matched anywhere in the histories of the higher civilizations: namely, as a relatively isolated development out of an initial Formative impulse of a preliterate civilization that can be compared to Egypt in the wonder of its monuments and with Rome in the organization of its culminating empire. Only toward the end, in the shaping of the Inca empire, do we find unmistakable evidence of a deliberate *political* emphasis in the shaping and enforcement of a mythology. There must have been something of the kind involved, also, in the structuring of the empire of Chimú. From what has been learned, on the other hand, of the period of Chavín de Huántar, there were evidently no fortifications, there was little weaponry, and of the possible social applications of the symbolized mythology, we have no evidence. The influence of the culture was nevertheless extensive and, in the full sense of the term, Formative. Bushnell describes it as "a religious cult which required imposing buildings...together with an elaborate form of pottery for ceremonial use...."[166]

"All the known sites of this period," he points out, "belong to some form of the Chavín Culture, of which the north coastal aspect is sometimes called Cupisnique. There is reason to believe that the new features were introduced by an immigrant people. The older inhabitants continued to live on and near some of their original sites, where their presence is shown by the persistence of the old types of utilitarian pottery, but the newcomers imposed their religious system on them."[167]

By what means imposed, no one can say; neither, indeed, whether it was imposed or, rather, caught on. Regardless, and notwithstanding all the historical obscurities surrounding its sudden appearance, the main impression is of a new level of metaphysical insight, which crystallized (c. 1000 B.C.) over a large part of the culture field of Peru, not only as an art form and local manner of life, but as the founding inspiration of a civilization. The precise whence and wherefore of it all remain to be learned.

South America: Languages and Distribution

	Arawakan
	Cariban
	Macro-Chibchan
	Macro-Ge
	Macro-Pano-Tacanan
	Quechumaran
	Tucanoan
	Tupian
	Isolates and unrelated languages
	Unclassified languages

CENTRAL
AMERICA

Caribbean   Sea

ATLANTIC OCEAN

Equator

Orinoco   River

Magdalena

Putumayo

Negro   River

Amazon   River

Ucayali

Tapajós

Madeira

Tocantins

Araguaia

São Francisco

Mamoré

Pilcomayo

Paraguay

Paraná

PACIFIC OCEAN

Tropic of Capricorn

Equator

Tropic of Capricorn

Strait of
Magellan

Map 43.

387

APPENDIX

ENDNOTES

AGRICULTURAL DEVELOPMENTS IN THE MESOAMERICAN MATRIX

[1]Susan Eger and Peter R. Collings, "Huichol Women's Art," in Kathleen Berrin, ed., Art of the Huichol Indians, Fine Arts Museums of San Francisco (New York: Harry N. Abrams, 1978), p. 35.

[2]Charles C. Di Peso, "Macaws…Crotals… and Trumpet Shells," Early Man, vol. 2, no. 3 (Autumn 1980), p. 5.

[3]Ibid., pp. 5 and 8.

[4]Ibid., p. 8.

[5]Ibid.

[6]Ibid., p. 11.

[7]Richard B. Woodbury, "Artifacts in the Guatemalan Highlands," in Robert Wauchope, ed., Handbook of Middle American Indians, 13 vols. (Austin: University of Texas Press, 1964–73), vol. 2, p. 169. The whole question of the hallucinogen in relation to religious visionary cults was introduced to modern anthropology largely through the researches of R. Gordon Wasson. See, for instance, V. P. Wasson and R. G. Wasson, Mushrooms Russia & History, 2 vols. (New York: Pantheon Books, 1957).

[8]Di Peso, op. cit., p. 11.

[9]Ibid., pp. 21–22.

[10]Ibid., p. 8.

[11]Richard I. Ford, "'Artifacts' That Grew: Their Roots in Mexico," Early Man, vol. 2, no. 3 (Autumn 1980), pp. 22–23. For detailed analyses of the matters here briefly reviewed, see J. Charles Kelley, "Mesoamerica and the Southwestern United States," and James B. Griffin, "Mesoamerica and the Eastern United States in Prehistoric Times," both in Wauchope, op. cit., vol. 4, pp. 95–110 and 111–131.

[12]Victor Wolfgang von Hagen, ed., The Incas of Pedro de Cieza de Leon (Norman: University of Oklahoma Press, 1959), opening maps.

[13]Oswald Spengler, Der Untergang des Abendlandes, 2 vols. (Munich: C. H. Beck'sche Verlagsbuchhandlung, vol. 1 in 1918, vol. 2 in 1922), vol. 2, pp. 51–52. Translation (slightly modified) by Charles Francis Atkinson, Decline of the West (New York: Alfred A. Knopf, 1926–1928), vol. 2, pp. 43–44.

[14]Jacques Soustelle, The Olmecs: The Oldest Civilization in Mexico, trans. Helen B. Lane (Garden City, N.Y.: Doubleday and Company, Inc., 1984), p. 1.

[15]Ibid., p. 25.

[16]Philip Drucker, Robert F. Heizer, and Robert Squier, Excavations at La Venta, Tabasco, 1955, Smithsonian Institution Bureau of American Ethnology Bulletin 170 (Washington, D.C., 1959), pp. 152–159 and plates 30–36.

[17]Ibid., pp. 93–95 and plates 14–17.

[18]Matthew W. Stirling, "Stone Monuments of the Rio Chiquito, Veracruz, Mexico," in Anthropological Papers, nos. 43–48, Smithsonian Institution Bureau of American Ethnology Bulletin 157 (Washington, D.C., 1955), pp. 8 and 19–20; also plates 2, 25, and 26.

[19]Ignacio Bernal, The Olmec World, trans. Doris Heyden and Fernando Horcasitas (Berkeley: University of California Press, 1969), p. 58.

[20]Michael D. Coe, "Olmec Jaguars and Olmec Kings," in Elizabeth P. Benson, ed., The Cult of the Feline, Dumbarton Oaks Research Library and Collections (Washington, D.C.: Trustees for Harvard University, 1972), pp. 10–11.

[21]Peter T. Furst, "The Olmec Were-Jaguar Motif in the Light of Ethnological Reality," in Elizabeth P. Benson, ed., Dumbarton Oaks Conference on the Olmec, October 28th and 29th, 1967, Dumbarton Oaks Research Library and Collection (Washington, D.C.: Trustees for Harvard University, 1968), p. 148.

[22]Soustelle, op. cit., p. 145.

[23]Bernal, op. cit., pp. 107–110.

[24]See, for example, Kent V. Flannery, "The Olmec and the Valley of Oaxaca: A Model for Inter-regional Interaction in Formative Times," in Benson, ed., Dumbarton Oaks Conference on the Olmec, pp. 79–177; also, David C. Grove, The Olmec Paintings of Oxtotitlan Cave, Guerrero, Mexico, Studies in Pre-Columbian Art and Archaeology Number 6 (Washington, D.C.: Dumbarton Oaks, Trustees for Harvard University, 1970), p. 32.

[25]Miguel Covarrubias, Indian Art of Mexico and Central America (New York: Alfred A. Knopf, 1957), p. 18.

[26]Paul Tolstoy, "Utilitarian Artifacts of Central Mexico," in Wauchope, op. cit., vol. 10, p. 271.

[27]Soustelle, op. cit., pp. 122–134.

[28]Ibid., p. 134.

[29]Ignacio Bernal, "Views of Olmec Culture," in Benson, ed., Dumbarton Oaks Conference on the Olmec, p. 137.

[30]Flannery, op. cit., pp. 98–102.

[31]From William H. Sears, "Seaborne Contacts between Early Cultures in the Lower Southeastern United States and Middle through South America," in Elizabeth P. Benson, ed., The Sea in the Pre-Columbian World, Dumbarton Oaks Research Library and Collections (Washington, D.C.: Trustees for Harvard University, 1977), p. 8.

[32]Gordon R. Willey, in discussion of Robert F. Heizer, "New Observations on La Venta," in Benson, ed., Dumbarton Oaks Conference on the Olmec, p. 40.

[33]Sears, "Seaborne Contacts," p. 9.

[34]Soustelle, op. cit., pp. 79–80.

[35]Ibid., p. 150.

AGRICULTURAL RITES AND MYTHS OF MIDDLE AMERICA

[1]Paul C. Mangelsdorf, Richard S. MacNeish, and Gordon R. Willey, "Origins of Agriculture in Middle America," in Robert Wauchope, ed., Handbook of Middle American Indians, 13 vols. (Austin: University of Texas Press, 1964–73), vol. 1, pp. 431–432.

[2]Carl O. Sauer, Agricultural Origins and Dispersals (New York: American Geographical Society, 1952), reedited and published with additional chapters as Seeds, Spades, Hearths & Herds: The Domestication of Animals and Foodstuffs (Cambridge, Mass.: M.I.T. Press, 1969), 2nd ed., p. 64.

[3]Gordon Vivian and Paul Reiter, The Great Kivas of Chaco Canyon and Their Relationships, The School of American Research Monograph 22 (Albuquerque: University of New Mexico Press, 1965), p.97, citing J. D. Jennings and E. K. Reed, eds., "Seminars in Archaeology, The American Southwest: A Problem in Cultural Isolation," in American Antiquity, vol. 22, no. 2, part 2, p. 86.

[4]Natalie Curtis, The Indians' Book: An Offering by the American Indians of Indian Lore, Musical and Narrative, to Form a Record of the Songs and Legends of Their Race (New York: Harper & Bros., 1907), p. 314.

[5]Vivian and Reiter, op. cit., pp. 97–99.

[6]Vivian and Reiter, op. cit., citing Gordon C. Baldwin, "A Basket Maker III Sandal Tablet," Southwestern Lore, vol. V, p. 49.

[7]Vivian and Reiter, op. cit., citing Paul S. Martin and John B. Rinaldo, Modified Basket Maker Sites in the Ackman-Lowry Area, Southwestern Colorado, Field Museum of Natural History Anthropological Series, vol. 23, no. 3 (1939), pp. 350–359.

[8]Vivian and Reiter, op. cit., p. 63.

[9]Stephen C. McCluskey, "The Astronomy of the Hopi Indians," Journal for the History of Astronomy, vol. 8 (October 1977), pp. 177–178.

[10]Anna Sofaer, Volker Zinser, and Rolf M. Sinclair, "A Unique Solar Marking Construct," Science, vol. 206, no. 4416 (October 19, 1979), pp. 283–291.

[11]Anna Sofaer, Rolf M. Sinclair, and L. E. Doggett, "Lunar Markings on Fajada Butte," in A. F. Aveni, ed., Archaeoastronomy in the New World (Cambridge: Cambridge University Press, 1982), pp. 169–186.

[12]Rolf M. Sinclair, Anna Sofaer, J. J. McCann, and J. J. McCann Jr., "Marking of Major Lunar Standstill at the Three-Slab Site on Fajada Butte," Bulletin of the American Astronomical Society, vol. 19, no. 4 (1987), p. 1043.

[13]Sofaer, Zinser, and Sinclair, op. cit., pp. 283–291; also Kendrick Frazier, "The Anasazi Sun Dagger," Science 80, vol. 1, no. 1 (November and December 1979), pp. 56–67.

[14]Anna Sofaer, M. P. Marshall, and R. Sinclair, "The Great North Road: A Cosmographic Expression of the Chaco Culture of New Mexico," in A. F. Aveni, ed., World Archaeoastronomy (Cambridge: Cambridge University Press, 1989).

[15]Anna Sofaer and Rolf Sinclair, "Astronomic and Related Patterning in the Architecture of the Chaco Culture ot New Mexico," Bulletin of the American Astronomical Society, vol. 18, no. 4 (1986), pp. 1044–1045.

[16]Recent findings by Anna Sofaer and her colleagues have shown that eighteen major Chaco buildings located across two thousand square miles were symmetrically and possibly astronomically organized about the ceremonial center of Chaco Canyon. See Anna Sofaer, Rolf Sinclair, and K. Williams, "A Regional Pattern in the Architecture of Chaco Culture of New Mexico and Its Astronomical Implications," Bulletin of the American Astronomical Society, vol. 19, no. 4 (1987), p. 1044.

[17]Frank Waters, Book of the Hopi (New York: Ballantine Books, 1969), pp. 188–254. Also, McCluskey, op. cit., pp. 176–191.

[18]Florence M. Hawley, "Pueblo Social Organization As a Lead to Pueblo History," American Anthropologist, vol. 39 (1937), pp. 504–522.

[19]Waters, op. cit., p. 168.

[20]Ibid., p. 183.

[21]Ibid., p. 170.

[22]Ibid., pp. 169–173.

[23]Ibid., pp. 168–179 and 422.

[24]See Alexander M. Stephen, Hopi Journal, Elsie Clew Parsons, ed., 2 vols., Columbia University Contributions to Anthropology, vol. 23, in two parts (New York: Columbia University Press, 1936), vol. 2, pp. 981–982. Stephen, whose great two-volume journal is a classic source for Hopi lore, lived among the Navaho and Hopi from about 1881 to the year of this death in 1894. His account of Wúwuchim, as observed at Walpi in 1891 (vol. 2, pp. 957–993) differs greatly in detail from Frank Waters' observations at Oraibi, over half a century later. Unfortunately, he missed the kiva ceremony of the Night of the Washing of the Hair altogether. As he laments: "I have missed the whole of the novice initiation" (p. 978).

[25]Waters, op. cit., pp. 185–187.

[26]Waters, op. cit., pp. 185 and 188–191. Elsie Clew Parsons, who watched the arrival of Soyál Kachina at Oraibi in 1920 was told, not that the kachina was tottering like a child, but that "He acts like an old man and wears old clothes because he is an old kachina" (in Stephen, op. cit., vol. 1, pp. 3–4, note 1). Waters' interpreters, on the other hand, declared that such an interpretation "negates the meaning of the whole Soyál ceremony" (p. 189, note 3). At Walpi, where Stephen observed the festival in 1982, the first kachina to appear was not Soyál, but Au'halani Kachina with his two sisters, Blue Corn Girl and Yellow Corn Girl (the female roles enacted by men); and here, too, the interpretation given was that the costume was "very old." Stephen comments, "and it surely looks it" (Stephen, op. cit., vol. 1, pp. 34–35).

[27]Waters, op. cit., p. 188.

[28]Ibid., pp. 188–201.

[29]Ibid., pp. 213–230.

[30]Ibid., p. 247.

[31]Ibid., p. 250.

[32]Ibid.

[33]Ibid., p. 255.

[34]James G. Frazer, The Golden Bough, one-volume edition (New York: The Macmillan Company, 1922), pp. 11–37.

[35]Waters, op. cit., pp. 272–273 and 448.

[36]Ibid., p. 277.

[37]Ibid., pp. 271–276.

[38]Ibid., pp. 257–265.

[39]Ibid., pp. 283–287.

[40]Ibid., pp. 283–291.

[41]Betty Bell, "Archaeology of Nayarit, Jalisco, and Colima," in Wauchope, op. cit., vol. 2, p. 695.

[42]Carl O. Sauer and D. D. Brand, "Aztatlan: Prehistoric Frontier on the Pacific Coast," Ibero-Americana, no. 1 (Berkeley: University of California Press, 1932), p. 41.

[43]Bell, op. cit., pp. 695–696.

[44]Peter T. Furst, "The Art of 'Being Huichol'," in Kathleen Berrin, ed., Art of the Huichol Indians (New York: Harry N. Abrams, Inc., 1978), a catalogue published in conjunction with an exhibition organized by the Fine Arts Museums of San Francisco, p. 22.

[45]Barbara G. Myerhoff, Peyote Hunt: The Sacred Journey of the Huichol Indians (Ithaca: Cornell University Press, 1974), pp. 125–126.

[46]See ibid., pp. 84–88 and 199–204, for a discussion of these mercurial figures.

[47]Ibid., pp. 130–132.

[48]Ibid., p. 133.

[49]Ibid., pp. 147–148.

[50]Barbara G. Myerhoff, "Peyote and the Mystic Vision," in Berrin, op. cit., p. 57.

[51]Myerhoff, Peyote Hunt, pp. 123–124.

[52]Ibid., p. 166.

[53]The account is greatly reduced from Myerhoff, Peyote Hunt, pp. 118–172.

[54]Myerhoff, Peyote Hunt, pp. 172–173.

[55]Ibid., p. 174.

[56]Ibid., p. 175, note 20.

[57]Susan Eger and Peter R. Collings, "Huichol Women's Art," in Berrin, op. cit., p. 44.

[58]Ibid.

[59]Ibid., p. 37.

[60]Ibid.; also Furst, op. cit., p. 22.

[61]Eger and Collings, op. cit., pp. 47 and 49.

[62]Ibid., p. 46.

[63]Ibid.

[64]Prem Das, "Initiation by a Huichol Shaman," in Berrin, op. cit., p. 138.

[65]Joseph Campbell, The Hero with a Thousand Faces, Bollingen Series XVII (Princeton: Princeton University Press, 1962).

[66]Furst, op. cit., p. 33.

[67]Ibid.

[68]Ibid., pp. 33–34.

[69]Ibid., p. 33.

[70]The phrase, "transparent to transcendence," I have borrowed from Karlfried Graf Durckheim, Erlebnis und Wandlung (Munich: Otto Wilhelm Barth Verlag, 1978).

[71]Myerhoff, Peyote Hunt, p. 210.

[72]Myerhoff, Peyote Hunt, pp. 210–213, adapted.

[73]"Journal of the First Voyage of Columbus," translated and edited, with an introduction and notes, by Cecil Jane, The Voyages of Christopher Columbus (London: The Argonaut Press, 1930), pp. 148–149. This so-called "Journal" is actually a redaction by Bartolomé de Las Casas of an already-edited version of the original account sent by Columbus to the king and queen, which original has been lost.

[74]The Bull "Inter Cetera" was issued by the newly elected Pope Alexander VI (Rodrigo Borgia) on May 4, 1493, on terms highly favorable to the Castillian crown. Several years later at the Treaty of Tordesillas, the line dividing Spanish and Portuguese hegemony in the New World was moved westward and Portugal gained possession of what is now Brazil. The translation is from Richard Eden, The History of Trauayle in the West and East Indies, and Other Countreys Lying Eyther Way, towardes the Fruitfull and Ryche Mollaccaes (London, 1577), pp. 455–457, abridged.

[75]Bartolomé de Las Casas, Historia de las Indias, ed. Agustín Millares Carlo, 3 vols. (Mexico: Fondo de Cultura Económica, 1951). The original manuscript was completed by Las Casas in Madrid in 1561, but was not printed until 1875–1876.

[76]Bartolomé de Las Casas, Brevíssima Relación de la Destrucción de las Indias (Mexico: Libros Luciernaga, 1957). Finished by Las Casas in 1542, and first printed in Seville in 1552.

[77]Andrés Bernáldez, Historia de los reyes católicos, Don Fernando y Doña Isobel (Seville: Sociedad Bibliófilos Andeluces, 1st Series, 1978), chapter 118; translation from Jane, op. cit., p. 314.

[78]Ramón Pane, Relación acerca de las antigüedades de los indios, ed. José Juan Arrom (Mexico: Siglo Veintiuno, 1977). Pane's account can be found in Hernando Colon [Ferdinand Columbus], Historie…della vita e de' fatti dell' Ammariglio D. Christoforo Colombo (Venice, 1571). A good English translation is by Benjamin Keen, The Life of…Columbus by His Son Ferdinand (New Brunswick, N. J.: Rutgers University Press, 1959).

[79]Bartolomé de Las Casas, Apologética historia sumaria cuanto a las cualidades, disposición, descripción, cielo y suelo destas tierras, y condiciones naturales, policías, repúblicas, manera de vivir e costumbres de las gentes destas Indias occidentales y meridionales cuyo imperio soberano pertenece a los Reyes de Castilla, ed. Edmundo O'Gorman, 2 vols. (Mexico: Universidad Nacional Autónoma de México, Insituto de Investigaciones Históricas, 1967). Completed by Las Casas in 1560 and first printed in full in Madrid in 1909.

[80]José Juan Arrom, Mitología y Artes Prehispánicas de las Antillas (Mexico: Siglo Veintiuno Editores, 1975), p. 16.

[81]Ibid., p. 19, citing Pane, chapter 1.

[82]Arrom, op. cit., pp. 19–22.

83Ibid., p. 22, citing Pane, chapter 19.

84See, for example, Jesse Walter Fewkes, "The Aborigines of Porto Rico and Neighboring Islands," Twenty-fifth Annual Report of the Bureau of American Ethnology (Washington, D.C., 1907), pp. 3–220, especially pp. 111–132, and plates xxxi–liii; and Frederick J. Dockstader, Indian Art in Middle America (Greenwich, Conn.: New York Graphic Society, 1964), caption to figure 199.

85Arrom, op. cit., pp. 22–30.

86Ibid., p. 26.

87Ibid., p. 44, citing Pane, parraio preliminar.

88Arrom, op. cit., p. 44, note 3, citing Las Casas, Apologética historia, chapter 120.

89Arrom, op. cit., pp. 44 47, citing Daniel G. Brinton, "The Arawak Language of Guiana in Its Linguistic and Ethnological Relations," Transactions of the American Philosophical Society, vol. XIV (1871), p. 444.

90Arrom, op. cit., p. 47.

91Arrom, op. cit., pp. 47–48, citing Vida de almirante don Cristobal Colon por su hijo Fernando, chapter 62.

92Arrom, op. cit., p. 55, citing Pane, chapter 11.

93Arrom, op. cit., pp. 55–56.

94Ibid., pp. 55–57.

95Ibid., p. 60.

96Frazer, op. cit., p. 436.

97Arrom, op. cit., pp. 128–129.

98Matthew 14:17 ff., Mark 6:38 ff., Luke 9:13 ff., John 6:9 ff.

99Arrom, op. cit., p. 129.

100Ibid., p. 137.

101Ibid., pp. 126–128, citing Pane, chapters 9–11.

102Arrom, op. cit., p. 142, citing Niels Fock, Waiwai, Religion and Society of an Amazonian Tribe (Copenhagen: National Museum, 1963), p. 47.

103Arrom, op. cit., p. 143.

104Julian H. Steward, ed., Handbook of South American Indians, 7 vols., Smithsonian Institution, Bureau of American Ethnology Bulletin 143 (Washington, D.C., 1944–1950); reissued in New York by Cooper Square Publishers, 1963.

105Ibid., vol. 4, p. 2.

106Ibid., p. 23.

107Ibid., p. 41; also, Irving Rouse, "The Ciboney," in ibid., pp. 497–503; and Pedro Garcia Valdes, "The Ethnogeography of the Ciboney," in ibid., pp. 503–505. The lengths of these last two articles are due to the number of culture traits enumerated and described which the Ciboney did not possess.

108Steward, op. cit., pp. 6–7.

109Rouse, "The Ciboney," pp. 533–534.

110Hartley Burr Alexander, Latin-American Mythology, in Louis Herbert Gray, ed., The Mythology of All Races, 13 vols. (Boston: Marshall Jones Co., 1920), vol. XI, p. 32.

111Girolamo Benzoni, Historia del Mondo Nuovo (Venice, 1565), translated and edited by W. H. Smyth as History of the New World by Girolamo of Milan: Shewing his Travels in America from A.D. 1541 to 1556; with Some Particulars of the Island of Canary (London, 1857).

112Alexander, op. cit., pp. 33–34, translating from Francisco López de Gómara, "Historia de las Indias," in A. Gonzales de Barcia, ed., Historiadores primitivas de las Indias Occidentales (Madrid, 1749).

113Alexander, op. cit., pp. 33–34, translating from Francisco López de Gómara, "Hispania Victrix. Primera y segunda parte de la historia general de las Indias," in Gonzales de Barcia, op. cit.

114Alexander, op. cit., p. 33.

115Irving Rouse, "The Carib," in Steward, op. cit., vol. 4, p. 558.

116Ibid., p. 560.

117Ibid., p. 558.

118Ibid., pp. 558–559.

119Alexander, op. cit., p. 39.

120Rouse, "The Carib," p. 548.

121See ibid., p. 549, and Alexander, op. cit., p. 352, for the catalogues of their sources.

122Diodorus Siculus, 5.14.1–3. See C. H. Oldfather, ed. and trans., Diodorus of Sicily, 12 vols. (Cambridge: Harvard University Press, 1939), vol. 3, p. 135.

123Strabo 3.4.17. See Horace Leonard Jones, ed. and trans., The Geography of Strabo, 8 vols. (Cambridge, Mass.: Harvard University Press, 1917), vol. 2, p. 113.

124E. Sidney Hartland, "Birth," in James Hastings, ed., Encyclopedia of Religion and Ethics (New York: Charles Scribner's Sons, 1928), vol. 2, pp. 635–636.

123Strabo 3.4.17. See Horace Leonard Jones, ed. and trans., The Geography of Strabo, 8 vols. (Cambridge: Harvard University Press, 1917), vol. 2, p. 113.

124E. Sidney Hartland, "Birth," in James Hastings, ed., Encyclopedia of Religion and Ethics (New York: Charles Scribner's Sons, 1928); vol. 2 pp. 635–636.

125Ibid., p. 636.

126Rouse, "The Carib," p. 557. Rouse comments: "The accounts of the couvade vary considerably from source to source. The above version is taken largely from [John] Davies [The History of the Caribby, London, 1666], pp. 336–338, with supplemental data from [Père de] La Borde [Voyage qui contient un relation exacte de l'origine, moeurs, coûtumes, réligion, guerres et voyages des Caraibes, sauvages des isles Antilles de l'Amérique, faite par le Sieur de la Borde, employé à la conversion des Caraïbes, et tirée du cabinet de Monsieur Blondel. A. Leide, Chez P. van de Aa, 1704. In Louis Hennepin, Voyage ou Nouvelle découverte, pp. 517–604. Amsterdam], 1886, pp. 249–250."

127Rouse, "The Carib," pp. 553–554.

SOUTH AMERICAN AGRICULTURAL RITES AND MYTHS

1Hartley Burr Alexander, Latin-American Mythology, in Louis Herbert Gray, ed., The Mythology of All Races, 13 vols. (Boston: Marshall Jones Co., 1920), vol. XI, pp. 38–39.

2"Satanam aliosque spiritus malignos, qui ad perditionem animarum pervagantus in mundo," from prayers at the foot of the altar at the conclusion of holy mass. Dom Gaspar Lefebure, Daily Missal (Abbey of St. Andre, Hophem-near-Bruges, Imprimatur, 1934), p. 78.

3The following is a radical abridgement of a few selected episodes from Marc de Civrieux, Watunna: Mitología Makiritare (Caracas: Monte Avila Editores, C.A., 1970), translated, with an introduction and glossary, by David M. Guss as Watunna: An Orinoco Creation Cycle (San Francisco: North Point Press, 1980).

4Guss, Watunna, pp. 21–22.

5Ibid., p. 28.

6Ibid.

7Ibid., pp. 28–36.

8Ibid., pp. 128–135.

9Ibid., pp. 47–50.

10Ibid., pp. 51–53.

11Ibid., pp. 55–61.

12Ibid., pp. 66–68.

13Ibid., pp. 80–82.

14Ibid., pp. 143–146.

15Ibid., pp. 147–153.

16Ibid., p. 161.

17Selections, greatly abridged and recast, from Gerardo Reichel-Dolmatoff, Amazonian Cosmos (Chicago: University of Chicago Press, 1971).

18Ibid., pp. 25–27 and 55–57.

19Ibid., pp. 28–29.

20Ibid., p. 26.

21Ibid., pp. 27–28.

22Ibid., p. 72.

23Ibid., pp. 29–30.

24Ibid., pp. 30–32.

25Ibid., p. 34.

26Ibid., p. 75.

27Ibid., pp. 36–37.

28Ibid., p. 172.

29Ibid.

30Ibid., pp. 172–174, 24–25.

31Ibid., p. 106.

32Ibid.

33Ibid., p. 135.

34Ibid., pp. 136–138.

35Ibid., p. 106.

36Ibid., pp. 138–139.

37Ibid., p. 139, note 6.

38Ibid., p. 127.

39Ibid., pp. 129–130.

40Ibid., pp. 64 and 130.

41Ibid., p. 81.

42Ibid., pp. 83–84.

43Ibid., p. 82.

44Ibid., pp. 82–83.

45Theodor Koch-Grünberg, Zwei Jahren unter den Indianern: Reisen in Nordwest Brazilien, 1903–1905, 2 vols. (Berlin: Ernst Wasmuth A.-G., 1909, 1910), vol. 2, pp. 292–293.

46Ibid., p. 293.

47Ibid., p. 293, note 317.

48Robert H. Lowie, "The Tropical Forests: An Introduction," in Julian H. Steward, ed., Handbook of South American Indians, 7 vols., Bureau of American Ethnology Bulletin 143 (Washington, D.C., 1944–48), vol. 3, "The Tropical Forest Tribes," pp. 1–56. 56.

49Ibid., p. 1.

50Stephen Hugh-Jones, The Palm and the Pleiades: Initiation and Cosmology in Northwest Amazonia, Cambridge Studies in Social Anthropology No. 24 (Cambridge: Cambridge University Press, 1979).

51Christine Hugh-Jones, From the Milk River: Spatial and Temporal Processes in Northwest Amazonia, Cambridge Studies in Social Anthropology No. 26 (Cambridge: Cambridge University Press, 1979).

52Christine Hugh-Jones, op. cit., pp. 6–9.

53Stephen Hugh-Jones, op. cit., p. 25.

54Ibid., pp. xiii–xiv.

55Ibid., p. 9.

56Ibid.

57Ibid., pp. 9–10.

58Ibid.

59Ibid., pp. 37–38.

60Ibid., p. 131.

61Ibid., p. 132.

62Ibid.

63Ibid.

64Ibid., p. 84. The whole above account is a radical abridgement of S. Hugh-Jones, op. cit., pp. 46–84.

65Emilio Estrada, Las Culturas pre-clássicas, formativas o arcaicas de Ecuador (Guayaquil: Publicación de Museo Victor Emilio Estrada, no. 5, 1958).

66Betty J. Meggers, "Did Japanese Fishermen Really Reach Ecuador 5,000 Years Ago?" Early Man, vol. 2, no. 4 (Winter 1980), p. 16.

67Ibid.

68Emilio Estrada, Betty J. Meggers, and Clifford Evans, "Possible transpacific contact on the coast of Ecuador," Science, no. 135 (1962), pp. 371–372.

69Meggers, op. cit., p. 17.

70Betty J. Meggers, Clifford Evans, and Emilio Estrada, Early Formative Period of Coastal Ecuador: The Valdivia and Machalilla Phases (Washington, D.C.: Smithsonian Institution Press, 1965).

71Ibid., p. 167.

72Chester S. Chard, Northeast Asia in Prehistory (Madison: University of Wisconsin Press, 1974), p. 111.

73Ibid.

74Ibid., p. 118.

75Ibid., p. 116.

76Ibid., p. 118.

77Edwin Doran, "The Sailing Raft as a Great Tradition," in Carroll L. Riley, J. Charles Kelly, Campbell W. Pennington, and Robert L. Rands, eds., Man across the Sea: Problems of Pre-Columbian Contacts (Austin: University of Texas Press, 1971), p. 131, citing R. H. Lane-Poole, "Primitive Craft and Medieval Rigs in South America," Mariner's Mirror, vol. 26 (1940), pp. 333–338; and p. 133, note 2, citing J. Hornell, Water Transport: Origins and Early Evolution (Cambridge, U.K., 1946).

78Stephen C. Jett, "Pre-Columbian Transoceanic Contacts," in Jesse D. Jennings, ed., Ancient Native Americans (San Francisco: W. H. Freeman, 1978), chapter 13, p. 606, citing his own paper, "Malaysia and Tropical America: Some Racial, Cultural, and Ethnobotanical Comparisons," Congreso Internacional de Americanistas, Actas y Memorias, vol. 37, no. 4 (1968), pp. 133–137.

79Jett, "Pre-Columbian Transoceanic Contacts," p. 606, citing his own paper, "The Development and Distribution of the Blowgun," Annals of the Association of American Geographers, vol. 60, no. 4 (1971), pp. 662–668.

80Jett, "Pre-Columbian Transoceanic Contacts," p. 606, citing Marcos Fulop, "Aspectos de la Cultura Tukana: Cosmología," Revista Colombiana de Antropología, vol. 3 (1954), pp. 97–137.

81Jett, "Pre-Columbian Transoceanic Contacts," p. 606.

82Ibid.

83J. Merrien, trans. J. H. Watkins, Lonely Voyages (New York: Putnam, 1954).

84Stephen C. Jett, "Diffusion versus Independent Development," in Riley et al., op. cit., pp. 17–18, abridged.

85Charles Wolcott Brooks, "Reports of Japanese Vessels Wrecked in the North Pacific, from the Earliest Records to the Present Time," Proceedings of the California Academy of Sciences, vol. 6 (1875), pp. 50–66.

86Robert von Heine-Geldern, "The Origin of Ancient Civilizations," Diogenes, vol. 13 (1956), p. 95.

87Jett, "Pre-Columbian Transoceanic Contacts," p. 603, citing Kuang-chih Chang, "Radiocarbon Dates from China: Some Initial Interpretations," Current Anthropology, pp. 525–528.

88Jett, "Pre-Columbian Transoceanic Contacts," p. 604, citing Paul Tolstoy, "Cultural Parallels between Southeast Asia and Mesoamerica in the Manufacture of Bark Cloth," Transactions of the New York Academy of Sciences, Series 2, vol. 25, no. 6 (1963), pp. 646–662.

89George F. Carter, "Pre-Columbian Chickens in America," in Riley et al., op. cit., p. 215.

90As reported in the San Francisco Chronicle (United Press International), Monday, December 1, 1980, p. 8.

91Meggers, op. cit., p. 16.

92Ibid.

93James A. Ford, A Comparison of Formative Cultures in the Americas (Washington, D.C.: Smithsonian Institution Press, 1969), charts 10, 3, 5, and 2.

94Betty J. Meggers, personal correspondence, 1982. She notes that "Ford refers especially to the ring plan. There are earlier ceremonial constructions on the coast of Peru."

95For a discussion of the value of calibrated versus uncalibrated dates see David H. Thomas, Archaeology (New York: Holt, Rinehart and Winston, 1979), s.v. "Calibration"; for a general discussion of dating techniques, see Ian Tattersall, Eric Delson, and John Van Couvering, eds., Encyclopedia of Human Evolution and Prehistory (New York: Garland Publishing, 1988), s.v. "Geochronometry."

96Clinton R. Edwards, "Commentary" in Riley et al., op. cit., Section II, p. 298.

97Jorge G. Marcos, Donald Lathrap, and James A. Zeidler, "Ancient Ecuador Revisited," Field Museum Bulletin (June 1976), pp. 3–8.

98The earlier start is suggested by Lathrap in his article on Formative Ecuador in Ancient Ecuador: Culture, Clay and Creativity 3000–300 B.C., catalogue of an exhibit organized by the Field Museum of Natural History, April 18 to August 5, 1975.

99Lathrap, Ancient Ecuador, p. 13.

100Ibid., p. 19.

101Ibid., p. 43.

102Meggers, personal correspondence, 1982.

103Lathrap, Ancient Ecuador, p. 21.

104Ibid., p. 43.

105Ibid., p. 45.

106Ibid., pp. 45 and 47.

107Ibid., p. 43.

108von Heine-Geldern, op. cit., p. 96.

109Juan R. Munizaga, "Skeletal Remains from Sites of Valdivia and Machalilla Phases," in Meggers, Evans, and Estrada, Early Formative Period of Ecuador, appendix 2, p. 228.

110Meggers, Evans, and Estrada, Early Formative Period of Ecuador, p. 39.

111Lathrap, Ancient Ecuador, pp. 22–23.

112Ibid., p. 73.

113John H. Rowe, "Diffusion and Archaeology," American Antiquity, vol. 31 (1966), p. 339.

114Lathrap, Ancient Ecuador, p. 27.

115S. G. Stephens, "Some Problems of Interpreting Transoceanic Dispersal of the New World Cottons," in Riley et al., op. cit., pp. 401 and 413, abridged.

116Ibid., p. 406.

117Ibid., p. 407.

118Meggars, Evans, and Estrada, Early Formative Period of Ecuador, p. 110.

119Munizaga, op. cit., pp. 232–233.

120Ibid., p. 229.

121Marcos, Lathrap, and Zeidler, "Ancient Ecuador Revisited," p. 4.

122Lathrap, Ancient Ecuador, p. 34.

123Ibid., pp. 23–25. Others suggest a later date: see Emilio Estrada and Betty J. Meggers, "A Complex of Traits of Probable Transpacific Origin on the Coast of Ecuador," American Anthropologist, vol. 63, no. 5 (October 1961), pp. 914–920.

124Garry J. Tee, "Evidence for the Chinese Origin of the Jaguar Motif in Chavín Art," Asian Perspectives, vol. XXI, no. 1 (1980), pp. 27–29.

125Garcilasso Inca de la Vega, *Royal Commentaries of the Incas*, Part I (Lisbon, 1609) and Part 2 (Cordova, 1616).

126The journals of Pedro de Cieza de León were published according to the following schedule (the titles are here given in English): Part I, *The Divisions and Description of the Province of Peru* (published in Seville, 1553); Part II, *The Government, Great Deeds, Origin, Policy, Buildings and Roads of the Incas* (in manuscript until published in London, 1873); Part III, *Discovery and Conquest of Peru by Pizarro, and the Rebellion of the Indians* (published in part [15 chapters] in Lima, 1946); Part IV, Book i: *The War between Pizarro and Almagro* (Madrid, 1923), Book ii: *The War of the Young Almagro* (Madrid, 1881; London, 1918), Book iii: *The Civil War of Quito* (Madrid, 1909; London, 1913), Book iv: *The War of Huarina* (lost), and Book v: *The War of Xaquixaguana* (lost); Commentary I, *Events from the Founding of the Audience to the Departure of the President* (possibly never written), and Commentary II, *Events to the Arrival of the Viceroy Mendoza* (possibly never written).

127As quoted by John Fiske, *Discovery of America* (Boston: Houghton Mifflin Company, 1892), vol. 2, p. 304, note 1, translation of Cieza by Clements Markham.

128Victor Wolfgang von Hagen, ed., *The Incas of Pedro de Cieza de León*, trans. Harriet de Onis (Norman: University of Oklahoma Press, 1959), pp. 25–26, from Cieza's *Chronicle*, Part I, chapter 38.

129From the May 3, 1493, Bull "Inter Cetera" of Pope Alexander VI.

130von Hagen, op. cit., p. 50; Cieza, Part II, chapter 67.

131According to von Hagen, op. cit., map.

132John M. Cooper, "The Araucanians," in Steward, op. cit., vol. 2, pp. 687–760.

133von Hagen, op. cit., p. 280, note 3.

134Ibid., pp. 280–281; Cieza, Part I, chapter 95.

135G. H. S. Bushnell, *Peru* (New York: Frederick A. Praeger, revised edition, 1963), pp. 133–134.

136von Hagen, op. cit., pp. 70–71; Cieza, Part I, chapter 19.

137Ibid., pp. 300–302; Cieza, Part I, chapter 101.

138Ibid., pp. 334–337; Cieza, Part I, chapter 116.

139Bushnell, op. cit., p. 89.

40Ibid., p. 89.

41Ibid., p. 91.

142Lathrap, *Ancient Ecuador*, p. 13.

43Ibid., p. 13.

44Wendell C. Bennett and Junius B. Bird, *Andean Culture History*, 2nd edition (New York: American Museum of Natural History, 1960), p. 105.

45Ibid., p. 114.

46Ibid., p. 135.

47Ibid., pp. 149–150.

48von Hagen, op. cit., p. 138; Cieza, Part II, chapter 15.

49Ibid., pp. 139–140; Cieza, Part II, chapter 21.

50Lathrap, *Ancient Ecuador*, p. 43.

51Bushnell, op. cit., p. 54.

152Lathrap, *Ancient Ecuador*, pp. 57 and 59.

153Donald W. Lathrap, "The Tropical Forest and the Cultural Context of Chavín," in Elizabeth P. Benson, ed., *Dumbarton Oaks Conference on Chavín, October 26th and 27th, 1968* (Washington, D.C.: Trustees for Harvard University, 1971), pp. 76–77.

154Stephen Hugh-Jones, op. cit., pp. 287–294.

155Lathrap, "The Tropical Forest and the Cultural Context of Chavín," p. 77.

156Ibid.

157See Miguel Covarrubias, *The Eagle, the Jaguar, and the Serpent* (New York: Alfred A. Knopf, 1954), p. 16. For the date, 1016 ± 300 B.C., see Frederick Johnson, "Radiocarbon Dating," *Memoirs of the Society for American Archaeology*, no. 8 (Salt Lake City, 1951), pp. 10–18, sample no. 321. Others have placed the date much earlier, c. 2000 B.C. (Peter Kvietok, personal communication, February 1989).

158*Mathews' Chinese-English Dictionary*, revised American edition (Cambridge, Mass.: Harvard University Press, 1960), p. 927, character 6392.

159William Willetts, *Foundations of Chinese Art* (New York: McGraw-Hill Book Company, 1965), pp. 96–97.

160*Skanda Purāṇa* II. Visnukānda, Kārtvkamasa, 17; as in Heinrich Zimmer, *Myths and Symbols in Indian Art and Civilization*, Joseph Campbell, ed., Bollingen Series VI (Princeton: Princeton University Press, 1972), pp. 175–184.

161Wendell C. Bennett, "The Archaeology of the Central Andes," in Steward, op. cit., vol. 2, p. 96.

162Wauchope, op. cit., vol. 4, p. 148.

163von Heine-Geldern, op. cit., p. 93.

164Ibid., p. 94.

165Ibid.

166Bushnell, op. cit., p. 43.

167Ibid., pp. 43–44.

CAPTIONS

1Maya Deren, *Divine Horsemen: The Living Gods of Haiti* (London: Thames and Hudson, 1953), pp. 37–38 and 107–108.

2Roman Pina Chan, "Preclassic or Formative Pottery and Minor Arts of the Valley of Mexico," in Robert Wauchope, ed., *Handbook of Middle American Indians*, 13 vols. (Austin: University of Texas Press, 1964–73), vol. 10, p. 177, chart 1.

3Miguel Covarrubias, *Indian Art of Mexico and Central America* (New York: Alfred A. Knopf, 1957), pp. 18–19.

4Ibid., pp. 24–27.

5Michael D. Coe, "San Lorenzo and the Olmec Civilization," in Elizabeth P. Benson, ed., *Dumbarton Oaks Conference on the Olmec, October 28th and 29th, 1967*, Dumbarton Oaks Research Library and Collection (Washington, D.C.: Trustees for Harvard University, 1968), p. 60.

6Ibid., p. 63.

7David C. Grove, "Olmec Monuments: Mutilation As a Clue to Meaning," in Elizabeth P. Benson, ed., *The Olmec and Their Neighbors*, Dumbarton Oaks Research Library and Collection (Washington, D.C.: Trustees for Harvard University, 1981), pp. 49–68.

8Ignacio Bernal, *The Olmec World*, trans. Doris Heyden and Fernando Horcasitas (Berkeley: University of California Press, 1969), pp. 56–57.

9Bernal, op. cit., citing Philip Drucker, Robert Heizer, and Robert Squier, *Excavations at La Venta, Tabasco, 1955*, Smithsonian Institution Bureau of American Ethnology Bulletin 170 (Washington, D.C., 1959), p. 170.

10Drucker, Heizer, and Squier, op. cit., p. 156.

11Ibid., p. 155.

12Ibid., p. 156.

13Ibid., p. 158.

14Jonas E. Gullberg, "Technical Notes on Concave Mirrors," in Drucker, Heizer, and Squier, op. cit., appendix 3, p. 280.

15Bernal, op. cit., p. 78, note 106.

16Gullberg, op. cit., p. 283.

17Drucker, Heizer, and Squier, op. cit., p. 196.

18Bernal, op. cit., p. 94.

19Jacques Soustelle, *The Olmecs: The Oldest Civilization in Mexico*, trans. Helen B. Lane (Garden City, N.Y.: Doubleday and Company, Inc., 1984), p. 137.

20Both the iconography and the nature of this object are a matter of contention: while some scholars are of the opinion that it is certainly a jaguar mask, others insist, according to personal correspondence of March 1985 from Jerald T. Milanich, Curator of Anthropology at the Florida State Museum, that "the tablet, one of more than 50 metal ones known (there are wooden ones as well), depicts a stylized spider (see Allerton, et al., 'Ceremonial Tablets and Related Objects from Florida,' *Florida Anthropologist* 37:5–54). The spider motif is very similar to spiders depicted on Southeastern Ceremonial Complex shell gorgets (see *Sun Circles and Human Hands*, by Fundaburk and Foreman; also, John Griffin, 'Historical Artifacts and the Buzzard Cult in Florida,' *Florida Historical Quarterly* 14:295–301). Recent documentary information and analysis of the Fort Center tablets suggests that the metal tablets were copies of earlier wooden plaques. The metal tablets were apparently being made in the early seventeenth century in Cuba for trade to the South Florida Indians. The date is consistent with other European items found with the tablets. I suspect that the spider is a cosmogonic symbol associated with high status individuals. Its origin may lie in the Southeast Indian myth regarding the role of the water spider in bringing fire to humans (e.g. James Mooney, 'Myths of the Cherokee,': *19th Annual Report*, Bureau of American Ethnology, pp. 240–242)."

21Campbell Grant, *The Rock Paintings of the Chumash* (Berkeley: University of California Press, 1965), plate 27, note.

22Barbara L. Moulard, *Within the Underworld Sky, Mimbres Ceramic Art in Context* (Pasadena, Calif.: Twelvetrees Press, 1984), pp. xi–xiii, abridged.

23Gordon Vivian and Paul Reiter, *The Great Kivas of Chaco Canyon and Their Relationships*, The School of American Research Monograph 22 (Albuquerque: University of New Mexico Press, 1965), pp. 62–65.

24T. Y. Canby, "The Anasazi," *National Geographic*, vol. 162, no. 5, pp. 554–592.

25Stuart J. Feidel, *Prehistory of the Americas* (Cambridge: Cambridge University Press, 1987), pp. 211–221.

26Barton Wright, essay in *Year of the Hopi*, catalogue accompanying a traveling exhibition, "Paintings and Photographs by Joseph Mora, 1904–1906," organized and circulated, 1979–1981, by the Smithsonian Institution Traveling Exhibition Service, p. 17.

27Ibid., p. 30.

28Following ibid., pp. 47 and 54, abridged.

29Ibid., p. 60.

30Frank Waters, *Book of the Hopi* (New York: Penguin Books, 1977), p. 208.

31Ibid., p. 210.

32Peter T. Furst, "The Art of 'Being Huichol'," in Kathleen Berrin, ed., *Art of the Huichol Indians* (New York: Harry N. Abrams, Inc., 1978) a catalogue published in conjunction with an exhibition organized by the Fine Arts Museums of San Francisco.

33Prem Das, "Initiation by a Huichol Shaman," in Berrin, op. cit., pp. 140–141, abridged.

34Following an interpretation furnished by the artist, Eligio Carrillos Vincente, obtained and translated courtesy of Prem Das.

35Barbara G. Meyerhoff, "Peyote and the Mystic Vision," in Berrin, op. cit., pp. 57–59.

36Ibid., p. 56.

37Ibid., p. 59.

38Furst, op. cit., p. 18, quoting Carl Lumholtz, *Symbolism of the Huichol Indians*, Memoirs of the American Museum of Natural History 1 (New York: American Museum of Natural History, 1900).

39Joseph Judge and James L. Stanfield, "Where Columbus Found the New World," *National Geographic*, vol. 170, no. 5 (November 1976), pp. 568–569.

40Frederick J. Dockstader, *Indian Art in Middle America* (Greenwich, Conn.: New York Graphic Society, 1964), pp. 128–132.

41Hartley Burr Alexander, *Latin-American Mythology*, in Louis Herbert Gray, ed., *The Mythology of All Races*, 13 vols. (Boston: Marshall Jones Co., 1920), vol. XI, pp. 33–34, translating from Francisco López de Gómara, "Historia de las Indias" (Anvers, 1554).

42Girolamo Benzoni, *Historia del Mondo Nuovo* (Venice, 1565), translated and edited by W. H. Smyth as *History of the New World by Girolamo of Milan: Shewing his travels in America from A.D. 1541 to 1556; with some particulars of the island of Canary* (London, 1857).

43Dockstader, op. cit., plate 193.

44José Juan Arrom, *Mitología y Artes Prehispánicas de las Antillas* (Mexico: Siglo Veintiuno Editores, 1975), p. 99, citing Ramón Pane, *Relación acerca de las antigüedades de los indios*, chapter 22 (here abridged).

45Arrom, op. cit., p. 106.

46David M. Guss, *To Weave and To Sing* (Berkeley: University of California Press, 1989), p. 1.

47Marc de Civrieux, *Watunna: Mitología Makiritare* (Caracas: Monte Avila Editores, C.A., 1970), translated, with an introduction and glossary, by David M. Guss as *Watunna: An Orinoco Creation Cycle* (San Francisco: North Point Press, 1980).

48Guss, *Watunna*, p. 12.

49Ibid.

50Guss, *To Weave and To Sing*, p. 21.

51Ibid., p. 27.

52Ibid., pp. 29–30.

53Ibid., p. 30.

54Ibid., p. 65.

55Gerardo Reichel-Dolmatoff, *Amazonian Cosmos* (Chicago: University of Chicago Press, 1971), pp. 80–81.

56Ibid., p. 11.

57Ibid., p. 81.

58Ermanno Stradelli, "Inscrizioni Indigene della regione dell'Uaupes," *Bolletino della Societe Geografica Italiana*, series 4, no. 1, p. 476.

59Thomas W. Whitaker, "Endemism and Pre-Columbian Migration of the Bottle Gourd, *Lagenaria siceraria* (Mol.) Stanal.," in Carroll L. Riley, J. Charles Kelly, Campbell W. Pennington, and Robert L. Rands, eds., *Man across the Sea: Problems of Pre-Columbian Contacts* (Austin: University of Texas Press, 1971), p. 232.

60Carl O. Sauer, "Cultivated Plants in South and Central America," in Julian H. Steward, ed., *Handbook of South American Indians*, 7 vols., Bureau of American Ethnology Bulletin 143 (Washington, D.C., 1944–48), vol. 6, p. 506.

61Herbert G. Baker, "Commentary" in Riley et al., op. cit., Section II, citing Whitaker in note I, pp. 431–432.

62Whitaker, op. cit., p. 327.

63Ibid.

64Donald W. Lathrap, *Ancient Ecuador: Culture, Clay and Creativity 3000–300 B.C.*, catalogue of an exhibit organized by the Field Museum of Natural History, April 18 to August 5, 1975, p. 43.

65Ibid., p. 23.

66Wendell C. Bennett and Junius B. Bird, *Andean Culture History*, 2nd edition (New York: American Museum of Natural History, 1960), p. 132.

67Feidel, op. cit., p. 333, citing M. E. Mosley and C. Mackey, "Chan Chan: Peru's Ancient City of Kings," *National Geographic*, vol. 152 (March 1973), pp. 319–345.

68Following Feidel, op. cit., pp. 319–320; also G. H. S. Bushnell, *Ancient Arts of the Americas* (New York: Frederick A. Praeger, 1965), pp. 152–154.

69G. H. S. Bushnell, *Peru*, revised edition (New York: Frederick A. Praeger, 1963), p. 48.

70Following Sat-cakra-nirūpana, verses 22–27, as translated and interpreted in Arthur Avalon (Sir John Woodroffe), *The Serpent Power* (Madras: Ganesh & Co.; London: Luzar and Co., 1931), pp. 369–381.

71Ibid., verse 30, p. 386.

72Meister Eckhart, "Sermons and Collations," no. 96, "Riddance," in Franz Pfeiffer, ed., D. de B. Evans, trans., *Meister Eckhart*, 2 vols., (London: John M. Watkins, 1947), vol. 1, p. 289.

73Miguel Covarrubias, *The Eagle, the Serpent, and the Jaguar* (New York: Alfred A. Knopf, 1954), p. 34, citing Carl Shuster, "Joint-marks, a Possible Index of Cultural Contact between America, Oceania, and the Far East," Med. XCLV, *Adfeling Culturele en Physische Antropologie*, no. 39, Koninklijl Instituut voor de Trpen, Amsterdam, 1951; also H. J. Spinden, "Ancient Civilizations of Mexico and Central America," American Museum of Natural History Handbook Series no. 3.

A NOTE ON THE INDEXES

*References to pages, captions,
maps, and map captions.*

In the Place Name Index and the Subject
Index, references to pages are page numbers, e.g.,

couvade, 320

which means that a reference to the practice of the couvade is to be found on page
320. In both indexes, commas, rather than
dashes, are used to indicate separate men-
tions of a topic on adjacent pages, e.g.,

358, 359

References to captions consist of a boldface caption number (or range of caption
numbers), followed by a hyphen and a
page number, e.g.,

444-328

338–390-286

References to maps consist of a boldface
capital "M" and a map number followed
by a hyphen and a page number, e.g.,

M42-369

Map captions are referred to similarly, but
with an additional letter "C," e.g.,

MC31-277

SUBJECT INDEX

INDEX OF PLACE NAMES

CREDITS AND ACKNOWLEDGEMENTS

PICTURES

Key:
AMNH = American Museum of Natural History, New York; **BB** = Barbara Brandli, Caracas; **BM** = British Museum, London; **BJM** = Betty J. Meggers, Smithsonian Institution, Washington, D.C.; **CUL** = Columbia University Libraries, New York; **DG** = David Guss, Piermont, NY; **DO** = Dumbarton Oaks Research Libraries and Collections, Washington, D.C.; **FAMSF** = Fine Arts Museums of San Francisco; **FGA** = Fundacion García Arévalo, Santo Domingo; **FMNH** = Field Museum of Natural History, Chicago; **GG** = courtesy of Gilett G. Griffin, Princeton, NJ; **JBT** = John Bigelow Taylor, New York; **JM/JRW** = Jacinto Mora/John R. Wilson, Tulsa; **LB** = Lee Boltin, Croton-on-Hudson, NY; **MAI** = Museum of the American Indian, New York; **ML** = Mennonite Library, North Newton, KS; **MMA** = Metropolitan Museum of Art, New York; **MNA** = Museo Nacional de Antropologia, Mexico City; **MNM** = Museum of New Mexico, Santa Fe; **NGA** = National Gallery of Art, Washington, D.C.; **NYPL** = New York Public Library; **PC** = Peter Collings, Moorpart, CA; **PF** = Peter Furst, Santa Fe; **PMA** = Philadelphia Museum of Art; **RD** = Gerardo Reichel-Dolmatoff, Bogotá; **SI** = Smithsonian Institution, Washington, D.C.

COVER: JBT, from the collection of Gilett G. Griffin

AGRICULTURAL DEVELOPMENTS IN THE MESOAMERICAN MATRIX

339 MNA; **340a–b** CUL; **341** GG; **342** JBT; **343** Muriel Porter Weaver, New York; **344** top, left to right: JBT, MNA, LB, MNA, JBT; bottom, left to right: JBT, MNA, JBT, JBT, MNA, JBT; **345–347** PF; **348** FAMSF; **349** Bibliothèque Nationale, Paris; **350–352** GG; **353** LB; **354** MNA; **355–356** GG; **357** Brooklyn Museum, New York; **358** AMNH; **359a** MNA; **359b** BM; **359c** SI; **359d** AMNH; **360** GG; **361** JBT, MNA; **362a–b** GG; **363** Florida State Museum, Gainesville

AGRICULTURAL RITES AND MYTHS OF MIDDLE AMERICA

364 NYPL; **365** PMA; **366a** MNM; **366b–c** Karl Kernberger, Santa Fe; **366d** Campbell Grant, Santa Barbara; **367–368** JBT; **369–370** MNM; **371** David and Barbara Anderson, Cochiti Lake, N.Y.; **372** Edward S. Curtis; **373** Anna Sofaer, Washington, D.C.; **374a–b** Mary Challinor, "Science 80"; **374c** Karl Kernberger, Santa Fe; **375** Barbara Bohrer, American Academy for the Advancement of Science, Washington, D.C.; **376** Peter Dechert, Santa Fe; **377** Cynthia Petrowski, Stamford, Conn.; **378** Arizona State Museum, Tucson; **379** JM/JRW; **380–381** ML; **382** Barton Wright, Phoenix; **383** California Academy of Sciences, San Francisco; **384–386** JM/JRW; **387** SI; **388** JM/JRW; **389** SI; **390** JM/JRW; **391** ML; **392** JM/JRW; **393** Southwest Museum, Los Angeles; **394** ML; **395** PMA; **396–397** Natural History Museum of Los Angeles County; **398** JM/JRW; **399** ML; **400–402** JM/JRW; **403** PF; **404** Museum of Cultural History, UCLA; **405** FAMSF; **406** PF; **407** Joseph Campbell; **408–410** PF; **411** Susan Eger-Valdez, Oakland; **412** PC; **413** Prem Das, Covelo, Calif.; **414** PC; **415–417** PF; **418** MNM; **419** FAMSF; **420–423** NYPL; **424** LB; **425a** MAI; **425b–c** SI; **425d** MAI; **426** FGA; **427–428** NYPL; **429** Museum of Anthropology, History, and Art, University of Puerto Rico; **430** FGA; **431** Museum für Völkerkunde, Munich; **432** MAI; **433–434** NGA; **435–436** NYPL; **437** NGA; **438** NYPL; **439** SI; **440** NGA; **441** DG

SOUTH AMERICAN AGRICULTURAL RITES AND MYTHS

442 Phillip Galgiani; **443–451** DG; **452** BB; **453–454** DG; **455** BB; **456** DG; **457** BB; **458** Phillip Galgiani; **459–468** DG; **469** BB; **470** DG; **471** NYPL; **472** Jacques Jangoux/Peter Arnold, New York; **473–477** RD; **478** Albert E. Stevens, "The Amazon, Father of Waters," *National Geographic*, vol. 64, no. 4 (April 1926); **479–483** RD; **484** FMNH; **485** RD; **486** Loren McIntyre/Woodfin Camp, New York; **487a** DG; **487b** RD; **487c–e** Steven Hugh-Jones, Cambridge, U.K.; **488** Theodor Koch-Grünberg, *Zwei Jahren unter den Indianern: Reisen in Nordwest Brazilien, 1903–1905*, 2 vols. (Berlin: Ernst Wasmuth A.-G., 1909, 1910); **489** Brian Moser, London; **490** Steven Hugh-Jones, Cambridge, U.K.; **491** RD; **492** Brian Moser, London; **493** FMNH, NMA; **494–499** NYPL; **500–503** BJM; **504** BJM, FMNH; **505** FMNH; **506–509** FMNH; **510** FMNH, MAI; **511** George J. Fery, Miami; **512** MAI; **513** Sally Black, Charlottesville, Virg.; **514** FMNH; **515** BJM; **516–517** FMNH; **518** JBT, AMNH; **519** FMNH; **520** Art Resources, New York; **521** Thomas Gilcrease Institute of American History and Art, Tulsa; **522–526** NYPL; **527** DO; **528** Hamlyn Picture Library, London; **529** Evan Hadingham, Cambridge, Mass.; **530–531** Michael Holford, London; **532** Victor Englebert, Cali, Colombia; **533** DO, MAI; **534–535** GG; **536** FMNH; **537** GG; **538** Cambridge Museum of Archaeology and Ethnology, Cambridge, U.K.; **539** AMNH; **540** MMA; **541–542** AMNH; **543** MMA, GG, RD; **544** G. H. S. Bushnell, *Peru* (New York: Praeger, 1963); **545** GG; **546** FMNH; **547** MMA; **548** AMNH; **549** William Y. Willets, *Foundations of Chinese Art from Neolithic Pottery to Modern Man* (New York: McGraw-Hill, 1965), as redrawn by Sally Black, Charlottesville, Virg.; **550** ACSAA Project, Ann Arbor, MI; **551** Musée Cernuschi, Paris; **552** Fernand Anton, Munich; **553** Musée de l'Homme, Paris; **554** FMNH; **555** Miguel Covarrubias, *The Eagle, the Jaguar, and the Serpent* (New York: Alfred A. Knopf, 1954); **556** AMNH; **557** DO

EXTRACTS

From Jacques Soustelle, *The Olmecs: The Oldest Civilization in Mexico*, Helen B. Lane, trans. (Garden City, N.Y.: Doubleday & Co., 1984).

From Prem Das, "Initiation by a Huichol Shaman," in Kathleen Berrin, ed. *The Art of the Huichol Indians* (New York: Harry N. Abrams, Inc., 1978) a catalogue published in conjunction with an exhibition organized by the Fine Arts Museums of San Francisco.

From Peter Furst, "The Art of 'Being Huichol'," in Kathleen Berrin, ed. *The Art of the Huichol Indians* (New York: Harry N. Abrams, Inc., 1978) a catalogue published in conjunction with an exhibition organized by the Fine Arts Museums of San Francisco.

From Barbara G. Myerhoff, *Peyote Hunt: The Sacred Journey of the Huichol Indians* (Ithaca: Cornell University Press, 1974).

From Marc de Civrieux, *Watunna: Mitología Makiritare* (Caracas: Monte Avila Editores, C.A., 1970), translated, with an introduction and glossary, by David M. Guss as *Watunna: An Orinoco Creation Cycle* (San Francisco: North Point Press, 1980).

From Gerardo Reichel-Dolmatoff, *Amazonian Cosmos* (Chicago: University of Chicago Press, 1971).

From Stephen Hugh-Jones, *The Palm and the Pleiades: Initiation and Cosmology in Northwest Amazonia*, Cambridge Studies in Social Anthropology No. 24 (Cambridge: Cambridge University Press, 1979).

From Donald Lathrap, *Ancient Ecuador: Culture, Clay and Creativity, 3000–300 B.C.*, catalogue of an exhibit organized by the Field Museum of Natural History, April 18 to August 5, 1975.

From Victor Wolfgang von Hagen, ed., *The Incas of Pedro de Cieza de León*, Harriet de Onis, trans. (Norman: University of Oklahoma Press, 1959).

MAPS

Map 26. Based in part on information adapted from Michael Coe et al., eds., *Atlas of Ancient America* (New York: Facts on File Publications, 1986).

Map 27. Based in part on information adapted from Michael Coe et al., eds., *Atlas of Ancient America* (New York: Facts on File Publications, 1986); Robert Wauchope, ed., *Handbook of Middle American Indians*, 13 vols. (Austin: University of Texas Press, 1964-73), vol. 3; Jacques Soustelle, *The Olmecs: The Oldest Civilization in Mexico*, trans. Helen B. Lane (Garden City, N.Y.: Doubleday and Company, Inc., 1984); *Past Worlds: The Times Atlas of Archaeology* (London: Times Books Ltd., 1988); and Michael Wood, ed., *The World Atlas of Archaeology* (Boston: G. K. Hall and Company, 1985).

Map 28. Based in part on information adapted from Jacques Soustelle, *The Olmecs: The Oldest Civilization in Mexico*, trans. Helen B. Lane (Garden City, N. Y.: Doubleday and Company, Inc., 1984); and Michael Coe et al. eds., *Atlas of Ancient America* (New York: Facts on File Publications, 1986).

Map 29. Based in part on information adapted from Michael Coe et al., *Atlas of Ancient America* (New York: Facts on File Publications, 1986); H. P. Walker and D. Bufkin, *Historical Atlas of Oklahoma* (Norman: University of Oklahoma Press, 1979); W. A. Beck and Y. D. Haase, *Historical Atlas of New Mexico* (Norman: University of Oklahoma Press, 1969); James M. Goodman, *The Navajo Atlas* (Norman: University of Oklahoma Press, 1982); *Historical Atlas of the United States* (Washington, D.C.: National Geographic Society, 1988); and Gordon R. Willey, *An Introduction to American Archaeology*, 2 vols. (Englewood Cliffs, N.J.: Prentice-Hall Inc., 1966), vol. 1, "North America."

Map 30. Based in part on information adapted from R. H. Lister and F. G. Lister, *Chaco Canyon: Archaeology and Archaeologists* (Albuquerque: University of New Mexico Press, 1981).

Map 31. Based in part on information adapted from Douglas Anderson and Barbara Anderson, *Chaco Canyon: Center of a Culture* (Globe, N.M.: Southwest Parks and Monuments Association, 1984); and "Complex Culture in a Harsh Land" (map), *National Geographic*, vol. 162, no. 5 (November 1982).

Map 32. Based in part on information adapted from M. Benzi, *Les Derniers Adorateurs du Peyotl* (Paris: Gallimard, 1972).

Map 33. Based in part on information adapted from R. H. Fuson, trans., *The Log of Christopher Columbus* (Camden, Me.: International Marine Publishing Co., 1987); G. Roberts, *Atlas of Discovery* (New York: Crown Publishers, 1973); J. Engel, *Grosser Historischer Weltatlas* (Munich: Bayerischer Schulbuch Verlag, 1967); F. W. Putzger, *Historischer Weltatlas* (Berlin: Velhagen und Klassing Verlag, 1968); C. L. Lombardi and J. V. Lombardi, *Latin American History: A Teaching Atlas* (Madison: University of Wisconsin Press, 1983); Joseph Judge, "Where Columbus Found the New World," *National Geographic*, vol. 170, no. 5 (November 1986); and "Where Did Columbus Discover America?" (map), *National Geographic*, vol. 170, no. 5 (November 1986).

Map 35. Based in part on information adapted from *Academic American Encyclopaedia* (Princeton, N.J.; Arete Publishing Co., 1980); and National Geographic Society, *Indians of South America*, map (Washington, D.C.: National Geographic Society, 1982).

Map 38. Based in part on information adapted from Gerardo Reichel-Dolmatoff, *Amazonian Cosmos* (Chicago: University of Chicago Press, 1971); Stephen Hugh-Jones, *The Palm and the Pleiades: Initiation and Cosmology in Northwest Amazonia*, Cambridge Studies in Social Anthropology No. 24 (Cambridge: Cambridge University Press, 1979); and Christine Hugh-Jones, *From the Milk River: Spatial and Temporal Processes in Northwest Amazonia*, Cambridge Studies in Social Anthropology No. 26 (Cambridge: Cambridge University Press, 1979).

Map 39. Based in part on information adapted from Michael Coe et al. eds., *Atlas of Ancient America* (New York: Facts on File Publications, 1986); and *Past Worlds; The Times Atlas of Archaeology* (London: Times Books Ltd., 1988).

Map 40. Based in part on information adapted from Edwin Doran Jr., "The Sailing Raft As a Great Tradition," chapter 7 in C. L. Riley et al., eds., *Man across the Sea; Problems of Pre-Columbian Contacts* (Austin: University of Texas Press, 1971).

Map 41. Based in part on information adapted from Society cf Ancient Pacific Cultures, *Yasei-Gô III: An Experimental Voyage and Archaeological Research by the Double Canoe in the Pacific Ocean* (Tokyo: Kadokawa Publishing Co., 1982); and Thor Heyerdahl, *Early Man and the Ocean* (Garden City, N.Y.: Doubleday and Co., 1979).

Map 42. Based in part on information adapted from Michael Coe et al. eds., *Atlas of Ancient America* (New York: Facts on File Publications, 1986).

Map 43. Based in part on information adapted from Michael Coe et al. eds., *Atlas of Ancient America* (New York: Facts on File Publications, 1986).

HISTORICAL ATLAS OF
WORLD MYTHOLOGY

Developed and first published in part by
Van der Marck Editions, New York

Editorial Director: *Robert Walter*

Designer: *Jos. Trautwein/Bentwood Studio*

Art Editor: *Rosemary O'Connell*

Associate Editor: *Antony Van Couvering*

Indexer: *Maro Riofrancos*

Maps and Charts: *Cartographic Services Center of R. R. Donnelley & Sons Company*

Map Design: *Sidney P. Marland III*

Map Research, Compilation, and Project Coordination: *Luis Freile*

Map Drafting and Production: *Robert Hoover*

Type Composition: *Typographic Art, Inc.*

Printing and Binding: *Royal Smeets Offset, B.V., The Netherlands*

Grateful acknowledgement is made to the following for their noted contributions to this volume: John Bigelow Taylor; Spencer Throckmorton; John R. Wilson; Dr. Peter T. Furst; Cathleen Baxter, Smithsonian Institution, Washington, D.C.; Barbara Mathé, American Museum of Natural History, New York; Nina Cummings, Field Museum, Chicago; James Foerster, Field Museum, Chicago; Peter Kvietok, American Museum of Natural History, New York; and Drew Dutcher.